The Amazing World of Rice

OTHER BOOKS BY MARIE SIMMONS

The Good Egg
(James Beard Award 2000)

Fresh & Fast

Lighter, Quicker, Better
with Richard Sax
(James Beard and Julia Child Awards 1995)

Holiday Celebrations

A to Z Puddings
A to Z Pancakes
A to Z Muffins
A to Z Bar Cookies

The Light Touch

Italian Light Cooking

Rice, the Amazing Grain

365 Ways to Cook Pasta

The Amazing World of Rice

with 150 Recipes for Pilafs, Paellas, Puddings, and More

Marie Simmons

WM
WILLIAM MORROW
An Imprint of HarperCollins Publishers

HarperCollins books may be purchased for educational, business, or sales promotional use. For information please write: Special Markets Department, HarperCollins Publishers Inc., 10 East 53rd Street, New York, NY 10022.

FIRST EDITION

Designed by Lee Fukui

Printed on acid-free paper

Library of Congress Cataloging-in-Publication Data

Simmons, Marie.
The Amazing World of Rice / Marie Simmons.—1st ed.
p. cm.
Includes index.
ISBN 0-06-093842-0
1. Cookery (Rice) 2. Rice. I. Title.

TX809.R5 .S463 2003
641.6'318—dc21
2002068574

03 04 05 06 07 WBC/QW 10 9 8 7 6 5 4 3 2 1

FOR THE COOKS IN MY FAMILY

Nana (in memory), my mentor

Mom, my inspiration

Aunt Tess, my idol

Aunt Rita, my role model

Stephanie, my guiding light

Seraphina, the brightest light in my life

Contents

Acknowledgments

More than ten years ago I spent several years exploring the world of rice while working on *Rice, the Amazing Grain.* I became fascinated with rice because I didn't know very much about it. At the time risotto was new to me and pilaf exotic. I realized that even stir-fries, salads, and puddings were dishes I yearned to explore in depth. I turned that curiosity into a book, researching and gathering a treasury of information and experimenting endlessly with rice recipes. Along the way I not only learned to cook rice but also learned to love it.

My fascination with rice did not end in 1991 when *Rice, the Amazing Grain* was published. Nor did it end, a decade later, when the book went out of print.

Over the years my rice education continued to grow. In my travels to Asia, the Mediterranean region, and South America I have eaten rice, learned to cook more rice dishes, and tried new (to me) varieties of rice. Meanwhile at home demographics have radically changed the profile of the restaurants where we eat and the markets where we shop. I don't have to go to Bangkok to eat coconut rice pudding with mango or to Delhi to find baby basmati rice. To add to the excitement, the United States is producing more varieties of rice, and many exotic rices are being imported from Asia and other parts of the world.

With so many new recipes and new rice information "milling" about in my head, writing a second book was inevitable. But I did it only because Harriet Bell, an editor and friend, said decisively, "Let's do it," over a glass of iced tea when I casually mentioned that "maybe some day I should write another book about rice."

A cookbook is never a solitary task. Recipes, stories, and information come from many sources—colleagues, new friends, old friends, and family.

Revisiting my decade-plus old notes and dog-eared fat files (there are some advantages to being a pack rat) reminded me of the kindness and generosity of the people who were there to advise and encourage me through the process of writing and researching *Rice, the Amazing Grain,* my first "real" cookbook. They are Susan Herner, Elizabeth Crossman, Kris O'Brien, and Gloria Spitz.

Thank you to the experts and growers in the industry who have continued to help me over the years with my various rice projects: Richard Long and Mark Denman at RiceTec, Inc., in Alvin, Texas, Donna Bayliss of Bayliss Ranch in Biggs, California, Michael Martin at the Martin Rice Company in Bernie, Missouri, the Lundberg Family Farms in Richvale, California, and Timothy Johnson of the California Rice Commission.

Now, many years—and cookbooks later—I am fortunate to have more people to whom I express my gratitude: Judith Weber, my stalwart agent and loyal confident, Ken Lee and Caryl Levine of Lotus Foods, who keep me supplied with their incredibly beautiful exotic grains, and Dr. Henry Beachell, rice expert at RiceTec who patiently vetted my new rice glossary. Special thanks to Kim Park, the National Consumer Education Director at USA Rice Federation, and Kasma Loha unchit, friend, cookbook author, and excellent Thai cooking teacher who taught me to cook rice, Thai-style.

Thank you to Brooke Jackson for expertly retesting many of my recipes, to Libby Connolly at The Spanish Table in Berkeley, California, for her paella advice, to Judith Sutton for correcting my mistakes and asking all the right questions, and to book designer Lee Fukui for such a beautiful book.

Finally, but not least, I thank our good friends and our neighbors for putting up with all the rice leftovers that I plied them with (or left on their doorsteps if they happened not to be at home). And an especially loving thank you to John for being there at the table, uncomplaining, as I fed him meal after meal of rice, rice, and more rice.

The Amazing World of Rice

Introduction

How nice
Is rice!
How gentle and how very free from vice
Are those whose fodder is mainly Rice.
Yes: Rice! Rice!
Beautiful Rice!
All the wrong in the world would be right in a trice
If everyone fed upon nothing but Rice.

Of all the foods in the world, rice as this little poem expresses, is the gentlest of foods. The grains, gracefully curved on two sides, come together in a soft point at each end. The absence of any true color is in itself a small comfort. When cooked, its softness soothes both hunger and soul.

Rice, a staple for billions of people on earth, is more than food. Rice is rich in legend and folklore that reaches far beyond the bags and boxes found in the kitchens of the world. In Southeast Asia especially, people believe rice is the link between heaven and earth. Intertwined in the customs, language, and arts of Asian culture, rice is the symbol of fertility, beauty, sensitivity, prosperity, energy, and life.

Throughout Asia rice is an integral part of the Creation myth and a gift from the gods, as these two tales illustrate:

In the Philippines, a legend about a beautiful young girl named Bright Jewel and the handsome god who loved her has been told and retold for centuries. Bright

1

Jewel insisted that the young god go into the great beyond in search of a food more delicious than she had ever tasted and bring it back to her as a token of his love. When a very long time had passed and he hadn't returned, Bright Jewel, filled with grief, died of a broken heart. The first rice plant grew from her grave.

In Indonesia, the following legend is a favorite: The god Anta was very poor, and he had no gift for the temple of the great god Batara Guru. He wept three tears. Each tear turned into an egg. Anta had to fight to protect the eggs from a fierce eagle, and before it could destroy the third one, the egg cracked and hatched a lovely female baby named Samyam Sri. The god's wife nursed the baby, who grew into a lovely maiden. Batara lusted for Samyam Sri; tragically, the other goddesses killed her to save her from being ravaged by Batara. As the goddesses mourned Samyam Sri, plants and grasses grew from her grave. Rice was among the plants and for this reason rice in Indonesia is often called, with great reverence, Samyam Sri.

Where Rice Grows

Rice is so ancient that the exact time and place of its first cultivation may never be known. However, grains of rice found imprinted in pottery shards unearthed in Thailand have been carbon dated to 4000 B.C. There, as throughout Southeast Asia, in China, and in India, rice is the primary agricultural crop and is consumed at every meal.

Rice grows throughout the world, from the low hot plains of Texas to the high cold mountains in Bhutan, from the foot of the Andes Mountains in central Argentina to the flood waters of Bangladesh, and from the humid tropics of India to the semi-arid dry lands of Australia. Antarctica is the only continent on the earth where rice does not grow.

In North America, the colonists first planted rice along the coast of the Carolinas in the late 1600s. By the 1700s, rice was firmly established as a valuable export commodity that had made some plantation owners very wealthy. During this time "Carolina Gold Rice" was being shipped to England. Then, as now, the United States exported more rice than it consumed. By the late 1800s, the once thriving rice industry was diminished by the ravages of the Civil War. But, with the birth of the Industrial Revolution, the industry moved inland to Arkansas, Louisiana, Mississippi, Missouri, and Texas. Eventually the Gold Rush brought the rice industry to California. Today Arkansas and California are the top two rice producers in the

United States, and the United States continues to be a major exporter in the world rice market.

How Rice Grows

Rice, *Oryza sativa,* is a very simple grain. It mostly grows in paddies flooded with water. At first the paddies look like blankets of soft green grass. When the plants grow tall and the grains mature, the water is drained. The rice is ready for harvest when the plants turn from green to the color of straw. In some parts of the world, the rice is still planted and harvested by hand. In more technologically advanced countries, lasers are used to level the fields, airplanes or mechanical grain drills are used for planting, and huge air-conditioned combines harvest the rice. In the Indian state of Kerala, I saw rice spread along the side of the road to dry in the hot sun. In Texas and California, the rice is dried and its moisture content reduced in enormous atmospherically controlled dryers.

When the rice is ready for milling, the inedible hull is rubbed off by friction between two rubber rollers, called a sheller. What remains is rice with the bran layers intact, or brown rice. All rice is brown before it is further processed. The brown bran is also removed from the rice by friction. The rice is then sorted for imperfections. In Texas, I watched a laser scanner spot discolored kernels and almost simultaneously blast them aside with a stream of pressurized air.

Rice experts say there are 40,000 or more varieties of rice worldwide. There are two major classifications: *indica* and *japonica.* A smaller classification is *javanica.*

The Science of Rice

Rice is composed of two types of starch: amylose, or dry starch, and amylopectin, or sticky starch. Indicas are long-grain rices that contain a greater proportion of amylose. Generally, long-grain rice elongates as it cooks into dry and separate grains. An exception to this rule is jasmine rice, a long-grain rice with a higher proportion of the sticky starch.

Japonicas are medium- to short-grain rices that contain a greater proportion of amylopectin. Generally, medium- to short-grain rice has a soft texture and clings together when cooked. It becomes wider rather than longer as it cooks. Some short-grain rice is entirely round and when cooked it turns soft and sticky, sometimes losing its shape.

Rice and Nutrition

Rice is a complex carbohydrate with a trace of fat and no sodium. A half-cup serving of white rice provides 103 calories; brown rice has 106 calories. Ninety percent of the calories in rice come from carbohydrates. Rice is a good source of iron and the B vitamins thiamin and niacin. A source of protein, rice contains all eight essential amino acids. It is low in the amino acid lysine, which is found in beans, making the classic combination of rice and beans a particularly healthful dish. Most of the

---

Rice Is More Than a Grain

This straw appears small and light, and most people do not really know how weighty it is. If most people knew the true value of this straw, a human revolution could occur, which would become powerful enough to move the country and the world.

—Masanobu Fukuoka, *The One Straw Revolution*

The straw, hulls, and bran of rice are all used. Rice straw is used to make tatami mats, sandals, and sun hats; particle board, compost; wattles and blankets to protect soil from erosion; ethanol; and newsprint. Bales of the straw are also used to construct energy efficient housing.

Rice hulls, which are composed of silica, are burned as fuel to generate electrical power; added to fertilizer; and used to create rice marbling on paper, make fabric, and provide animal bedding in the agricultural industry.

Rice bran is used as a dietary supplement, as animal feed, in rice bran oil, and in breakfast cereals.

Rice is used to make beer, sake, brandy, wine, syrup, vinegar, milk, flour, noodles, and starch (with its many uses, including candy, snacks, cereal, and baked goods).

It is turned into glue, and used in pharmaceuticals, cosmetics, and as a stabilizer in commercially prepared foods.

---

nutrients in rice are contained in the bran; therefore, when rice is milled, the nutrients are lost. But almost all white rice sold in the United States is enriched with thiamin, niacin, iron, riboflavin, vitamin D, and calcium, making it almost as nutritious as brown rice. Enriched white rice contains more iron and thiamin than brown rice. Brown rice, however, has five times more vitamin E, three times more magnesium, and twice as much fiber. White rice is also enriched with folic acid, a nutrient not naturally found in rice. The enrichments are applied as a coating, which is why rice milled in the United States should not be rinsed.

A Rice Glossary

There are dozens and dozens of varieties of rice, and many can be found in American markets. This glossary identifies those varieties and defines some of the many words and terms related to rice and its production.

Amasake: a thick beverage made from cooked brown rice and *koji* (a mold used in making sake, miso, and soy sauce). Amasake has a fermented taste. It is available in health-food stores.

Amylopectin: one of two types of starch typically found in medium- and short-grain rices (*see also* amylose). It is the waxier of the two starches and gives the cooked rice grains a stickier, softer consistency and tendency to cling. In some varieties, the uncooked grains appear translucent except for a solid white center, or pearl, as in rice used for risotto.

Amylose: one of two types of starch found in long-grain rice. The drier of the two starches, it makes the rice cook into firm separate grains. The uncooked grains appear opaque.

Arborio: the most popular Italian rice, used to make risotto. The grains are medium (although it is often called short-grain) and translucent, with a white center that remains firm to the bite when cooked, while the rest of the grain softens and lends a creamy consistency to the risotto. Once grown exclusively in Italy, it is now raised in the United States as well.

Aromatic rice: a broad term for a group of long-grain rices with a pronounced nutty aroma that comes from a naturally occurring compound (2-acetyl 1-pyrroline) found, in varying degrees, in all rice. Basmati, Della, and jasmine are a few examples of aromatic rice.

Baldo: an Italian medium-grain rice sometimes used for risotto and, in some parts of Turkey, for pilaf. It cooks up soft and tender. Baldo rice is now being grown in limited quantity in Missouri.

Basmati: a long-grain aromatic rice highly regarded for its fragrance, taste, long slender shape, and ability to elongate when cooked. *Basmati* means "queen of fragrance." True basmati is grown in India and Pakistan, but many hybrids are grown elsewhere, including the United States. It's typically used in Indian pilaf.

Black rice: found in both medium- and short-grain varieties, also called black japonica or black sticky rice. Grown mostly in Southeast Asia and in limited quantity in California and Italy, these rices are black from the layers of black bran that surround the endosperm, or kernel. Sometimes the kernel under the bran is white, so when it is cooked, the rice turns purple or lavender. Black rice is considered a delicacy in Asia and is reserved for celebrations or funerals. In Thailand, it is cooked with coconut milk and served with mango as a dessert. Use it in salads or stir-fries, but cook it separately and combine with other ingredients just before serving to prevent discoloring them. A nonsticky black rice, imported by Lotus Foods, is especially good in salads.

Bomba: highest-quality medium-grain Spanish rice (though marketed as a short-grain rice), used in paella and other Spanish rice dishes. It is prized for its ability to absorb a large amount of liquid resulting in large, plump grains of highly flavored rice.

Brewer's rice: broken rice used in beer brewing. Rice-based beer is light in flavor and golden in color. In the United States, 4 pounds out of the almost 27 pounds per person of rice consumed each year is utilized in beer production.

Brown rice: All rice is brown before it is processed. Brown rice is rough paddy rice with the hull removed and the bran layers left intact. The bran, which contains vitamins, minerals, and fiber, gives the rice a chewy texture and a nutty flavor. Brown rice requires longer cooking because the bran acts as a shield against the cooking liquid.

Calasparra: a high-quality medium-grain Spanish rice (marketed as a short-grain rice) used in paella and appreciated for its tender bite and ability to absorb a large amount of liquid. *See* Bomba.

California medium-grain rice: a japonica rice with a high level of sticky starch (amylopectin). It is used for sushi, paella, risotto, and desserts. Over 90 percent of California rice production is in medium-grain rice, much of it raised and milled to specification for export to Asia and Turkey (where it is used in pilaf).

Calriso: from Bayliss Ranch in California, an Arborio-type rice that is a cross between a premium California medium-grain rice and Italian varieties. Use in risotto, soft pilafs, puddings, and paella.

Carolina gold: a rare rice first cultivated in South Carolina during colonial times, named for its golden yellow kernels.

Camargue: a medium-grain rice from the Camargue region in the southwest corner of Provence. It is uncommon in the United States, but when available here it has a red bran. In Europe, it can be found as a brown, red, and white rice. It is good served simply with olive oil, garlic, and herbs.

Christmas rice: a speckled medium-grain rice with a red bran and an earthy taste from the creative Lundberg Family Farms in California. Use it in stir-fries, salads, and pilaf.

Converted rice: a registered trademark of Uncle Ben's. *See* parboiled rice.

Della: a long-grain aromatic rice. These rices are sold under such names as Texmati, Wild Pecan, Konriko, and Delta Rose, among others. Use them to make pilaf, steamed rice, or baked rice. Often compared to basmati, but they do not elongate.

Enriched rice: when the bran is removed, many nutrients are stripped from rice. In the United States, white rice is enriched with a thin topical coating of nutrients, including iron, niacin, thiamin, and folic acid. If the rice is rinsed before cooking, or cooked in a large amount of water and then drained, this enrichment is lost.

Golden rice: a controversial new type of rice genetically engineered to contain beta-carotene, the precursor of vitamin A.

Glutinous rice: A term used to describe waxy rice with 100 percent amylopectin, and a sticky texture. Also called sticky, sweet, or waxy rice. A specialty of Thailand and other Asian countries. The name is confusing because glutinous refers to the gluey texture of the rice, not its gluten content. (Rice does not contain gluten, a protein found in wheat.) *See* sticky rice, sweet rice, or waxy rice.

Indica: one of the two main groups of *Oryza sativa* (the other is japonica). Indica rices are generally long-grain with a higher percentage of amylose, or dry starch, than japonicas. They are successfully grown in hot tropical and semitropical conditions. Della, basmati, and other aromatic rices are all considered indicas.

Jasmine: a fragrant medium- to long-grain rice that cooks into a moist, tender grain. Considered the rice of choice in Thailand, it has more amylopectin, or sticky starch, than dry starch. Native to Asia, it is also grown in the United States.

Japonica: one of the two main groups of *Oryza sativa* (the other is indica). Japonica rices are generally medium- to short-grain, with a higher percentage of amylopectin, or waxy starch, than indicas. They are grown in cooler climates and mountainous regions. Japanese rices (many not exported to the United States), Arborio, and other risotto rices, Kokuho Rose, CalRose, Nishiki, and other Japanese-style rices grown in California are all japonicas.

Kalijira: also called baby basmati and known in India as *gobindavog*. The grains look like miniature basmati rice grains, and, when cooked, have the same pleasant aroma and firm but tender texture. Available from Lotus Foods.

Long-grain rice: refers to rice varieties that are four to five times longer than they are wide. Long-grain rices contain more amylose, or dry starch; the grains cook up dry and separate. Basmati is a type of long-grain rice.

Medium-grain rice: refers to rice varieties that are less than two to three times longer than they are wide. Contain more amylopectin, or sticky starch; the grains cook up soft and tender. These rices readily absorb other flavors, which is why they are popular for paella and risotto. Examples are Arborio and Baldo.

Mochi: a sweet treat made in Japan from soaked and cooked short-grain sweet rice that is pounded until perfectly smooth, then rolled into small balls or other shapes.

Oryza sativa: Latin botanical name for rice, a semiaquatic member of the grass family.

Paddy rice: *See* rough rice.

Parboiled rice: rice that is steam pressure–treated before milling, forcing all the nutrients from the bran layer into the endosperm. Hundreds of years ago the process of parboiling was practiced in India and Asia by soaking the rice and then heating it over hot coals. The United States industrialized parboiling during World War II to provide a nutrient and stable grain to the United States armed forces. It was marketed commercially by Uncle Ben's as converted rice, a registered trademark. Parboiling greatly reduces breakage during milling, but many cooks, especially in food service, prefer it because it always cooks firm and can stand for long periods of time without getting sticky. It has a creamy tan color and a less sweet, starchy flavor than plain milled rice. *See also* rosematta.

Paella: a popular rice dish that originated in Valencia in southeast Spain. It can be a simple dish of rice, beans, snails, and duck or rabbit, or a more elaborate one with shellfish, sausage, artichokes, and saffron. Bomba, Calasparra, and Valencia, three Spanish rices available in the United States, traditionally are used to make paella, but any medium-grain rice can be used.

Pilaf: a Middle Eastern dish of rice sautéed in fat (butter or oil) and then cooked in broth that often includes vegetables and/or meats. Typically it is made with long-grain rice, but medium-grain rice is sometimes used in Turkish pilaf. Pilaf is from the Turkish word *pilau* or *pilaw*.

Popcorn: a term used to describe the aroma of aromatic rices. The aroma comes from a naturally occurring compound—2-acetyl 1-pyrroline—found in all rice, popcorn, and some nuts.

Red rice: aromatic rice with a reddish-brown bran layer, a nutty taste, and a chewy consistency. Look for American-grown Wehani, Bhutanese red rice (imported by Lotus Foods), or red Camargue (from southern France) in specialty markets. Excellent in salads, pilaf, soups, and side dishes.

Retrogradation: a term describing what takes place when cooked rice is refrigerated and its texture changes from soft and tender to hard and chewy. Technically, the starch cells collapse, squeezing out the moisture and causing the realignment of the

> **To Reheat Cold Rice**
>
> - On the stovetop: place in a skillet or shallow saucepan, sprinkle with 1 to 2 tablespoons water, cover, and heat over low heat just until heated through.
>
> - In the microwave: Place in a microwaveproof dish, sprinkle with 1 to 2 tablespoons water, cover, and microwave on high for 2 to 3 minutes. Let stand for 2 minutes before serving.
>
> - In the oven: Wrap in foil and place in a preheated 350°F oven for 10 to 15 minutes, or until heated through. (Only use this method if the oven is already on for another dish.)

starch molecules. The process cannot be prevented but it can be reversed by reheating the rice.

Rice bran: the tan nutrient-rich outer layer that gives brown rice its color. High in nutrients such as thiamin, niacin, vitamin B_6, iron, potassium, and fiber, rice bran is used in cereals, baked goods, and vitamins. Studies suggest that the oil in rice bran may have cholesterol-reducing properties. Rice bran is perishable; buy it at a reputable health-food store with a good turnover and refrigerate once the package is opened.

Rice flour: finely ground rice, used in baked goods, breakfast cereals, pancake or waffle mixes, pasta, and snack foods. It is gluten-free and therefore cannot be substituted for wheat flour without adjusting the recipe.

Rice hull: rice's inedible outside covering, or husk. Rice hulls are burned as a source of fuel, used as mulch, and are also used in manufacturing.

Rice paper: edible rice paper is made from rice flour and water, formed into translucent sheets that are supple when wet, brittle when dry; used as wrappers in Vietnamese and Thai cooking. Rice paper also refers to a decorative paper known for its textural beauty; it is made from the pulp of a scrub called the rice paper tree, related to the mulberry bush. Rice straw and hulls are also used to make decorative papers.

Rice syrup: a mildly sweet syrup with the consistency of honey, made from rice fermented with enzymes from sprouted barley. Mostly used in the food industry as a coating for snack foods.

Rice vinegar: vinegar made from fermented rice. Japanese rice vinegar is light and mild. Chinese rice vinegar is sharp and sour.

Rice wine: wine made from fermented steamed rice. Sake and mirin (a sweet wine used in cooking) are two Japanese rice wines. China and other rice-growing cultures make a variety of alcoholic beverages, including beer and brandy, as well as wine, from fermented rice.

Risotto: a northern Italian dish prepared by constantly stirring rice while adding small amounts of simmering broth until the consistency is creamy. Italians prefer medium-grain Vialone Nano, Carnaroli, and Arborio rices for risotto because they have a distinctive core, called the pearl, that remains just slightly firm when cooked. Baldo and California medium-grain rices can also be used.

Rosematta: a parboiled rice from the Indian state of Kerala. The grains are large and almost round, about the size of barley, with a reddish bran and an earthy, meaty taste and aroma.

Rough rice: Rice with its rough hull still intact; also called paddy rice.

Sake: a Japanese wine made from carefully selected rice and the purest water. Premium sake is served chilled; lower-grade sake is served warm. In cooking, it is used in marinades and sauces. Today sake is made in the United States in California, Colorado, and Oregon.

Samba: a tiny, almost round, rice grown in southern India and Sri Lanka. The sample I tasted had a unique herbaceous flavor and aroma. Samba can have either sticky or dry starch, depending on its genetic makeup, although high amylose (dry starch) rice is typical of Sri Lanka.

Short-grain rice: refers to rice varieties with almost round grains that are soft and cling together when cooked. Sushi rice is considered a short-grain rice. The term can be confusing, because in Italy and Spain the rices used for risotto and paella are called short-grain although they are technically medium-grain. Also used in soups and puddings.

Socarrat: the caramelized rice clinging to the bottom of the paella pan. The word comes from the Spanish verb *socarrar*, "to toast lightly."

Sticky rice: term used for waxy, sweet, or glutinous rices, but confusing because there are so many different types of rice within this category. Domestically grown sticky rice, which does not hold its shape when cooked, is used as a stabilizer in processed foods. Asian sticky rice is a whole different world of long- and short-grain rices that may be white, black, or even red. Some need to be soaked before cooking; some don't. The sticky rice, also called sweet rice, is opaque white, as opposed to translucent, with a small oval shape. It is 100 percent amylopectin, the waxy starch, which means it is very sticky. It is used in many Asian desserts, which is probably why it is called sweet rice.

Sushi rice: a short-grain rice with smooth glassy grains. When cooked the rice is sticky. Sushi is the preparation of cooked rice seasoned with rice vinegar and sugar (see page 92). The rice is shaped into ovals and topped with raw fish, wrapped in nori, or prepared in a wide variety of preparations.

Rice Yields

1 cup uncooked white rice	= 3 cups cooked
1 cup uncooked brown rice	= 3½ cups cooked
1 cup wild rice	= 3½ to 4 cups cooked

Sweet rice: a rice with round, chalky, opaque grains that become very soft and lose their shape when cooked; it must be soaked before cooking. The cooked rice is pounded into a sticky glutinous mass to make the Japanese confection called *mochi*.

Sweet rice is also used in food production as a binder, especially in frozen products, because it doesn't break down when thawed. Also called waxy or glutinous rice.

Tah-dig: the Persian name for the crusty bottom layer of caramelized rice in pilaf dishes. Considered a delicacy.

Texmati: an aromatic rice with an aroma and texture similar to basmati; it is available as both brown and white rice. Used in pilaf, puddings, and side dishes.

Valencia: a short- to medium-grain Spanish rice of everyday quality, with the ability to absorb 3 cups of liquid for each cup of raw rice. Used in paella.

Waxy rice: *See* glutinous rice, sticky rice, or sweet rice.

Wehani: a long-grain rice with a dark russet bran and a distinctive nutty taste and aroma grown by Lundberg Family Farms in California. Good in salads, fried rice dishes, pilaf, and stuffing.

Wild rice: looks like rice and grows like rice, but has a different botanical classification (*Zinzania aquatica*). It is the only grain native to North America and was an important food to Native Americans living in the regions where it grew. Today, most wild rice is cultivated in man-made paddies in Minnesota, California, and central Canada. When it is cooked, the dark chewy hull expands and the kernel pops, exposing the soft white center. Cooking times will vary from 35 to 55 minutes, or longer, depending on the way the rice is cured. Good in salads, stuffing, and side dishes.

How to Cook Rice

The question I am most frequently asked about cooking rice is, "Do you rinse it?" I usually don't rinse rice, but in many countries, because of tradition and cultural preferences of taste and texture, rice is always rinsed.

The practical reason to rinse rice is to wash off dirt and debris. In less-developed parts of the world, rice is milled in less than sanitary conditions. The result is rice containing pieces of hull and other matter. It is sometimes dried out in the open or stored in open sacks or containers that collect dust, leaves, and insects.

Rinsing rice also washes off excess starch and any polishing compounds that may have been used. Sometimes during milling a layer of ground rice is left clinging to the grains, causing the rice to be overly starchy. In Asian countries, rice is sometimes coated with cornstarch to rid the grains of any oily bran that might spoil. At one time rice was coated with talc, but this practice is now outlawed in the United States.

Rinsing rice also leaches out some of its aroma: some cultures don't like the perfume of aromatic rice, preferring to rinse and soak it to diminish this aspect.

The philosophical reasons for rinsing rice are difficult to define. In Asian homes, rinsing the rice is a ritual that signals the beginning of the preparation of the day's sustenance. Traditionally the rice is stirred only in one direction as it is rinsed, presumably to appease the symbolic rice mother. (It also keeps the grains from breaking.) A Japanese friend says his parents believe that rinsing and soaking the rice releases its life force and gives the eater a more peaceful soul. In some Asian households, the eldest member of the family ritualistically rinses and cooks the rice every morning.

To rinse rice, place it in a large bowl and cover with water. Slowly stir the rice so any debris will float to the top. Pour off the water. More water can be added to help release the starch from the rice; repeat two or three times, depending on how much starch you want to release. Pour the rice into a sieve to drain.

Sometimes rice should be soaked. The soaking time can be as little as twenty minutes or as long as one hour or more. Soaked rice will absorb some of the water and will cook more quickly and in less water. When basmati is soaked, the cooked grains are fluffier and less starchy. When medium- or short-grain rice is soaked, the cooked rice is soft without being too sticky. Because excess starch will leach out of the rice during soaking, the cooked rice will have a clean, fresh, less starchy taste. Generally 1 cup dry rice requires 1½ to 2 cups of water to cook, while rice that has been soaked will need only 1 to 1½ cups water.

I never rinse American-grown rice, because it is clean. I also prefer the taste, aroma, and texture of rice that has not been rinsed or soaked. Furthermore, 99 percent of domestically grown rice is enriched; washing it will rinse off the vitamins and minerals.

The Absorption Method for Perfectly Cooked Rice

- Use a heavy wide shallow saucepan, deep skillet, or sauté pan with a tight-fitting lid.
- Heat the water to a boil over high heat. For 3 cups firm cooked white rice, use 1 cup raw rice and 1½ to 2 cups water; for soft-cooked white rice, use 1 cup raw rice and 2 to 2¼ cups water. For 3½ to 4 cups firm cooked brown rice, use

1 cup raw rice and 2¼ cups water; for soft cooked brown rice, use 1 cup raw rice and 2½ to 2¾ cups water.

- Add the rice and salt, if using, to the boiling water; stir once to distribute evenly. Return to a boil; stir again.

- Cover and reduce the heat to low. Cook the white rice for about 15 minutes and the brown rice for 45 to 55 minutes, or until all the liquid is absorbed.

- When the rice is cooked, carefully lift the lid, so the condensation on the underside of the cover does not drip into the rice. Look at, do not touch, the rice. Little steam holes all over the surface indicate that the water has been absorbed. If the water has not been absorbed, continue to cook over low heat, covered, for 2 to 3 more minutes.

- When the rice is cooked, let it stand, covered, for 5 to 10 minutes before serving.

- Fluff the rice with a large fork, never a spoon. Turn into a serving dish.

- When cooking medium-grain brown rice for a salad, turn the cooked rice into a strainer and rinse with cold water to remove excess starch and stickiness. Drain well.

The right pan A narrow saucepan does not provide enough space for the rice to cook evenly or allow for enough surface evaporation. My favorite rice pan is a large (10½- by 2-inch-deep) heavy skillet with a tight-fitting lid.

Why not stir the rice while it is cooking? Stirring the rice releases the starch and makes the rice stick together. Exceptions are risotto and rice pudding, because you want the starch to combine with the liquid and create a creamy consistency.

Why shouldn't the lid be lifted during cooking? There is a delicate balance between the steam heat in the saucepan and its ability to cook the rice. If you lift the lid, you allow the steam, along with the heat, to escape. Also, if there is condensation on the lid, it is likely to drip into the pan and you run the risk of having wet, overcooked rice. (In Indian and Persian cooking, a rice cloth sits under the lid to collect the condensation so the rice won't become too wet.) If not looking makes you anxious, buy a pan with a glass lid.

Rice Troubleshooting

As with human beings, not all rices are the same. Besides being long or short, sticky or dry, soft, chewy, black, brown, red, and white, they may have other characteristics that are not so obvious. Freshly harvested rice (prized in Japan) has a higher moisture level and requires much less water for cooking than older rice. Aged rice (favored in India) has a much lower moisture level, requiring more water. Your favorite brand of rice, which *always* cooks just the way you like it, may suddenly need a few more minutes, or a few tablespoons more water—or a few tablespoons less water. What's a cook to do?

As you cook more rice and experiment with different types of rice and various cooking methods you will develop a certain amount of rice intuition. The ratios of water to rice on pages 17–18 are only a guide. There will always be variables among different brands, especially in rice bought in bulk. But rice is pretty hard to ruin—unless you burn it!

Here are some problems and quick fixes:

- You uncover the pan and the water has been absorbed but the rice is undercooked.

  Reason: You didn't add enough water; the heat was too high; and/or the rice was drier than usual.

  Quick Fix: Sprinkle 1 to 2 tablespoons water on the surface, cover, and cook for 2 or 3 minutes more. Let stand off the heat, covered, for 5 to 10 minutes.

- You uncover the pan and the rice hasn't absorbed the water but is tender.

  Reason: You added too much water; the heat was too low; or the rice was moister than usual.

  Quick fix: Pour off the excess water and put the pan back on the flame, uncovered, for a minute or two to cook off the excess moisture. Then cover and let stand off the heat for 5 minutes.

Uncovered/Covered Method

Standing in the airport in a small town in Texas one hot summer day, I struck up a conversation with a fellow passenger. The conversation, not surprisingly, turned to rice. The gentleman from Texas cooks his rice this way: Spread the rice in the bottom of a wide pot; add just enough water to cover the rice by ½ inch, or the thickness of your hand; heat to a gentle boil; stir once; and cook, uncovered, for 5 minutes, or just until almost all the water has been absorbed. Then cover the rice and cook, without lifting the lid, for 15 to 20 minutes, until the rice is tender and fluffy. Subsequently, I learned that this technique is popular in the American South, throughout South and Central America, and in parts of Europe.

Boiling Water Method

Cooking rice uncovered in plenty of boiling water (like cooking pasta) until it reaches the consistency desired and then draining it in a strainer is an especially popular method among chefs. This method provides a certain amount of control, as you can easily dip into the pot to check the progress of the rice as it boils. But because all the enrichment is washed off the rice (if you are using domestically grown rice), it is wasteful. This method also leaches flavor from the rice, which goes down the drain with the water and the enrichment unless you are smart enough to catch it in a pot for soup or some other use. I do use this method when I precook rice for pudding and in Persian-style pilaf recipes. I also like it for medium-grain brown rice, which tends to be very sticky when cooked using the covered method.

Thai-Style Steamed Rice

This is an unusual method for steaming rice taught to me by Kasma Loha unchit, a Thai cookbook author, teacher, and friend. Like Kasma, I have only used it for Thai jasmine rice. Jasmine rice is sticky; steaming fluffs it up and also helps it to retain its natural aroma. Set a kettle of water on to boil. Select a large wide pot and a heat-proof bowl that fits inside. Set a small rack in the bottom of the pot. Place the rice (2 cups, or whatever amount you will need) in the bowl, add cold tap water, and swish it around; drain. Repeat once or twice more. Return the drained rice to the bowl. Add 2 or 3 inches boiling water to the pot. Place the bowl of rice on the rack and add boiling water to the rice to cover it by ¾ inch. Cover the pot and steam the rice over medium heat—you should hear the water boiling against the bowl and there should be steam pushing at the lid—for 20 to 25 minutes.

Microwave Method

Although it doesn't save time, rice can be cooked in the microwave. Combine 1 cup long-grain white rice with 1¾ to 2 cups water (use 1½ to 1¾ cups water for short- or medium-grain rice) and 1 teaspoon salt in a microwave-safe dish; stir once to distribute rice evenly. Cover and microwave on high power for 5 minutes, then on medium (50%) power for 15 minutes. Let stand for 5 minutes, covered, before serving. For long-grain or short-grain brown rice, use 2¼ cups water and ½ teaspoon salt; microwave on high power for 5 minutes, then on medium (50%) power for 30 minutes.

Baked Rice

Baking rice is a foolproof method that saves you from worrying about whether the heat under the pan is too high or too low. Because it is in the oven and out of sight, you won't be tempted to lift the lid and stir it while it is cooking. It is also energy-efficient if you are cooking the rest of the meal in the oven at the same time.

To make plain oven-baked white or brown rice, preheat the oven to 350°F. Combine 1 cup long-grain white rice and 1¾ to 2 cups boiling water or broth; 1 cup medium-grain white rice with 1½ cups boiling liquid; or 1 cup brown rice with 2¼ cups boiling liquid. Add salt to taste; stir once to distribute the rice evenly. Bake covered, for 25 to 30 minutes for white rice, or 1 hour for brown rice. Makes 4 servings.

Simple Rice-Cooker Pilaf

Makes 4 servings

This recipe works in rice cookers that have a liner with a nonstick surface.

2 tablespoons extra virgin olive oil
¼ cup chopped onion
1 cup long-grain white rice

½ teaspoon minced garlic
1¾ cups reduced-sodium chicken broth
1 tablespoon finely chopped walnuts

1. Preheat the rice cooker. Add the olive oil and onion to the rice cooker liner. Heat until sizzling; cook, stirring, until the onion is tender. Stir in the rice and garlic. Add the chicken broth; stir once to distribute the rice evenly.

2. Cover and start cooking. The bell will alert you when the liquid is absorbed. Sprinkle with the walnuts and serve.

Soups

I have vivid childhood memories of blowing on the steaming surface of a bowl of my mother's chicken and rice soup, mesmerized by the swollen rice grains swirling in the hot broth.

Adding small amounts of cooked rice to soup is the perfect way to use leftover cooked rice, especially for light broth-based soups like my mom's chicken soup. It adds creaminess without fat and makes a thin soup more nutritious. But rice can also be just one of many ingredients in hearty main dish soups like the recipes for Peruvian chowder and Shiitake, Beef, and Red Rice Soup.

Mom usually added uncooked rice to her homemade chicken broth. This might seem like the slow way to make a soup heartier, but her technique has two advantages. As the rice cooks and slowly swells it absorbs the fragrant broth, adding flavor while the rice releases its starch, giving the soup body and substance.

Either way, Mom's example taught me to make soups rich in flavor, and in memories.

Peruvian-Style Shrimp and Rice Chowder

Makes 4 to 6 main-dish servings

After a day hiking around Machu Picchu, the famed site of a mysterious Inca settlement, my companions and I enjoyed steaming bowls of a shrimp and rice chowder similar to this one. For strong-flavored shrimp stock, buy large shrimp with the heads on. Often there is coral under the heads that will add a rosy color and extra flavor to the stock. The recipe has several steps, but it can be prepared in stages and then put together just before serving.

Shrimp Stock

2 tablespoons extra virgin olive oil

¼ cup minced shallot

¼ cup minced celery

¼ cup minced carrot

1½ pounds shrimp, preferably with heads on, shells (and heads) removed and reserved

1 cup dry white wine

¼ cup extra virgin olive oil

2 garlic cloves, minced

1 tablespoon finely chopped seeded jalapeño

2 teaspoons ground cumin

One 14½-ounce can diced tomatoes, with their juices

8 ounces boneless and skinless cod, halibut, sea bass, or other firm white fish fillet, about ½ inch thick

1 teaspoon dried oregano

Kosher salt and freshly ground black pepper

½ cup fine dry bread crumbs

1 medium Yukon Gold potato, peeled and diced (about 1 cup)

¾ cup uncooked Arborio, Baldo, or other medium-grain white rice

½ cup frozen petite green peas, thawed

1 ear corn, husked, ends trimmed, cob cut into ½-inch-thick disks

4 to 6 large eggs (1 per serving)

2 ounces *queso fresco*, or other lightly salted white cheese such as ricotta salata, or a very mild feta (see Notes), cut into thin slivers

½ cup chopped cilantro

½ cup heavy cream, at room temperature (see Notes)

1. ***For the shrimp stock:*** Heat the olive oil in a large wide saucepan. Add the shallot, celery, and carrot. Cook, stirring, over medium-low heat until tender, about 5 minutes. Add the shrimp shells and their heads, if you have them. Cook, stirring, over medium-high heat until the shells turn dark red, about 5 minutes. Add the wine and boil until reduced by half, about 5 minutes. Add 6 cups water; heat

to a boil. Reduce the heat and simmer, uncovered, for about 15 minutes. Let cool to room temperature.

2. Working in batches, puree the shells with the liquid in a blender. Set a strainer over a large bowl and strain the pureed stock; discard the solids. There should be about 5 cups stock. Refrigerate until ready to use. (The stock can be prepared up to 1 day ahead.)

3. In a large wide saucepan, combine 2 tablespoons of the olive oil, the garlic, and jalapeño. Heat over medium heat, stirring, until sizzling. Add the cumin; cook for 1 minute. Add the shrimp stock and tomatoes. Heat to a boil. Reduce the heat and simmer, covered, for 20 minutes. (The recipe can be prepared to this point up to 1 day ahead.)

4. *For the fish:* Sprinkle the fish on both sides with the oregano and salt and pepper to taste; rub into the fish. Coat with the bread crumbs, pressing them on with fingertips; shake off excess. Heat the remaining 2 tablespoons olive oil in a large nonstick skillet. Add the fish and cook, turning once, until lightly browned and just cooked through, about 8 minutes. Set aside, covered with foil, until ready to serve.

5. Reheat the tomato and shrimp stock mixture to a boil. Add salt to taste, about 2 teaspoons. Add the potatoes and rice; cover and cook over low heat until tender, about 15 minutes. Add the shrimp, peas, and corn. Cover and cook for 5 minutes.

6. While the rice and potatoes are cooking, warm the soup bowls in an oven set at the lowest temperature. Poach the eggs: Half-fill a large deep skillet or sauté pan with water. Heat to a boil; reduce to a simmer. One at a time, break the eggs into a small cup and slip into the simmering water. Cook the eggs until the whites are set, about 5 minutes. Gently lift from the water with a slotted spoon and drain on a plate lined with a double thickness of paper towels.

7. Divide the fish into portions and place a portion in each bowl. Place the poached eggs on top of the fish. Add the cheese and the cilantro, dividing them evenly.

8. Ladle some of the hot soup into a small bowl and stir in the heavy cream, then add to the soup. Reheat for 1 minute; do not boil. Add a generous grinding of black pepper. Ladle the hot soup into the bowls, dividing the ingredients evenly. Serve piping hot.

NOTES: Feta cheese of any kind will be too salty here. To tame the saltiness, drain off the brine and rinse the cheese well under cold running water. Place the cheese in a clean container, cover with milk or water, and marinate for at least 1 day before using; drain well.

In Peru, canned evaporated milk is used in place of heavy cream. If watching calories, do not hesitate to use evaporated skim milk.

Golden Yellow Spring Vegetable Soup

Makes about 10 cups; 4 to 6 servings

Saffron adds a sophisticated flavor and golden hue to this otherwise simple soup. It is best to make the soup and serve at once because the vegetables will lose their fresh taste if reheated.

10 cups reduced-sodium chicken broth
¼ teaspoon crushed saffron threads
½ cup uncooked medium- or long-grain white rice
2 cups packed torn (1-inch pieces) escarole
8 ounces slender green beans, trimmed and cut into ¼-inch pieces (about 2 cups)
1 cup diced (¼-inch) carrots

1 cup diced zucchini or yellow squash (about 1 small)
½ cup frozen petite peas, thawed, or fresh, if available
½ cup diced, seeded, peeled, fresh or canned tomato
Kosher salt and freshly ground black pepper
Freshly grated Parmigiano-Reggiano

1. Heat the chicken broth to a simmer in a large saucepan.

2. Meanwhile, toast the saffron in a small saucepan or skillet, about 20 seconds. Add ½ cup of the hot broth to the saffron; cover and let steep for 10 minutes.

3. Reheat the broth to boiling; add the steeped saffron and the rice. Cook, uncovered, until the rice is almost tender, about 10 minutes.

4. Stir in the escarole, green beans, and carrots; cook, stirring, until the rice and vegetables are very tender, about 8 minutes. Add the zucchini, peas, and tomato. Simmer, uncovered, until the zucchini is tender, about 5 minutes. Season to taste with salt and pepper.

5. Ladle into bowls and sprinkle generously with grated Parmesan.

Broccoli and Rice Soup with Red Pepper Oil and Golden Garlic

**Makes about
8 cups;
4 servings**

This robust, easy-to-make soup is the perfect quick supper. I make it with Arborio or Baldo rice, but any white rice will do. Use broccoli or broccoli rabe.

8 cups reduced-sodium chicken broth

1 medium carrot, thinly sliced

½ cup uncooked medium- or long-grain white rice

4 cups coarsely chopped broccoli florets and tender
stems or broccoli rabe tops and ½-inch lengths
peeled broccoli rabe stems

Kosher salt and freshly ground black pepper

Red Pepper Oil

2 tablespoons extra virgin olive oil

¼ cup thin slivers (approximately ⅛ × ½-inch) red
bell pepper

¼ teaspoon red pepper flakes

1 tablespoon thinly slivered garlic

1. Heat the broth to a boil in a large saucepan; add the carrot and rice. Cook, covered, over low heat for 10 minutes. Add the broccoli; cook, uncovered, until the broccoli is tender and the soup has thickened, about 8 minutes more. Season to taste with salt and pepper.

2. *Meanwhile, for the red pepper oil:* Heat the oil in a small skillet. Add the red bell pepper slivers and red pepper flakes; cook for 3 minutes, or until the bell pepper begins to brown. Remove from the heat and, with a slotted spoon, transfer the pepper to the soup.

3. Add the garlic to the hot oil and cook over very low heat just until the garlic is golden, about 1 minute; immediately stir the hot oil and garlic mixture into the simmering soup.

4. Ladle into bowls and serve.

Shiitake, Beef, and Red Rice Soup with Spinach

Makes 6 cups; about 4 servings

Soy sauce, mushrooms, and red rice, especially the variety imported from Bhutan, all have a meaty taste. In this hearty soup, they are complemented by the richness of the beef broth and the herbal quality of the spinach.

2 tablespoons peanut oil

8 ounces shiitakes, stems discarded, caps wiped clean and cut into ⅛-inch slices

½ cup chopped white part of scallions, plus ¼ cup thinly sliced scallion greens for garnish

1 teaspoon minced garlic

4 cups reduced-sodium beef broth

1 cup cooked red rice or short-grain brown rice

8 ounces spinach, washed and trimmed (about 2 cups lightly packed)

1 tablespoon soy sauce or tamari

1 teaspoon toasted sesame oil

2½ teaspoons grated fresh ginger

Kosher salt, optional

2 teaspoons brown sesame seeds (see Note)

1. Heat the oil in a large heavy saucepan. Add the mushrooms; cook over medium heat, stirring, until tender, 3 to 5 minutes. Add the scallion whites; cook, stirring, over low heat for 5 minutes. Add the garlic; cook for 1 minute.

2. Add the broth and the rice. Bring to a simmer; simmer, covered, over medium heat for 15 minutes. Stir in the spinach. Add the soy sauce, sesame oil, and ginger. Taste and add salt if needed.

3. Ladle into four bowls. Sprinkle each with ½ teaspoon sesame seeds and 1 tablespoon scallion greens.

NOTE: Sesame seeds come in white, brown, black, and red; the white are the most common. If they are the only ones you can find, toast them in a small heavy skillet over low heat, shaking the pan constantly, until they begin to turn golden, then remove from the heat and the pan. They will color very quickly, within 2 or 3 minutes; do not leave them unattended. I prefer the nutty taste of brown sesame seeds. They are often sold in jars (labeled as roasted sesame seeds) wherever Asian products are sold. To preserve freshness, store sesame seeds in the refrigerator or freezer.

Roasted Tomato, Mushroom, and Rice Soup

**Makes
8 cups;
6 servings**

A rather elegant rendition of a basic tomato soup; serve it as a first course or as a light supper with Italian whole wheat bread that has been drizzled with extra virgin olive oil. Almost any mushroom can be used in this soup: white, cremini, or shiitake. I prefer cremini for their deep, earthy flavor. Roast plum tomatoes, no matter what time of the year, to concentrate their flavor.

2 pounds ripe plum tomatoes, halved lengthwise

6 tablespoons extra virgin olive oil

Kosher salt and freshly ground black pepper

2 garlic cloves, minced

½ cup finely chopped onion

1 pound cremini mushrooms, trimmed and chopped (about 4 cups)

2 tablespoons chopped Italian parsley

2 tablespoons thyme leaves

4 cups reduced-sodium vegetable, beef, or chicken broth

1½ cups cooked medium- or long-grain white or Arborio rice

2 tablespoons heavy cream, sour cream, or low-fat or whole milk yogurt

1. Preheat the oven to 400°F.

2. Arrange the tomatoes in a single layer on a baking sheet. Drizzle with ¼ cup of the olive oil. Sprinkle with salt and pepper. Roast for 30 minutes, stirring once.

3. Remove from the oven and sprinkle the tomatoes with the garlic, making sure it is on the tomatoes so it won't brown. Roast for 15 to 20 minutes more, until the tomatoes have given up a lot of their juices and some of their skins are blackened. Set aside to cool.

4. Meanwhile, heat the remaining 2 tablespoons oil in a large skillet. Add the onion and cook, stirring, over low heat, until golden, about 5 minutes. Add the mushrooms and cook, stirring, over medium heat until golden, about 10 minutes. Meanwhile, finely chop the parsley and 1 tablespoon of the thyme together. Add the chopped herbs to the mushrooms. Sprinkle with salt and pepper; remove from the heat.

5. Spoon out about 1 cup of the mushrooms and reserve. Combine the remaining mushrooms and the roasted tomatoes. Puree the tomatoes and mushrooms in a blender in batches, using some of the broth to help liquefy the mixture; it should be a smooth puree.

6. Transfer the pureed tomatoes and mushrooms to a large saucepan. Add the remaining broth and heat to a simmer. Cover and cook over low heat for 5 minutes. Stir in the cooked rice and the reserved mushrooms; heat through.

7. Ladle the soup into bowls and garnish the top of each with a swirl of heavy cream or stirred sour cream or yogurt. Sprinkle with the remaining 1 tablespoon thyme leaves, dividing evenly.

Curried Tomato Soup with Ginger and Black Rice

Makes 8 cups; 6 servings

Any type of rice is good stirred into this soup, but the presentation is most dramatic when black rice is spooned into the red broth. Look for black rice in upscale supermarkets or Asian markets. Or, try any of the aromatic blends like Wehani, a rice with a rust-brown bran and a texture similar to wild rice.

Cilantro Cream
1 cup low-fat or whole milk yogurt
½ cup chopped cilantro leaves and tender stems

2 tablespoons vegetable oil
1 cup thin lengthwise slices sweet yellow onion
1 garlic clove, minced
1 tablespoon Madras-style curry powder
2 teaspoons ground cumin

Two 28-ounce cans plum tomatoes, with their juices
1 teaspoon grated fresh ginger
8 ounces spinach, washed and trimmed (about 2 cups packed)
1 cup cooked long-grain black rice or Wehani or wild rice
1 cup reduced-sodium chicken or vegetable broth, or as needed
Kosher salt and freshly ground black pepper

1. ***For the cilantro cream:*** Puree the yogurt and cilantro together in a blender. Refrigerate until ready to use. (It will thicken upon standing.)

2. Heat the oil in a large saucepan. Add the onion and cook, stirring, over low heat until golden, about 10 minutes. Add the garlic; cook for 1 minute. Stir in the curry powder and cumin; cook, stirring, for 1 minute.

3. Meanwhile, press the tomatoes through a sieve or food mill; discard the solids. Add the pureed tomatoes and ginger to the onion; cover, and cook over low heat for 20 minutes.

4. Stir in the spinach. Heat until the spinach is wilted, about 5 minutes. Stir in the rice; heat through. Add the broth as needed to thin the soup. Season to taste with salt and pepper.

5. Ladle the soup into bowls. Swirl a spoonful of the cilantro cream into each bowl, dividing evenly.

Black Bean, Chipotle Chile, and Rice Soup with Cilantro Cream

Makes about 9 cups; 4 to 6 servings

The secret ingredient in this soup, inspired by a remarkable black bean salad I ate many years ago at the Lark Creek Inn in Larkspur, California, is Guinness stout. The stout, says chef/proprietor Bradley Ogden, adds a distinctive depth of flavor. Plan ahead; the beans need to be soaked overnight, and the soup only improves upon standing.

1 pound small black beans, sorted and rinsed
2 tablespoons vegetable oil
2 cups chopped onions
1 cup chopped red bell peppers
½ cup chopped celery
½ cup chopped carrot
2 tablespoons minced seeded jalapeños
2 garlic cloves, minced
2 teaspoons ground cumin
½ teaspoon red pepper flakes
½ teaspoon dried thyme
One 12-ounce bottle Guinness stout
1 cup chopped, drained, peeled, canned, or fresh
   tomatoes

1 bay leaf
2 cups cooked long-grain white rice
1 tablespoon pureed chipotle chile in adobo sauce
   (see box on page 230)
1 to 2 teaspoons salt

Cilantro Cream
1 cup sour cream or ½ cup each sour cream and
   low-fat or whole milk yogurt
1 cup loosely packed cilantro leaves and minced
   stems
1 jalapeño, seeded and chopped

1. Place the beans in a large bowl and cover generously with water. Soak overnight; drain. (If the weather is warm, refrigerate the beans while soaking.)

2. Heat the oil in a large wide saucepan over medium-low heat. Add the onions, bell peppers, celery, and carrot; cook, stirring, until the vegetables are golden, about 15 minutes. Add the jalapeños and garlic; cook for 1 minute. Add the cumin, red pepper flakes, and thyme; cook for 1 minute. Add the stout, tomatoes, and bay leaf; heat to a boil. Reduce the heat and simmer, uncovered, for 10 minutes.

3. Add the beans and 8 cups water to the saucepan; cook, uncovered, at a gentle simmer until the beans are very tender and the soup is thickened, 2½ to 3 hours; add more water if needed to keep beans moist.

4. With a slotted spoon, transfer 1 cup of the beans to a food processor; add about ½ cup bean liquid. Process until smooth; return to the saucepan. Add the rice, pureed chipotle chile, and salt. Cook, covered, for 10 minutes.

5. *Meanwhile, for the cilantro cream:* Puree the sour cream, cilantro, and jalapeño in a food processor. Transfer to a bowl; cover and refrigerate until ready to serve. (The cream will thicken upon standing.)

6. To serve, ladle the soup into bowls and add 1 tablespoon of the cilantro cream to each bowl. Serve the remaining cilantro cream on the side to add to taste.

Roasted Eggplant and Lentil Soup with Brown Rice and Roasted Red Pepper Puree

Makes about 8 cups; 4 servings

The roasted eggplant and vegetables make a delicious side dish served solo, or cut into chunks and spooned on top of hot cooked rice.

1 medium eggplant (about 1 pound), trimmed and quartered lengthwise

1 large sweet yellow onion, quartered

1 large tomato, quartered

1 jalapeño or other hot chile, halved, stem and seeds removed

½ large green bell pepper, stem and seeds removed

½ large red bell pepper, stem and seeds removed

3 garlic cloves, bruised with the side of a knife

3 tablespoons extra virgin olive oil

Kosher salt and freshly ground black pepper

6 cups reduced-sodium chicken broth (or half broth and half water), plus up to 1 cup more if needed

1 cup lentils, sorted and rinsed

½ cup uncooked long-grain brown rice

2 teaspoons ground cumin

1 bay leaf

Red Pepper Puree

3 tablespoons extra virgin olive oil

¼ cup chopped onion

½ teaspoon chopped garlic

One 7-ounce jar roasted red peppers, drained and rinsed

Freshly ground black pepper

1½ to 2 cups half-and-half, at room temperature

1. Preheat the oven to 400°F.

2. Place the eggplant, onion, tomato, jalapeño, bell peppers, and garlic in a single layer in a large roasting pan; drizzle with the oil and sprinkle with salt and pepper. Roast the vegetables, turning every 15 minutes until tender and the edges are browned, about 45 minutes. Let cool.

3. Carefully scoop the eggplant from the skin; discard the skin. Cut all the vegetables into 1-inch pieces and combine in a bowl. Add about 1 cup of the broth to the roasting pan; set over low heat and scrape any charred bits from the bottom and sides of the pan. Add this deglazing liquid to the roasted vegetables.

4. Set a food mill over a large saucepan and puree the vegetables with the liquid; discard the solids. Stir the remaining broth, the lentils, brown rice, cumin, and bay leaf into the puree. Cook uncovered, over medium-low heat, stirring occasionally, until the lentils and rice are very tender, about 1½ hours. Add up to 1 cup additional liquid if the soup thickens too much, but keep in mind that the soup will be thinned with the half-and-half.

5. *Meanwhile, for the red pepper puree:* Heat 1 tablespoon of the oil in a small skillet; add the onion and cook, stirring, until tender. Stir in the garlic; cook for 30 seconds. Process the red pepper, the onion mixture, and the remaining 2 tablespoons olive oil in a food processor to a smooth puree. Transfer to a small bowl; add pepper to taste.

6. Remove the bay leaf from the soup. Stir in the half-and-half until blended. Add salt and pepper to taste. Heat gently; do not boil.

7. Ladle the soup into bowls. Stir a spoonful of the red pepper puree into each bowl.

Chicken and Rice Soup

**Makes
10 cups;
4 to 6
servings**

My mom's chicken soup was a multi-pot affair: one pot for simmering the chicken and making the broth, another for cooking the rice in some of the broth, and another for the greens. Mom made the soup with or without escarole or romaine lettuce. She often served greens in soup or as a softly cooked vegetable side dish seasoned with olive oil, garlic, and red pepper flakes.

1 chicken (about 3 pounds), thoroughly rinsed and
  excess fat removed
1 garlic clove, bruised with the side of a knife
1 bay leaf
1 large carrot
½ cup uncooked medium- or long-grain white or
  Arborio rice
Kosher salt

1 small head escarole or romaine lettuce (about
  1 pound), trimmed, rinsed, and leaves torn into
  bite-sized pieces
½ cup drained, chopped, peeled, seeded fresh or
  canned tomato, optional
Freshly ground black pepper
Freshly grated Parmigiano-Reggiano, optional

1. Place the chicken in a medium pot and add 3 quarts water, the garlic, and bay leaf. Heat to a gentle simmer over medium heat; skim the foam from the top. Reduce the heat to medium-low and cook, uncovered, without boiling, for 1 hour.

2. Add the carrot; cook for 30 minutes more, or until the chicken is falling from the bones. Remove the chicken and carrot; set aside to cool. Discard the garlic and bay leaf.

3. Ladle 2 cups of the broth into a medium saucepan; heat to a boil. Stir in the rice and ½ teaspoon salt; cover and cook over low heat for 20 minutes, or until the rice is very tender. Remove from the heat and set aside, still covered.

4. While the rice is cooking, remove and discard the skin and bones from the chicken. Tear the chicken into thin shreds; set aside. Cut the carrot into thin slices or small dice.

5. Season the remaining broth with salt to taste; heat to a boil. Add the escarole; cover and cook until tender, about 15 minutes. (Or wilt the greens in a separate

pot, covered, over low heat, with just the water left clinging to the leaves; add to the simmering broth.)

6. Just before serving, add the chicken, carrot, and cooked rice to the broth; add the tomato, if using. Add pepper to taste. Heat until very hot.

7. To serve, ladle the soup into bowls, distributing the ingredients evenly. Sprinkle generously with Parmesan cheese, if desired.

Rice Noodles, Bok Choy, and Shrimp in Ginger-Chicken Broth

Makes 10 cups; 4 to 5 servings

This is my version of *pho* (pronounced "far"), the hearty Vietnamese rice-noodle soup that is served in enormous bowls with a fork to eat the noodles and vegetables and a dipping spoon for the rich broth.

3 ounces dried rice vermicelli (rice sticks; see Note)

8 cups reduced-sodium chicken broth

2 tablespoons minced fresh ginger

1 scallion, trimmed

1 garlic clove, bruised with the side of a knife

3 ounces shiitakes, stems discarded, caps wiped clean and cut into ⅛-inch slices

4 ounces baby bok choy (about 4), outside leaves and stems trimmed, cut across into ½-inch strips (2 to 3 cups)

4 ounces frozen small cooked shelled shrimp, thawed and blotted dry (about 1½ cups)

1 tablespoon soy sauce or tamari

1 tablespoon toasted sesame oil

1 tablespoon unseasoned Japanese rice vinegar

½ teaspoon chile oil, or to taste, or a pinch of red pepper flakes

Kosher salt

Garnishes (choose at least 3)

1 cup fresh bean sprouts, rinsed and crisped in ice water

½ cup thin diagonal slices scallion greens

Mint leaves

Cilantro leaves

Thai basil leaves

1. Place the rice vermicelli in a large bowl and cover with room-temperature tap water. Let stand for about 1 hour, checking for tenderness occasionally. When the noodles are soft but still slightly firm to the bite, drain. (They should yield about 3 cups.)

2. ***Meanwhile, for the broth:*** Combine the broth, ginger, scallion, and garlic in a large saucepan; heat to a boil. Cover and cook over low heat for 15 minutes. Set a strainer over a large bowl and strain the broth. Discard the solids.

3. Pour the seasoned broth back into the saucepan. Add the shiitakes; cover and simmer for 10 minutes.

4. Stir the bok choy, shrimp, and drained noodles into the simmering broth. Cover and cook for 5 minutes. Add the soy sauce, sesame oil, rice vinegar, and chile oil. Season to taste with salt.

5. Ladle the soup into deep soup bowls, distributing the ingredients evenly. Sprinkle with the garnishes.

NOTE: Rice vermicelli, also called rice sticks, are thin (about $\frac{1}{16}$ inch), brittle strands often folded into loose wads. The packages are large (often about 14 ounces) and the vermicelli are tough and hard to break apart. I use heavy-duty poultry shears to cut them into the amount needed. When soaked, they soften, unravel, and expand. Soak them in room-temperature tap water; some package directions say to soak them in boiling water, but I find that can make them gummy. They take about 1 hour to soften enough to be pliable and just slightly firm to the bite. They will continue to soften in the simmering soup.

Chinese Rice Soup with Egg Threads

**Makes 8 cups;
4 to 6 servings**

This pretty, flavorful soup has traveled a long way from its original inspiration. It has a thick, almost porridge-like consistency typical of the Chinese soup called *congee* or *jook*. Congee is traditionally served as a breakfast dish, but this soup is particularly soothing if you are feeling tired or under the weather.

1 slice (about ¼-inch-thick) fresh ginger
¼ cup uncooked long-, medium-, or short-grain (sushi) white rice
¼ cup chopped white part of scallions, plus 1 tablespoon slivered scallion greens
Kosher salt
8 ounces boneless, skinless chicken breast, trimmed and cut crosswise into ¼-inch slices

1 teaspoon minced seeded jalapeño or other hot chile
1 large egg
1 teaspoon toasted sesame oil
½ cup packed, thinly sliced spinach leaves, optional
1 tablespoon finely chopped red bell pepper, optional
½ to 1 cup reduced-sodium chicken broth or water, if needed

1. In a large saucepan, heat to a boil 6 cups water, the ginger, rice, scallion whites, and 1 teaspoon salt; stir well. Cover and cook over low heat, stirring occasionally, for 45 minutes, or until the rice is swollen and the soup is very thick.

2. Stir the chicken and jalapeño into the soup. Cover and cook over low heat for 15 minutes; do not boil.

3. Whisk the egg and sesame oil in a small bowl. Heat the soup to a rolling boil. Gently stir in the egg in a slow, steady stream; the egg will cook into short threads.

4. Stir in the spinach and red pepper, if using; cover and cook over very low heat for 2 minutes. Add broth if needed to thin the soup. Season to taste with more salt. Ladle into bowls and garnish with the scallion greens before serving.

Wild Rice, Acorn Squash, and Mushroom Soup

Makes about 10 cups; 6 to 8 servings

The colors of the ingredients in this soup—orange acorn squash, red tomatoes, and brown mushrooms—remind me of autumn leaves. A thick, hearty soup, it is ideal for cool fall days. Spread the preparation out over a couple of days. Make the beef broth one day. Cook the wild rice the next and finish the soup. Cooling and reheating the soup intensifies the flavors and adds even more body. Served with a loaf of crusty whole-grain bread, this is a meal in itself.

3 tablespoons extra virgin olive oil

About 1½ pounds (1 or 2 pieces) meaty beef shin, cut about 1 inch thick

½ onion, skin left on

2 garlic cloves, 1 bruised with the side of a knife, 1 minced

1 carrot, peeled

1 bay leaf

Kosher salt

½ cup uncooked wild rice, rinsed in warm water and drained

½ cup diced onion

8 ounces small white button or cremini mushrooms, trimmed and quartered or cut into ½-inch pieces (about 2½ cups)

¼ cup chopped Italian parsley, plus more for garnish

Freshly ground black pepper

2 cups peeled, cubed (about ½ inch) acorn squash (about 1 pound)

1 cup chopped, seeded, peeled, fresh or canned tomatoes

1 tablespoon tomato paste (see Note)

1. Heat 1 tablespoon of the olive oil in a large heavy saucepan. Add the beef, onion, and bruised garlic; brown over medium-low heat, turning once. Add 3 quarts water, the carrot, and bay leaf. Cook over low heat (for a clear broth, do not allow to boil) until the broth is reduced to about 8 cups and the meat is falling off the bone, 2½ to 3 hours.

2. Lift the shin from the broth and set aside to cool. Strain the broth; discard the solids. If the broth doesn't equal 8 cups, add water.

3. Pull the meat from the bone and shred or chop fine; discard the gristle, fat, and bone(s). Push the marrow from the center of the bone, dice, and set aside with

the meat. Carefully blot any fat from the surface of the broth with a double thickness of paper towels. Reserve the meat and marrow separately. (Or, if making this soup over 2 days, pour the broth into a bowl; place the meat and marrow in a separate bowl. Cover and refrigerate. The next day, remove the solid fat from surface of the chilled broth.)

4. In a large saucepan, heat the broth to a boil; season to taste with salt. Stir in the wild rice; cover and cook until the grains are beginning to burst and are tender to the bite, 45 to 55 minutes.

5. Meanwhile, heat the remaining 2 tablespoons olive oil in a large skillet. Add the onion, cook, stirring, until golden, about 5 minutes. Add the mushrooms; cook, stirring, until lightly browned. Stir in the minced garlic and the parsley. Cook, stirring, for 1 minute. Season with salt and pepper to taste. Set aside.

6. When the wild rice is cooked, add the shredded beef and marrow, the sautéed mushroom mixture, the squash, tomatoes, and tomato paste. Cover and cook over medium-low heat until the squash is tender, about 20 minutes. Season to taste with salt and pepper.

7. To serve, ladle into bowls and sprinkle with chopped parsley.

NOTE: What to do with the rest of the can when a recipe calls for 1 tablespoon of tomato paste from a 6-ounce can? I make 1-tablespoonful mounds on a cookie sheet and freeze until firm. Then I lift them off and store them in a freezer bag or plastic container in the freezer.

Carrot and Sake Soup

Makes 6 cups; 4 to 6 servings

A bunch of short, squat French carrots from our local farmers' market inspired this simple soup. Basically a puree of carrots cooked in sake and broth, it is very simple to prepare.

1 tablespoon canola or other flavorless
  vegetable oil
¼ cup minced shallots
1½ pounds carrots, cut into ½-inch cubes (about
  4 cups)
2 cups sake (see page 46)

2 cups reduced-sodium chicken broth
2 teaspoons grated fresh ginger
Kosher salt
6 tablespoons heavy cream or crème fraîche
¼ cup minced chives

1. Combine the oil and shallots in large saucepan; cook, stirring, over low heat, until the shallots are wilted, about 5 minutes. Stir in the carrots; cook, stirring, about 5 minutes. Add the sake and heat to a boil. Cook, uncovered, over medium-low heat until the sake is reduced by two-thirds, 15 to 20 minutes.

2. Add the chicken broth and 2 cups water; cover and cook for 20 minutes, or until the carrots are very soft. Remove from the heat and let cool.

3. Working in batches, puree the carrots with the cooking liquid in a food processor. Pour into a saucepan; add the ginger. Taste and add salt as needed. Reheat over low heat.

4. Ladle the soup into soup plates. Swirl a tablespoon or so of heavy cream across the top of each bowl. Garnish with the minced chives.

Sake

Sake is made from rice and pure water. The rice is specially selected and milled in an ancient process that is believed to have originated in China in 4800 B.C. but which eventually made its way to Japan. The brewing process has been highly refined over the centuries. It is fairly complex because it requires two chemical processes: saccharification, which turns the starch in the rice into sugar, and fermentation, which turns the sugar into alcohol. First a special type of rice is milled, polished, and steamed. Next the rice is injected with *koji*, a rice mold that facilitates the fermentation process. Next sake yeast and then carefully filtered water, containing only the specific minerals useful in fermentation, are added. Usually, the sake is briefly aged, pasteurized, and then blended.

There is a wide range of styles and flavors (some say there are more than 40,000 labels worldwide) of sake from which to choose. Today imported and domestic sakes are widely available in the United States.

In Japan, sake is used in cooking, especially in marinades and sauces. It has a distinctive musky, herbaceous aroma and taste that goes well with seafood and vegetables, and, of course, rice. Use sake in cooking in place of wine:

• When making risotto, especially with seafood, mushrooms, or vegetables

• To deglaze the pan for a quick sauce for fish or chicken breasts

• To marinate salmon or other fish steaks (equal parts sake and soy sauce)

• To splash on fresh strawberries, orange slices, peaches, or a medley of fresh fruits

• To moisten stir-fried chicken, seafood, or vegetables

• To steam open clams or mussels

Salads

I prefer rice salad made with freshly cooked rice because rice that has been refrigerated tightens and becomes firm and waxy. (This process, called retrogradation, is explained on page 11.) Reheating the rice to room temperature by steaming it in a foil packet in a low oven or heating it for about 2 minutes in the microwave will soften it slightly, but the grains will never be as moist and tender as when the rice is just cooked.

White rice takes only 15 minutes to cook, just enough time to prepare a dressing and chop a few vegetables. If you need to prepare the salad ahead of time, this can be a problem, but rice salad that doesn't contain meats or dairy products that might spoil can be stored safely in a cool dark place (e.g., a kitchen cabinet) for several hours. Another option is to prepare and refrigerate the perishable ingredients and then add them to the freshly cooked and cooled rice before serving.

If you must make the salad ahead, know that green vegetables like broccoli, sugar snap or snow peas, green peas, and green beans lose their color and texture when exposed to salad dressing for any length of time. To avoid drab green vegetables, refrigerate them separately and add them to the salad just before serving. Refrigerated leftover rice salad can be rescued by letting it warm to room temperature for 20 minutes or so before serving. Rice has the capacity to absorb flavors quickly, flattening the overall flavor of the salad. Make sure to taste the salad before serving. If it needs a jolt of flavor, add a squeeze of fresh lemon or lime juice, a dash of vinegar, a sprinkling of fresh herbs, a drizzle of olive oil, or a pinch of kosher salt.

Tuscan Rice Salad

**Makes 6
first-course or
4 main-course
servings**

Tuscan rice salad presents a canvas for endless variations. Use cut green beans instead of peas; substitute shredded chicken or diced pork roast for the prosciutto; or make the dressing with red wine vinegar instead of lemon juice. Serve as a main dish, or as part of a buffet of other room-temperature dishes.

3 large eggs

¼ cup plus 1 teaspoon extra virgin olive oil

¼ teaspoon minced garlic

Kosher salt and freshly ground black pepper

⅓ cup fresh lemon juice

3 cups cooked Arborio, Baldo, or other medium- or long-grain white rice

½ cup diced (¼-inch) carrot

½ cup frozen petite peas, thawed

¼ cup diced (¼-inch) red onion

2 tablespoons finely chopped Italian parsley

2 tablespoons chopped basil, plus a few sprigs for garnish

2 ounces prosciutto or other flavorful baked or cured ham, cut into thin slivers

Red or oak leaf lettuce leaves

1 large ripe tomato, cored and cut into ½-inch wedges

Small chunks of Parmigiano-Reggiano

1. Whisk the eggs in a medium bowl, then whisk in 1 teaspoon of the olive oil, the garlic, a pinch of salt, and a grinding of black pepper. Heat a small skillet, preferably nonstick, over medium-low heat. Add the eggs and cook, stirring, until scrambled into large clumps. Remove from the heat; set aside until ready to use.

2. Whisk the lemon juice, the remaining ¼ cup olive oil, ¼ teaspoon salt, and ⅛ teaspoon pepper in a large bowl. Add the rice, scrambled eggs, carrot, peas, red onion, parsley, basil, and prosciutto. Gently toss to mix.

3. Line a platter with the lettuce leaves. Spoon the rice into the center. Garnish with the tomato wedges, chunks of Parmesan cheese, and basil sprigs.

Yellow Basmati Rice and Black Bean Salad with Toasted Cumin and Lime Dressing

Makes 4 to 6 servings

The aroma and flavor of cumin is enhanced when it is lightly toasted before it is added to the salad dressing. The rice is toasted in oil, pilaf-style, before it is cooked. Ground turmeric turns the rice a brilliant yellow, a dramatic background for the black beans.

2 tablespoons canola or other flavorless vegetable oil

2 cups uncooked basmati rice

1 teaspoon ground turmeric

½ teaspoon ground cumin

2 teaspoons kosher salt

Dressing

1 teaspoon ground cumin

¼ cup canola or other flavorless vegetable oil

¼ cup fresh lime juice, or more to taste

½ teaspoon kosher salt, or more to taste

1 garlic clove, minced

Two 15-ounce cans black beans, rinsed and drained

½ cup thinly sliced scallions (white and green parts)

½ cup diced (¼-inch) red bell pepper

½ cup diced (¼-inch) seedless cucumber

¼ cup chopped cilantro, plus a few sprigs for garnish

1 tablespoon minced seeded jalapeño, or more to taste

One ½-pint small cherry tomatoes, stemmed

Lime wedges

1. Heat the oil in a wide saucepan or deep skillet over low heat. Add the rice; cook, stirring, for 2 minutes. Sprinkle with the turmeric and cumin; heat, stirring, for 1 minute. Add 3½ cups water and the salt; heat to a boil. Stir once. Reduce the heat to low; cover and cook until the water is absorbed and the surface is dotted with small steam holes, about 15 minutes. Uncover and let cool to room temperature.

2. *For the dressing:* Sprinkle the cumin into a small skillet. Heat over low heat just until fragrant, about 30 seconds. Remove from the heat. Add the olive oil, lime juice, salt, and garlic; stir to blend. Set aside.

3. Combine the cooled rice, dressing, black beans, scallions, bell pepper, cucumber, cilantro, and jalapeño in a large bowl. Toss lightly to blend. Taste and add more salt and lime juice if necessary. Spoon onto a deep platter or a shallow bowl. Garnish with cilantro sprigs, cherry tomatoes, and lime wedges.

Black Rice and Snow Pea Salad with Grilled Chicken

Makes 4 to 6 servings

Revered in Asia, black rice is reserved for auspicious occasions like births, marriages, and other celebrations. It has a chewy texture, a nutty flavor, and a dramatic black color. Look for black rice imported from China that retains its ebony color when it is cooked (the cooking water will turn black).

1½ cups uncooked black rice, rinsed and drained well

Chicken
2 tablespoons fresh lime juice
1 tablespoon canola or other flavorless
   vegetable oil
2 teaspoons grated fresh ginger
4 boneless, skinless chicken breasts, fillets
   separated
Kosher salt and freshly ground black pepper

4 ounces snow peas
Kosher salt

Dressing
¼ cup canola or other flavorless vegetable oil
2 tablespoons fresh lime juice

2 tablespoons unseasoned Japanese rice vinegar
1 tablespoon soy sauce
1 tablespoon toasted sesame oil
½ teaspoon grated fresh ginger
½ teaspoon minced garlic
½ teaspoon kosher salt

2 medium carrots, peeled and coarsely shredded
   (about 1 cup)
½ cup thinly sliced scallions (white and green
   parts)
½ cup finely chopped red bell pepper
1 tablespoon brown sesame seeds (see Note,
   page 30)

1. Cook the rice in plenty of boiling salted water until the grains are soft to the bite, 25 to 35 minutes. Drain well.

2. *Meanwhile, for the chicken:* Combine the lime juice, oil, and ginger in a shallow dish. Add the chicken and turn to coat. Sprinkle with salt and pepper. Cover and marinate at room temperature for about 15 minutes (or longer in the refrigerator).

3. Heat the grill, or heat a grill pan or a nonstick skillet until hot enough to sizzle and evaporate a drop of water. Add the chicken and cook, turning, once until

golden and cooked through, 3 to 4 minutes per side (fillets will take 2 minutes per side). Transfer to a plate; set aside at room temperature until ready to serve.

4. Meanwhile, soak the snow peas in a bowl of ice water for 10 minutes.

5. Drain the snow peas and trim them. Stack and cut into ¼-inch slices on the diagonal. Heat a small saucepan of water to a boil; add ½ teaspoon salt. Add the snow peas and blanch for 20 seconds; drain well and plunge into iced water to crisp. Drain again. Set aside.

6. *For the dressing:* Combine the oil, lime juice, rice vinegar, soy sauce, sesame oil, ginger, garlic, and salt in a bowl, whisk until well blended.

7. In a large serving bowl, combine the cooked rice, snow peas, carrots, scallions, and red bell pepper. Add the dressing and toss to blend. Spoon onto a deep platter or shallow bowl.

8. Slice the chicken on the diagonal and arrange on the salad. Sprinkle with the sesame seeds. Serve at room temperature.

BLACK RICE AND SNOW PEA SALAD WITH GRILLED SALMON. Lightly brush 1 pound thick salmon steaks or fillets with soy sauce. Grill or broil turning once, until cooked through, about 10 minutes. Let cool. Remove the skin and any bones. Break the salmon into 1-inch chunks. Make the rice salad, skipping steps 2 and 3. Place 4 cups lightly packed torn salad greens on a large platter, spoon the rice salad in the center, and place the salmon around the edges. Sprinkle the salad and salmon with sesame seeds and garnish with lime wedges.

Bhutanese Red Rice Salad with Edamame, Tamari Walnuts, and Ginger and Rice Wine Dressing

Makes 4 to 6 servings

Red rice imported from Bhutan has a distinctive earthy, almost mineral flavor compared to other red rices. As a result, it complements, rather than dominates, the sweet, nutty taste of the edamame and the tamari-coated walnuts. This makes an excellent side dish with seafood, but it can also stand on its own as a main-dish salad. You could use medium- or long-grain brown rice instead of the red rice, or a combination of separately precooked red, black, and brown rices. Substitute broccoli for the edamame if preferred.

1 cup uncooked red rice

Tamari Walnuts

1 cup broken walnuts

1 teaspoon canola or other flavorless vegetable oil

3 tablespoons tamari or soy sauce

2 cups frozen shelled edamame (soybeans; see Notes)

Dressing

5 tablespoons canola or other flavorless vegetable oil

¼ cup unseasoned Japanese rice vinegar

1 teaspoon grated fresh ginger

½ teaspoon minced or pressed garlic

½ teaspoon salt

½ cup thinly sliced scallions (white and green parts)

1 tablespoon minced jalapeño, or to taste

¼ cup cilantro leaves, optional

1. Cook the rice in plenty of boiling salted water until the grains are tender, 20 to 25 minutes (or 45 minutes or longer for brown rice); drain. (If using medium-grain brown rice, rinse with cold water to remove excess starch.) Let cool to room temperature.

2. ***For the tamari walnuts:*** Combine the walnuts and oil in a medium heavy skillet over medium heat; stir-fry just until fragrant, about 20 seconds. Sprinkle with the tamari and stir-fry until the walnuts are coated with the thickened tamari, adjusting the heat as necessary to keep the tamari from burning, about 1 minute. Turn out onto a double thickness of paper towels to blot, then transfer to a small bowl. (Do not cool the walnuts on the paper towels; they will stick to them.)

3. Place the edamame in a vegetable steamer; cover and steam over boiling water for 3 minutes. Remove from the steamer and let cool to room temperature.

4. ***For the dressing:*** Whisk the oil, rice vinegar, ginger, garlic, and salt in a large bowl until blended.

5. Add the rice, edamame, scallions, and jalapeño to the dressing; toss to coat. Sprinkle with the walnuts; toss. Garnish with the cilantro leaves, if desired. Serve at room temperature.

NOTES: Edamame is the immature green pod of the soybean plant. The Japanese serve edamame as a snack food, still in the pods. Their sweet, slightly nutty taste is irresistible. Look for them in the frozen food section of Asian markets and some supermarkets. Sometimes called sweet beans, they are available either raw or cooked in their shells and conveniently shelled.

If desired, substitute 3 cups broccoli florets for the soybeans. Steam for 4 minutes, or until crisp-tender.

Brown Rice, Mango, and Smoked Chicken Salad with Lime-Tamari Dressing

Makes 4 servings

Medium-grain brown rice has a pleasant nutty taste and chewy texture. It can be sticky, so for salads I usually rinse the cooked rice with cold water before using. This salad is also excellent with russet-colored Wehani or red rice from Bhutan. Substitute smoked turkey, plain cooked chicken, pork loin, or shrimp for the smoked chicken.

Dressing

¼ cup canola oil

3 tablespoons fresh lime juice

1 tablespoon tamari or soy sauce

1 teaspoon grated fresh ginger

1 garlic clove, minced

3 cups cooked medium-grain brown rice (rinse the cooked rice to remove excess starch)

6 ounces smoked chicken breast, skin removed and cut into ¼-inch dice (about 1 cup)

1 ripe mango, peeled, pitted, and cut into ¼-inch dice (about 2 cups)

½ cup thinly sliced scallions (white and green parts)

1 jalapeño, seeded and minced

½ cup roasted unsalted cashews, chopped

1. ***For the dressing:*** Whisk the oil, lime juice, tamari, ginger, and garlic in a large bowl.

2. Add the rice, smoked chicken, mango, scallions, and jalapeño. Toss to blend. Sprinkle with the cashews. Serve at room temperature.

Italian Tuna, Caper, and Rice Salad in Tomato Cups

Makes 4 servings

With its moist texture and mild taste, imported Italian tuna packed in olive oil is the only tuna to use in this salad. When tomatoes are in season, I like to serve the salad in hollowed-out tomatoes using half yellow and half red tomatoes. Alternatively, you can spoon the salad onto a platter and garnish with wedges of tomato.

2 large ripe red tomatoes (about 12 ounces each)
2 large ripe yellow tomatoes (about 12 ounces each)
Kosher salt and freshly ground black pepper
1½ cups cooked long- or medium-grain white rice
One 7-ounce can Italian tuna packed in olive oil, well drained
½ cup finely chopped celery

¼ cup finely chopped Parmigiano-Reggiano
2 tablespoons finely chopped red onion
2 tablespoons finely chopped Italian parsley, plus a few leaves for garnish
2 tablespoons capers, rinsed and drained
2 tablespoons extra virgin olive oil
1 tablespoon red wine vinegar
¼ teaspoon minced garlic

1. Cut the tops off the tomatoes, about ½ inch down from the crowns. Scoop the pulp from the tomatoes with a grapefruit knife or spoon or a tablespoon. Chop ½ cup of the pulp for the salad. Reserve the remainder for another use. Sprinkle the inside of the tomatoes lightly with salt and pepper. Set aside.

2. Combine the rice, tuna, tomato pulp, celery, Parmigiano-Reggiano, red onion, parsley, capers, olive oil, vinegar, and garlic in a large bowl; stir to blend. Add salt and pepper to taste.

3. Use a ½-cup measure to fill the tomatoes with the rice salad. Garnish with parsley leaves. Serve at room temperature.

Brown Rice, Shrimp, and Corn Salad with Cilantro-Lime Dressing

Makes 4 servings

The perfect salad for an August supper, when corn and tomatoes are at their peak. Substitute strips of grilled chicken for the shrimp, or serve it as a side dish, omitting the shrimp. I like this with medium-grain brown rice (make sure to rinse the cooked rice to remove excess starch), but white rice is good too.

Dressing

½ cup extra virgin olive oil

2 tablespoons minced fresh cilantro

½ teaspoon grated lime zest

¼ cup fresh lime juice

1 garlic clove, minced

½ teaspoon kosher salt

Freshly ground black pepper

1 teaspoon ground cumin

3 cups cooked brown or white rice (or use half of each color)

1 pound small frozen peeled and deveined shrimp, thawed and drained

3 cups corn kernels (from 4 to 5 ears)

½ cup thinly sliced scallions (white and green parts)

½ cup diced green bell pepper

½ cup diced red bell pepper

2 teaspoons minced seeded jalapeño, or more to taste

Curly or red leaf lettuce leaves

1 lime, cut into wedges

Cilantro sprigs, optional

1. *For the dressing:* Whisk the oil, cilantro, lime zest, lime juice, garlic, salt, and pepper to taste in a large bowl. Sprinkle the cumin into a small dry skillet and heat over low heat, shaking the pan frequently, until fragrant, about 30 seconds. Add to the dressing; whisk to blend.

2. Add the rice, half of the shrimp, the corn, scallions, green and red peppers, and jalapeño to the dressing; toss to blend.

3. Line a large shallow bowl with lettuce leaves. Spoon the salad into the center; garnish with the remaining shrimp and the lime wedges. Add a few sprigs of cilantro, if desired. Serve at room temperature.

Wehani Rice, Spinach, Bacon, and Toasted Almond Salad

Makes 4 servings

Spinach salad with bacon, toasted nuts, and hard-cooked eggs, once a ladies' lunch special, is updated with the addition of rice. The texture of Wehani, somewhere between crunchy and chewy, is perfect in this hearty main-dish salad. Cooked brown rice, either medium- (rinsed with cold water to remove stickiness) or long-grain, or even wild rice, could be used as well.

5 thick slices bacon
½ cup sliced natural (skin-on) almonds
⅓ cup canola or other flavorless vegetable oil
3 tablespoons red wine vinegar
1 garlic clove, minced
½ teaspoon kosher salt
Freshly ground black pepper

3 to 4 cups cooked Wehani rice
4 cups cut-up spinach (about 10 ounces)
½ cup thinly sliced celery
½ cup thin wedges (about ¼-inch) red onion
½ cup thin slivers (1-inch lengths) red bell pepper
2 hard-cooked eggs, peeled and quartered
1 cup small cherry tomatoes, stems removed

1. Preheat the oven to 350°F.

2. Cook the bacon in a large heavy skillet over medium-low heat, turning, until browned; drain on absorbent paper. When the bacon is cool, cut crosswise into ¼-inch pieces; set aside.

3. Spread the almonds in a small baking pan; bake until toasted, stirring once, about 5 minutes. Set aside.

4. Whisk the oil, vinegar, garlic, salt, and pepper to taste in a large bowl. Add the rice, spinach, celery, red onion, red pepper, and half of both the bacon and the almonds; toss to combine.

5. Spoon the salad onto a deep platter or shallow serving bowl. Arrange the egg quarters and cherry tomatoes around the edges. Sprinkle the salad with the remaining bacon and almonds. Serve at once.

Mussels and Saffron Rice Salad

Makes 6 first-course or 4 main-course servings

The white wine–based broth the mussels are cooked in is later used to cook the rice, giving the entire salad a pleasant briny seafood flavor. Serve the salad as a first course or a main course. Leave at least two dozen of the mussels in their shells to use as garnish.

Mussels

1 cup dry white wine

1 small onion, thinly sliced

A few sprigs each basil, parsley, and thyme, plus more for garnish

1 garlic clove, bruised with the side of a knife

½ teaspoon kosher salt

4 pounds mussels, scrubbed and beards removed

Rice Salad

¼ teaspoon crumbled saffron threads

1 cup uncooked long-grain white rice

½ cup seeded and diced (⅛-inch) plum tomato

½ cup diced (⅛-inch) red bell pepper

¼ cup minced green bell pepper

¼ cup minced red onion

¼ cup minced tender inside celery stalk, plus 1 tablespoon minced tender pale green celery leaves

¼ cup finely chopped Italian parsley

2 tablespoons chopped basil

⅓ cup extra virgin olive oil

3 tablespoons fresh lemon juice

1 garlic clove, minced

Freshly ground black pepper

1. *For the mussels:* Combine 1 cup water, the wine, onion, basil, parsley, and thyme sprigs, garlic, and salt in a very large saucepan or deep skillet with a tight-fitting lid. Heat to a boil; simmer, uncovered, for 5 minutes.

2. Add the mussels to the simmering broth. Cover and cook over high heat for 5 minutes, without lifting the cover. Remove the opened mussels with a slotted spoon. Continue to cook until the remaining mussels open; discard any that refuse to open. Let the mussels and broth cool separately.

3. Strain the broth through a fine sieve into a 2-cup measure. Add enough water to equal 2 cups. Reserve 2 dozen of the mussels in their shells; set aside in a bowl. Remove the remaining mussels from their shells and set aside.

4. Heat the mussel broth and the saffron in a wide saucepan or deep skillet to a boil; stir in the rice. Cover and cook over medium-low heat until the broth is absorbed and the rice is tender, about 15 minutes. Let stand, uncovered, until cooled.

5. Combine the tomato, bell peppers, red onion, celery, celery leaves, parsley, and basil in a large bowl. Add the shelled mussels, and cooled rice.

6. Whisk the olive oil, lemon juice, garlic, and a grinding of black pepper in a small bowl until blended. Add to the rice mixture; toss gently to combine.

7. Spoon the salad into a large shallow bowl. Arrange the reserved mussels in their shells around the edges. Garnish with basil, parsley, and thyme sprigs. Serve at once.

Crispy Rice Vermicelli Salad with Chicken and Snow Peas

Makes 4 servings

Fish sauce, lime juice, sugar, and jalapeño represent salty, sour, sweet, and hot, the four prominent flavors of Southeast Asian cooking. Fried rice sticks give this salad crunch. Use the very fine ones—they look like clear wires all wound together—sold in clear bags in Asian markets. I am always amazed to see the tangle of noodles magically—and instantly—expand to many times their original size when plunged into hot oil. Test a small portion before you proceed so you won't be overwhelmed with too many crispy rice threads at once.

Marinade

2 tablespoons Asian fish sauce
2 teaspoons sugar
½ teaspoon red pepper flakes

12 ounces boneless, skinless chicken breasts, pounded thin
Vegetable oil for deep-frying
2 ounces dried rice vermicelli (rice sticks), separated into thin webs
6 ounces snow peas, ends trimmed on a diagonal
1 teaspoon toasted sesame oil
1 teaspoon black or brown sesame seeds
Kosher salt

Dressing

6 tablespoons fresh lime juice
2 tablespoons Asian fish sauce
1 tablespoon canola or other flavorless vegetable oil, plus additional for coating the skillet
1 tablespoon minced seeded jalapeño
1 teaspoon sugar
1 teaspoon minced garlic
1 teaspoon grated fresh ginger

½ small head romaine lettuce, trimmed and cut crosswise into ½-inch strips
½ large red bell pepper, stem and seeds removed, cut into very thin half-circles
½ large red onion, cut into very thin half-circles
¼ cup cilantro leaves, plus tender stems, coarsely chopped
¼ cup mint leaves, coarsely chopped
¼ cup Thai basil leaves, coarsely chopped, optional

1. *Marinate the chicken:* Combine the fish sauce, sugar, and red pepper flakes in a pie plate or shallow bowl; stir to blend. Add the chicken; turn to coat. Refrigerate for 15 minutes.

2. Heat 2 inches vegetable oil in a large wide saucepan (with plenty of room for the noodles to expand) to 375°F or hot enough to sizzle and puff up a single rice

stick used as a test. Toss half of the rice sticks into the hot oil: they will expand instantly. Turn over with tongs. The frying will take about 2 seconds per side. Immediately transfer to a plate lined with doubled paper towels. Repeat with the remaining rice sticks.

3. Heat a saucepan of water to a boil. Add the snow peas and cook for 2 minutes (no longer—they overcook quickly); immediately drain and rinse under cold water until cool. Spread out on a kitchen towel to dry.

4. Toss the snow peas with the sesame oil, sesame seeds, and a pinch of salt. Set aside.

5. *For the dressing:* Whisk the lime juice, fish sauce, oil, jalapeño, sugar, garlic, and ginger in a small bowl; set aside.

6. Heat a large nonstick skillet over medium-high heat. Drizzle with a thin film of canola oil. Add the chicken and sear on both sides until cooked through, about 2 minutes per side. Transfer to a side dish. When cool enough to handle, cut the chicken into ¼-inch-thick diagonal slices.

7. In a large shallow bowl, combine the chicken, snow peas, lettuce, red pepper, red onion, cilantro, mint, and basil, if using. Add the dressing; toss to coat. Lightly crush the fried rice sticks and sprinkle over the top of the salad. Serve at once.

Roasted Chickpea and Rice Salad with Lemon-Parsley Dressing

Makes 6 servings

Addictive crunchy roasted chickpeas are easy to make with good-quality canned chickpeas, or dried chickpeas cooked from scratch, if you prefer. (Dried chickpeas need to soak overnight and will take at least 2 hours to cook until tender.) Simply roast the chickpeas in a hot oven with olive oil, garlic, salt, and pepper. Serve them as a snack or in this rice salad. For an all-vegetable meal, serve this salad with a platter of sliced tomatoes and an assortment of grilled vegetables.

Two 15-ounce cans chickpeas, rinsed and well
    drained (or about 4 cups cooked dried chickpeas)
¼ cup extra virgin olive oil
Kosher salt and freshly ground black pepper
2 garlic cloves, chopped
3 cups cooked long-grain white rice
1 cup diced (¼-inch) celery
1 cup diced (¼-inch) plum tomatoes

½ cup diced (¼-inch) red onion
3 tablespoons finely chopped celery leaves

Dressing
6 tablespoons extra virgin olive oil
2 tablespoons fresh lemon juice
¼ cup finely chopped Italian parsley
½ teaspoon kosher salt

1. Spread the chickpeas on a clean kitchen towel and blot dry.

2. Preheat the oven to 400°F.

3. Spread the chickpeas in a 13 × 9-inch baking pan. Drizzle with the olive oil. Sprinkle with salt and pepper. Roast for 10 minutes. Sprinkle with the garlic; stir to blend. Roast until the chickpeas are crisp and browned, about 10 minutes more. Let cool.

4. Combine the rice, roasted chickpeas, celery, tomatoes, red onion, and celery leaves in a large bowl.

5. *For the dressing:* Whisk the olive oil, lemon juice, parsley, and salt in a small bowl.

6. Pour the dressing over the rice salad. Toss to blend. Taste and add more salt and a grinding of black pepper if needed. Serve at room temperature.

Basmati Rice, Mango, and Toasted Coconut Salad

Makes 4 servings

Inspired by three ingredients I adore: fragrant basmati rice, lush ripe mango, and naturally sweet crunchy toasted coconut. Serve with chicken that has been marinated in a paste of yogurt, curry powder, and grated ginger, and then grilled.

½ cup unsweetened dried coconut

Dressing
5 tablespoons canola or other flavorless
   vegetable oil
2 tablespoons unseasoned Japanese rice
   vinegar
½ teaspoon grated fresh ginger

¼ teaspoon finely chopped garlic
¼ teaspoon kosher salt

3 cups cooked basmati rice
1 mango, peeled, pitted, and cut into ⅛-inch dice
2 scallions, trimmed and thinly sliced
¼ cup chopped cilantro, optional

1. Preheat the oven to 325°F.

2. Spread the coconut in a pie plate or small baking pan. Bake, stirring once, until golden, about 5 minutes. Let cool.

3. *For the dressing:* Whisk the oil, rice vinegar, ginger, garlic, and salt in a large bowl.

4. Add the rice, mango, scallions, and toasted coconut. Toss to combine. Top with chopped cilantro, if using. Serve at room temperature.

Sushi Rice Salad with Cucumber and Toasted Sesame Seeds

Makes 4 servings

Sushi is technically a Japanese dish made with cooked short- (or medium-) grain rice and sweetened rice vinegar. But for this recipe the rice is used to make a refreshing salad that is dressed with rice vinegar. Soy-glazed broiled or grilled salmon is the ideal accompaniment.

2 cups uncooked sushi rice
1 teaspoon kosher salt

Dressing
½ cup unseasoned Japanese rice vinegar
3 tablespoons canola or other flavorless
  vegetable oil
1 tablespoon tamari or soy sauce
2 tablespoons toasted sesame oil

1 teaspoon grated fresh ginger
½ teaspoon minced garlic

1 cup 1 × ⅛-inch julienne strips peeled seedless
  cucumber (cut into thin slices, stack, and cut
  across into julienne)
¼ cup minced red onion
1 tablespoon brown sesame seeds (see Note,
  page 30)

1. Place the rice in a bowl, add cold water to cover, and stir gently; drain. Repeat two more times. Combine the rice, 2½ cups water, and the salt in a rice cooker and cook according to the manufacturer's directions. Or combine in a saucepan, cover, and cook over low heat until the water is absorbed, 10 to 12 minutes; let the rice stand, still covered, for 10 minutes. Carefully remove the lid, to prevent condensation from dripping onto the rice. Let cool to room temperature.

2. *For the dressing:* Whisk the rice vinegar, oil, tamari, sesame oil, ginger, and garlic in a small bowl until blended.

3. Combine the cooled rice, cucumber, red onion, and sesame seeds in a large bowl. Add the dressing; toss gently until blended. Serve at room temperature.

Parsley and Rice Salad with Parmigiano-Reggiano, Pignoli, and Dried Tomatoes

Makes 4 servings

This unusual salad was inspired by a display of bunches of freshly harvested Italian parsley with small tender leaves at my local farmers' market. Here half of the parsley is pureed with the oil and vinegar dressing, which gives the salad a bright green color.

⅓ cup plus 1 tablespoon extra virgin olive oil

1½ cups uncooked medium- or long-grain white rice

2 garlic cloves, minced

Kosher salt

4 cups lightly packed tender Italian parsley leaves

3 tablespoons red wine vinegar

½ cup pignoli (pine nuts)

½ cup diced (¼-inch) sun-dried tomatoes in olive oil (rinsed and blotted dry, then diced)

½ cup freshly grated Parmigiano-Reggiano

Freshly ground black pepper

1. Heat 1 tablespoon of the oil in a large wide saucepan or deep skillet over medium-low heat. Add the rice; cook, stirring, until some of the grains turn from translucent to opaque (the rice will look tweedy), about 10 minutes. Add half the minced garlic; cook for 1 minute. Add 2¾ cups water and 1 teaspoon salt. Heat to a boil over high heat; stir once. Reduce the heat to low; cook, covered, until the water is absorbed and the rice is tender, about 15 minutes. Remove from the heat. Uncover—do not stir—and let cool to room temperature.

2. Place half the parsley, the remaining ⅓ cup olive oil, the vinegar, ½ teaspoon salt, and the remaining garlic in a food processor; process until the parsley is finely chopped.

3. Toast the pignoli in a small skillet over low heat, stirring constantly, until golden, about 2 minutes.

4. Transfer the rice to a large serving bowl. Add the parsley vinaigrette; stir to combine. Finely chop the remaining parsley. Add the parsley, dried tomatoes, pignoli, cheese, and pepper to taste; toss to blend. Serve at room temperature.

Brown Rice Salad with Two Sesame Flavors

Makes 4 to 6 servings

I make this salad whenever I have a piece of tuna, brushed with soy, waiting to be grilled, or chicken cutlets marinating in ginger, garlic, and lime juice to sear in a hot skillet on top of the stove.

2 tablespoons canola or other flavorless vegetable oil

2 tablespoons fresh lime juice

2 teaspoons toasted sesame oil

3 to 4 cups cooked medium-grain brown rice (rinse the cooked rice to remove excess starch)

1 cup coarsely shredded carrots

½ cup thinly sliced scallions (white and green parts)

½ cup chopped dry-roasted peanuts

2 teaspoons brown sesame seeds (see Note, page 30)

Whisk the oil, lime juice, and sesame oil in a large bowl. Add the rice, carrots, and scallions. Toss to blend. Sprinkle with the peanuts and sesame seeds. Toss once and serve.

Brown Rice and Broccoli Salad with Tamari Almonds

Makes 4 servings

This salad is a long-time favorite, especially made with medium-grain brown rice. (Rinse the cooked rice to remove excess starch.) The starchy grains absorb the flavors of the lemon dressing and the tamari on the nuts. Ideal as part of a vegetarian summer menu with a platter of steaming corn on the cob and thick slices of ripe tomatoes. Or, it goes well with grilled soy- or tamari-marinated flank steak, jumbo shrimp, or fish steaks. You can use either tamari or soy to glaze the nuts. Use walnuts instead if you like; both are good. Make extra nuts and keep them on hand to sprinkle on green beans, toss with mixed greens, or just nibble as a snack. If making the salad ahead, reserve the broccoli and tamari almonds and add just before serving.

Tamari Almonds

½ cup natural (skin-on) whole almonds

1 teaspoon canola or other flavorless vegetable oil

2 tablespoons tamari or soy sauce

1 pound broccoli, tough stems trimmed, stems sliced into ¼-inch-thick rounds, florets separated into 1-inch clusters (about 4 cups florets)

Dressing

¼ cup canola or other flavorless vegetable oil

2 tablespoons fresh lemon or lime juice

1 tablespoon tamari or soy sauce

1 teaspoon grated fresh ginger

½ teaspoon grated lemon zest

½ teaspoon minced garlic

3 to 4 cups cooked medium-grain brown rice (rinse the cooked rice to remove excess starch)

½ cup thin diagonal slices scallions (white and green parts)

1. *For the tamari almonds:* Combine the almonds and oil in a medium heavy skillet over medium heat; stir-fry just until fragrant, about 20 seconds. Sprinkle with the tamari and stir-fry until the almonds are coated with the thickened tamari, adjusting the heat as necessary to prevent burning, about 1 minute. Turn out onto a double thickness of paper towels to blot, then transfer to a small bowl. (Do not cool the almonds on the paper towels; they will stick to them.)

2. Place the broccoli in a vegetable steamer, cover, and steam over gently boiling water until tender, about 4 minutes. Rinse the broccoli with cool water to stop the cooking.

3. *For the dressing:* Whisk the oil, lemon juice, tamari, ginger, lemon zest, and garlic in a large bowl.

4. Add the cooked rice, tamari almonds, broccoli, and scallions; toss to blend. Serve at room temperature.

Asparagus, Egg, and Arborio Rice Salad with Lemon Dressing

Makes 4 to 6 servings Serve this simple spring salad crowned with curls of Parmigiano-Reggiano. (Use a vegetable peeler to shave thick curls from a wedge of cheese.) Served with other salads as part of a buffet, it is a great party dish. The recipe can easily be doubled.

1 cup uncooked Arborio or other medium-grain white rice

Kosher salt

1 pound asparagus, trimmed and cut into ½-inch diagonal pieces

2 large eggs

1 teaspoon olive oil

Pinch of kosher salt

¼ cup pignoli (pine nuts)

3 tablespoons fresh lemon juice

¼ teaspoon minced garlic

½ teaspoon kosher salt

Freshly ground black pepper

½ cup thin diagonal slices scallions (white and green parts)

Thick curls Parmigiano-Reggiano

Dressing

¼ cup extra virgin olive oil

1 teaspoon grated lemon zest

1. Heat 2 cups water to a boil in a medium saucepan. Stir in the rice and 1 teaspoon salt; cover and cook over low heat until the water is absorbed and the rice is tender, about 15 minutes. Let stand, uncovered, until cooled to room temperature.

2. Place the asparagus in a vegetable steamer; cover and steam over simmering water until crisp-tender, about 3 minutes. Rinse the asparagus with cool water; drain and let cool.

3. Whisk the eggs, in a small bowl. Whisk in 1 tablespoon water, the olive oil, and salt. Heat a small skillet, preferably nonstick, over medium-low heat; add the

eggs and cook, stirring gently with a rubber spatula, until scrambled into large clumps. Remove from the heat and set aside.

4. Toast the pignoli in a small skillet over low heat, stirring constantly, until golden, about 2 minutes.

5. *For the dressing:* Whisk the oil, lemon zest, lemon juice, garlic, salt, and pepper to taste in a large bowl.

6. Add the rice, asparagus, eggs, and scallions; fold together to blend. Spoon onto a large deep platter or shallow bowl. Sprinkle with the toasted pignoli and curls of Parmigiano-Reggiano.

Summer Rice Salad

Makes 4 servings

The best dishes are often the simplest. Here freshly cooked rice is folded into a colorful mix of tomatoes, cucumber, green beans, and basil. Add a little crumbled cheese, such as ricotta salata or a mild feta, if you like. Cooked shrimp or strips of poached chicken make it a complete meal.

1 cup uncooked long-grain white rice
6 tablespoons extra virgin olive oil
¼ cup red wine vinegar
½ teaspoon minced garlic
Kosher salt and freshly ground black pepper
1 cup corn kernels (from 2 ears)
1 large ripe tomato, seeded, cored, and cut into
 ¼-inch dice

1 cup diced (¼-inch) seedless cucumber
½ cup diced (¼-inch) red onion
¼ cup packed torn basil leaves
1 cup thawed frozen shelled cooked shrimp,
 shredded cooked chicken, and/or crumbled or
 chopped cheese (Parmigiano-Reggiano, ricotta
 salata, mild feta, or goat cheese), optional

1. Heat 1¾ cups water to a boil in a shallow saucepan or deep skillet. Add the rice and salt; cook, covered, over low heat until the liquid is absorbed and the rice is tender, about 15 minutes. Let stand, uncovered, until cooled. Fluff with a fork.

2. *For the dressing:* Whisk the olive oil, vinegar, garlic, ¼ teaspoon salt, and a grinding of black pepper in a large bowl. Add the rice, corn kernels, tomato, cucumber, red onion, and basil; toss to blend. Add the shrimp (and/or chicken and/or cheese), if using. Serve at room temperature.

Tabbouleh-Style Basmati Rice Salad

Makes 4 servings

The dish has the flavors of tabbouleh, with basmati rice instead of the traditional bulgur. Use all white basmati or a mixture of white and brown (cooked separately).

1 cup uncooked basmati rice
½ teaspoon kosher salt

Dressing
¼ cup extra virgin olive oil
3 tablespoons fresh lemon juice
1 tablespoon tahini
½ teaspoon minced garlic
½ teaspoon kosher salt
Pinch of cayenne

2 cups diced (¼-inch) seeded tomatoes
1 cup diced (¼-inch) seedless cucumber
1 cup finely chopped, tender, curly leaf parsley, including stems
½ cup thinly sliced scallions (white and green parts)
¼ cup finely chopped mint, plus a few sprigs for garnish
Cherry tomatoes for garnish

1. Heat 1¾ cups water to a boil in a shallow saucepan or deep skillet. Add the rice and ½ teaspoon salt; cook, covered, over low heat until the liquid is absorbed and the rice is tender, about 15 minutes. Let stand, uncovered, until cooled. Fluff with a fork.

2. *For the dressing:* Whisk the olive oil, lemon juice, tahini, garlic, ½ teaspoon salt, and the cayenne in a large bowl. Add the rice, tomatoes, cucumber, parsley, scallions, and mint. Toss to blend.

3. Spoon the salad onto a platter. Garnish with cherry tomatoes and mint sprigs. Serve at room temperature.

Jasmine-Tea Rice Salad with Snow Peas

Makes 4 servings

Jasmine tea imparts a sweet floral note to the tender grains of jasmine rice. Serve this salad with seafood, such as shrimp, salmon, or halibut.

2 teaspoons loose jasmine tea leaves or 1 tea bag jasmine tea
1 cup uncooked jasmine rice
½ teaspoon kosher salt
4 ounces snow peas, trimmed

Vinaigrette
⅓ cup canola or other flavorless vegetable oil
3 tablespoons unseasoned Japanese rice vinegar

1 teaspoon grated fresh ginger
½ teaspoon kosher salt

¼ cup thinly sliced scallion greens
¼ cup minced carrot
1 teaspoon sesame seeds, toasted

1. In a 2-cup glass measure, combine 1¾ cups boiling water and the tea; cover with a saucer and let steep for 5 minutes. Strain out the tea leaves or discard the tea bag; transfer the tea to a shallow saucepan or deep skillet. Add the rice and salt and heat to a boil; stir once. Cover and cook over low heat for 12 to 15 minutes, until the liquid is absorbed and the rice is tender. Uncover and let cool.

2. Steam the snow peas in a vegetable steamer over gently boiling water until crisp-tender, about 3 minutes. Rinse under cold water to stop the cooking; drain well. Cut the snow peas into ¼-inch slices.

3. *For the vinaigrette:* Whisk the oil, rice vinegar, ginger, and salt in a small bowl until blended.

4. Combine the cooled rice, snow peas, 3 tablespoons of the scallions, and the carrot in a large bowl. Add the dressing; toss to coat. Spoon into a serving bowl. Sprinkle with the sesame seeds and garnish with the remaining scallions. Serve at once.

Wild Rice and Smoked Turkey Salad with Dried Cranberries and Toasted Hazelnuts

Makes 4 servings

You could also make this salad with half wild and half long-grain brown or white rice. The recipe can be easily doubled (or tripled) for a large buffet supper. Substitute fully cooked corn- or apple-smoked ham for the turkey. Or add a cup or so of diced smoked mozzarella. When chopping the parsley, include the sweet, fragrant stems along with the leaves.

1 cup uncooked wild rice, rinsed in warm water and drained

½ cup canola or other flavorless vegetable oil

3 tablespoons fresh lemon juice

1 small garlic clove, minced

½ teaspoon kosher salt

Freshly ground black pepper

6 ounces sliced smoked turkey, cut into 1 × ⅛-inch slivers

1 cup small seedless green grapes

½ cup dried cranberries

½ cup toasted and peeled hazelnuts (see box)

¼ cup finely chopped Italian parsley

¼ cup thinly sliced scallions (white and green parts)

1. Heat 3 cups water to a boil in a large saucepan; stir in the rice. Cook, covered, over medium-low heat until tender, 35 to 55 minutes, depending on the rice. Uncover and cook to evaporate any excess liquid; or let stand, covered, until any remaining water is absorbed. Let cool to room temperature.

2. Whisk the oil, lemon juice, garlic, salt, and a grinding of black pepper in a large bowl. Add the rice, turkey, grapes, cranberries, hazelnuts, parsley, and scallions; toss to blend. Taste and add more salt and pepper, if needed. Serve at room temperature.

To Toast and Peel Hazelnuts

Preheat the oven to 350°F. Spread the hazelnuts in a single layer in a cake pan. Toast until the skins begin to blister, 10 to 15 minutes. Wrap the hot nuts in a towel and let cool for 15 minutes. Use the towel to briskly rub the nuts and loosen the skins (not all the skins will be removed—that's fine).

Quick Rice Salads

Makes 2 main-course or 4 side-dish servings

Two to three cups leftover cooked rice become a main or side dish salad with the addition of a simple dressing, fresh vegetables, and bits of seafood or meat.

Dressing

3 to 4 tablespoons canola or other flavorless vegetable oil or extra virgin olive oil

2 tablespoons fresh lemon juice, unseasoned Japanese rice vinegar, or mild red wine vinegar

Kosher salt and freshly ground black pepper

Optional Seasonings

½ teaspoon minced garlic

1 teaspoon grated lemon zest

Tomato, Corn, and Basil (use olive oil and lemon juice)

1 medium tomato, diced

½ cup corn kernels (from 1 ear)

2 tablespoons torn basil leaves

Carrot and Dry-Roasted Peanuts (use canola oil and rice vinegar)

1 medium carrot, coarsely shredded

¼ cup chopped dry-roasted unsalted peanuts

¼ cup dark raisins

Italian Tuna, Red Onion, and Green Olives (use olive oil and red wine vinegar)

One 7-ounce can Italian tuna in olive oil, well drained

½ cup chopped red onion

8 pitted green olives, coarsely chopped

2 tablespoons chopped Italian parsley

Confetti Vegetables (use olive oil and lemon juice)

¼ cup finely chopped red bell pepper

¼ cup finely chopped green bell pepper

¼ cup finely chopped carrot

¼ cup finely chopped red onion

Chicken and Coconut (use canola oil and lemon juice)

1 cup shredded cooked chicken

½ cup chopped cilantro

¼ cup toasted unsweetened flaked coconut

¼ cup roasted salted cashews

1 teaspoon grated fresh ginger

Whisk the oil, lemon juice or vinegar, salt, and pepper to taste, and any optional seasonings in a large bowl until blended. Add the rice and the ingredients for one of the salads. Toss to blend, and serve at once.

Japanese Rice Vinegar Salad Dressing

Makes about ½ cup

This is an all-purpose dressing that can be used on green salads as well as rice salads. Choose an unseasoned Japanese rice vinegar that says "light" or "mild" on the label.

¼ cup canola or other flavorless vegetable oil

3 tablespoons unseasoned Japanese rice vinegar

½ teaspoon kosher salt

½ teaspoon grated fresh ginger

½ teaspoon minced garlic

½ teaspoon toasted sesame oil, optional

Whisk the oil, rice vinegar, salt, ginger, garlic, and sesame oil, if using, in a small bowl. Use at once or in 1 to 2 days. Store in the refrigerator.

Little Dishes
and Sides

These recipes come under the heading of little rice dishes, not because they are small servings but because they can be served as a snack, appetizer, side dish, or light meal.

To cook rice in any form is to take a jaunt around the world, which is perhaps more evident in this chapter than it is in the others. From Japanese sushi rice balls to Greek-inspired stuffed grape leaves the recipes encompass the globe from Asia to the Mediterranean.

The recipes illustrate the amazing versatility of this unassuming grain. There are rice pancakes made from leftover risotto, Turkish- and Persian-style pilafs, classic Chinese fried rice, Greek-style stuffed vegetables, and Arancini deep-fried rice balls from Sicily.

Many recipes are reminders of the countries I have visited; others are from places I dream of visiting as I dip my cup into a sack of rice.

Tips for Making Little Rice Pancakes

- The technique for rice pancakes is similar to risotto, but one can be less vigilant about the stirring. I find that stirring each time you add more hot broth is sufficient.

- To ensure evenly sized pancakes, use a ⅓-cup measure. Or spread the cooked rice in a 13 × 9-inch baking pan. The thin layer of rice will cool quickly and easily can be divided into 12 equal portions. Scoop the portions up with a metal spatula and shape into pancakes.

- To avoid sticky hands, work near a sink and rinse and rewet your hands between pancakes.

- Place the formed pancakes on a baking sheet, cover, and refrigerate for 20 to 30 minutes (or longer) before browning. This helps them to dry out and set.

- Sauté the pancakes until well browned on the bottom, 10 to 15 minutes, before turning. The pancakes will fall apart if they are turned too soon; a crisp crust helps them to stay together.

- Pancakes can be cooked ahead and kept warm in an oven set at the lowest setting or refrigerated and reheated in a 350°F oven until hot, about 15 minutes.

- Feel free to experiment with different seasonings. Just remember to keep the additions to a minimum and the pieces of vegetable, cheese, or whatever you are adding small so they won't prevent the rice from sticking together.

- Leftover risotto makes excellent little rice pancakes as well. See Risotto al Salto, page 86.

Shiitake and Scallion Rice Pancakes with Sesame Seeds

Makes 12 to 16 pancakes; 4 to 6 servings

Serve these crunchy little rice pancakes as a nibble with wine before dinner or as a side dish with grilled fish or chicken. I also like them as a vegetarian main course, with a side dish of crisp cooked sugar snap peas tossed with a few drops of toasted sesame oil.

2 tablespoons canola or other flavorless vegetable oil, plus additional for cooking the pancakes

4 ounces shiitakes, stems discarded, caps wiped clean and cut into ⅛-inch slices

½ cup thinly sliced white part of scallions, plus ¼ cup thinly sliced scallion greens

1 garlic clove, minced

1 cup uncooked sushi rice or Arborio, Carnaroli, Vialone Nano, Baldo, or other medium-grain white rice

½ cup unseasoned Japanese rice vinegar

3 cups reduced-sodium chicken broth

1 tablespoon brown sesame seeds

1 teaspoon soy sauce or tamari

1 teaspoon toasted sesame oil

Kosher salt and freshly ground black pepper

1. Heat the oil in a large wide saucepan or deep skillet. Add the shiitakes; cook, stirring, until tender, about 5 minutes. Add the scallion whites and garlic; cook for 1 minute. Stir in the rice; cook, stirring, until blended. Add the rice vinegar and cook, stirring, until it has evaporated, about 3 minutes.

2. Meanwhile, heat the chicken broth to a simmer in a medium saucepan.

3. Stir 2 cups of the hot chicken broth into the rice. Cover and cook over low heat for 10 minutes. Add ½ cup more broth; stir for 30 seconds. Cover and cook for 5 minutes. Add the remaining ½ cup chicken broth; stir for 30 seconds. Cover and cook for 5 minutes.

4. Add the scallion greens, sesame seeds, soy sauce, and sesame oil. Stir until well blended. Add salt to taste and a grinding of black pepper. Spread the rice in a 13 × 9-inch baking pan, smoothing the top with a spatula. Place a piece of plas-

tic wrap directly on the rice. Refrigerate until cool enough to handle, about 30 minutes.

5. Using a small knife, cut the rice into 12 squares. Dampen your hands with water and shape each portion into a 2½-inch pancake about ½ inch thick. Rinse your hands frequently to prevent sticking. Refrigerate the pancakes, covered, for at least 20 minutes.

6. When ready to serve, heat a thin film of vegetable oil in a large heavy skillet or on a griddle. Add the pancakes and cook over medium to medium-low heat until the bottoms are set and golden brown, about 10 to 15 minutes. Using a wide spatula, carefully turn and brown the other sides. Serve hot.

Butternut Squash Rice Pancakes with Gruyère

Makes about 16 pancakes; 4 to 6 servings

Come fall, I am drawn to winter squash like a bee to a honeycomb. My favorite is butternut; I put it in everything—even rice pancakes. Keeping in the spirit of the season, I serve these with pork chops topped with sautéed apple slices, or with a pork loin stuffed with dried fruit. Easier than serving risotto to a large table of dinner guests, these can be made ahead, browned, and then reheated in a 350°F oven just before serving.

One 1-pound butternut squash, seeds discarded, peeled, and cut into ¼- to ½-inch dice (about 2 cups)
2 tablespoons unsalted butter
½ cup minced onion
1 garlic clove, minced
1 cup uncooked Arborio, Carnaroli, Vialone Nano, Baldo, or other medium-grain white rice

½ cup dry white wine
3 cups reduced-sodium chicken broth (or half broth and half water)
1 cup shredded Gruyère
2 tablespoons minced Italian parsley
Kosher salt and freshly ground black pepper
Canola or other flavorless vegetable oil for cooking the pancakes

1. Put the squash in a vegetable steamer, cover, and steam over boiling water until crisp-tender, 10 to 12 minutes. Set aside.

2. Melt the butter in a wide deep saucepan or deep skillet. Add the onion; cook over medium-low heat, stirring, until golden, about 10 minutes. Add the garlic; cook for 1 minute. Stir in the rice and cook for 1 minute. Add the wine; cook, stirring, until it has evaporated, about 3 minutes.

3. Meanwhile, heat the chicken broth to a simmer in a medium saucepan.

4. Stir 2 cups of the hot chicken broth into the rice. Cover and cook over low heat for 10 minutes. Add ½ cup more broth; stir for 30 seconds. Cover and cook for 5 minutes. Add the remaining ½ cup broth and the squash; stir for 30 seconds. Cover and cook for 5 minutes. The rice should be tender and moist.

5. Stir in the cheese and parsley until blended. Add salt to taste and a grinding of black pepper. Spread the rice mixture in a 13 × 9-inch baking pan, smoothing the top with a spatula. Place a piece of plastic wrap directly on the rice. Refrigerate until cool enough to handle, about 30 minutes.

6. Using a small knife, cut the rice into 12 squares. Dampen your hands with water and shape each portion into a 2½-inch pancake about ½ inch thick. Rinse your hands frequently to prevent sticking. Refrigerate the pancakes, covered, for at least 20 minutes.

7. When ready to serve, heat a thin film of vegetable oil in a large heavy skillet or on a griddle. Add the pancakes and cook over medium to medium-low heat until the bottoms are set and golden brown, about 10 to 15 minutes. Using a wide spatula, carefully turn and brown the other sides. Serve hot.

Sun-Dried Tomato, Parmesan Cheese, and Rice Pancakes

Makes 12 pancakes; 4 to 6 servings

Serve these little pancakes, crisp on the outside and soft and tender within, as an appetizer, with a salad for a light lunch, or as a side dish with roasted chicken.

½ cup chopped onion

1 tablespoon extra virgin olive oil, plus more as needed

1 cup uncooked Arborio, Carnaroli, Vialone Nano, Baldo, or other medium-grain white rice

¼ cup snipped and drained sun-dried tomatoes in olive oil

1 teaspoon snipped rosemary leaves or ½ teaspoon dried rosemary

2½ cups reduced-sodium chicken broth (or half broth and half water)

½ cup freshly grated Parmigiano-Reggiano

1 large egg yolk

1. Combine the onion and olive oil in a large wide saucepan or skillet with a tight-fitting lid. Cook, stirring, over low heat until the onion is tender, about 5 minutes. Stir in the rice, dried tomatoes, and rosemary; stir for 1 minute.

2. Meanwhile, heat the chicken broth to a simmer in a medium saucepan.

3. Stir 1½ cups of the hot chicken broth into the rice. Cover and cook for 10 minutes. Add ½ cup more broth; stir for 30 seconds. Cover and cook for 5 minutes. Add the remaining ½ cup chicken broth; stir for 30 seconds. Cover and cook for 5 minutes. The rice should be tender and moist. Stir in the cheese. Let cool.

4. Whisk the egg yolk in a large bowl. Add the cooled rice mixture and stir to blend. Spoon the rice into a 13 × 9-inch baking pan, smoothing the top with a spatula. Place plastic wrap directly on the rice and refrigerate until cold, about 30 minutes.

5. Using a small knife, cut the rice into 12 squares. Dampen your hands with water and shape each portion into a 2½-inch pancake about ½ inch thick. Rinse your hands frequently to prevent sticking. Refrigerate the pancakes, covered, for at least 20 minutes.

6. Coat a large nonstick skillet with a thin film of olive oil. Heat over medium heat. Add the pancakes and cook until the bottoms are set and golden brown, about 10 minutes. Using a wide spatula, carefully turn the pancakes and brown the other sides. Serve hot.

Risotto al Salto
Pancakes Made from Leftover Risotto

Makes 4 to 8 pancakes; 2 to 4 servings The Italian name for pancakes made with risotto translates as "jumping risotto," presumably because they are quickly turned in the pan or maybe because they are easy to pop right into your mouth. In Milan, where risotto reigns supreme, *risotto al salto* is made as one large pancake. I rarely have enough risotto left over to make a large pancake, so I usually make smaller ones. The formula is simple and the recipe can be doubled.

1 large egg, well beaten
1 to 2 cups cold leftover risotto

1 to 2 tablespoons unsalted butter
Freshly grated Parmigiano-Reggiano

1. Add the beaten egg 1 tablespoon at a time to the cold stiff risotto until it is softened. You may not need to add all of the egg.

2. Rinsing your hands frequently with cold water to prevent sticking, shape the risotto into patties about 2 inches in diameter; set aside on wax paper. (The patties can be made ahead of time, covered, and refrigerated.)

3. Melt the butter in a large heavy skillet, preferably nonstick, over medium heat and heat until the foam subsides. Add the risotto pancakes and cook until browned and crusty on the bottom. Carefully turn and cook the other sides.

4. Serve warm, or arrange on a heatproof platter and keep warm in an oven set on lowest temperature until ready to serve. Sprinkle with grated Parmesan just before serving.

Arancini with Spiced Meat Filling

Makes about 12 arancini (about 2½ inches in diameter); 6 servings

Arancini are balls of rice stuffed with meat or cheese and fried until crisp golden brown. In Sicily, they are a popular street food, fried right before your eyes. The rice is usually cooked with saffron, which turns it a pale orange color, perhaps the reason they are called *arancini*, "little oranges." In this recipe the arancini are stuffed with a mixture of beef or pork slowly simmered with tomato and seasoned with cinnamon and dried currants. The variation that follows is a simpler version that stuffs the rice with cubes of cheese or prosciutto.

Besides the saffron, the rice is seasoned generously with grated cheese. I prefer the taste of Parmigiano-Reggiano, but pecorino Romano, a sheep's milk cheese, is probably more authentic. This is a fairly labor intensive recipe, but the components can be made a day or two ahead. The meat filling makes enough for 24 arancini, double the amount that is needed. I usually freeze any portion I don't use if I can get it away from my husband, John, who likes it spooned onto a toasted roll. It is also delicious served over a platter of steaming hot rice. The arancini can be served as a snack or with a glass of wine before dinner. They can be fried ahead and served at room temperature or reheated in a 350°F oven for 10 to 15 minutes. Leftovers freeze well, but my guess is there won't be any to freeze.

Filling

1 tablespoon extra virgin olive oil

12 ounces boneless pork shoulder or beef round or chuck, cut into 1½-inch chunks

½ cup finely chopped onion

¼ cup finely chopped carrot

1 garlic clove, minced

2 cups reduced-sodium beef broth, or more if needed

2 tablespoons tomato paste

1 cinnamon stick

2 tablespoons dried currants

¼ cup frozen petite peas, thawed

Kosher salt and freshly ground black pepper

Rice

2½ cups reduced-sodium chicken broth

¼ teaspoon crushed saffron threads

2 tablespoons extra virgin olive oil

⅓ cup finely chopped onion

1 garlic clove, minced

1 cup uncooked Arborio, Vialone Nano, Carnaroli, Baldo, or other medium-grain white rice

½ cup freshly grated Parmigiano-Reggiano or pecorino Romano

2 large eggs, separated

1 cup all-purpose flour

About 2 cups fine dry bread crumbs

4 to 8 cups olive or other vegetable oil for deep-frying

1. **For the filling:** Heat the oil in a Dutch oven or deep heavy skillet with a tight-fitting lid. Add the meat and brown over medium-high heat. Stir in the onion and carrot; cook, stirring, over low heat until tender, about 10 minutes. Add the garlic; cook for 1 minute. Add the beef broth, tomato paste, and cinnamon stick; heat to a boil. Cover and cook over low heat for 1½ to 2 hours, or until the meat is very tender. Check the broth level occasionally and add more broth or water if needed. Use a slotted spoon to transfer the meat to a platter and let stand until cool; set the pot aside.

2. Cut the meat into thin slices, then shred it or chop into small pieces. Return the meat to the cooking juices and add the currants. Cook, uncovered, over medium heat, stirring occasionally, until the broth is almost completely reduced, about 10 minutes. Add the peas. Cook, stirring, until the mixture is very dry and thick, about 2 minutes. Remove from the heat and season to taste with salt and pepper. (The filling can be made up to 2 days ahead, covered, and refrigerated.)

3. **For the rice:** Heat the broth to a boil in a medium saucepan. Add the saffron and set aside to infuse.

4. Combine the oil and onion in a large wide saucepan; cook, stirring, over medium-low heat until the onion is tender, about 5 minutes. Add the garlic; cook for 1 minute. Add the rice; stir to coat with the oil. Stir in the saffron-infused broth; heat to a boil, stirring to keep the rice from sticking. Cover and cook over medium-low heat for 20 minutes, or until the broth is absorbed and the rice is very tender. Stir in the cheese. Let cool to room temperature.

5. **For the arancini:** Beat the egg yolks; stir into the rice mixture until well blended. Spread the rice in a 13 × 9-inch baking pan. Place a piece of plastic wrap directly on the rice. Refrigerate until cold and easy to shape, about 30 minutes.

6. When ready to shape the arancini, whisk the egg whites in a shallow bowl until foamy. Place the flour and bread crumbs on two separate sheets of wax paper. Have ready a tray or baking sheet. Use a knife to cut the rice mixture into 12 squares. Wet your hands with cold water. Lift a square of rice and place it in the palm of your hand. Place a half-tablespoon of the meat filling in the center.

Flatten the rice mound in the palm of your hand and spoon a rounded table-spoonful of the meat mixture in the center. Gently close your hand so that the meat is surrounded by rice. Repeat with the remaining rice, wetting your hands frequently to prevent the rice from sticking to them.

7. When all the arancini are formed, coat them one at a time with the flour; shake off excess. Dip into the beaten egg white; let the excess drip off. Roll in the bread crumbs, making sure to cover evenly; shake off excess. Place the arancini on the tray as they are prepared. Refrigerate for 20 to 30 minutes to set and dry out slightly.

8. *To fry the arancini:* Heat the oil in a deep-fryer or wide deep saucepan to 350°F, or hot enough to turn a crust of bread golden. Fry the arancini a few at a time, turning, until dark golden brown, 2 to 3 minutes. Remove with the fry bas-ket, if you used one, or slotted spoon and drain on paper towels. Serve warm or at room temperature.

NOTE: The arancini can be made smaller if preferred. Use a ¼-cup measure to portion out the rice, or spreading it into a pan as above, chill, and then cut the rice into small squares. Conversely, the arancini can be made larger by using about ½ cup rice for each or cutting the rice in the pan into larger squares.

ARANCINI WITH PROSCIUTTO AND CHEESE FILLING. This is a simple version of arancini with a filling of diced prosciutto and cheese instead of the more tra-ditional cooked meat filling.

Substitute about 4 ounces prosciutto cut ⅛ inch thick and 4 ounces pro-volone, mozzarella, Italian Fontina, or Gorgonzola for the meat filling. Cut the prosciutto and cheese into small dice and use a few pieces in the center of each arancini.

Grape Leaves Stuffed with Rice, Pignoli, and Mint

**Makes
24 stuffed
grape leaves:
4 servings**

Stuffed grape leaves, or *dolmades,* as they are called in Greece, are stuffed with rice, meat, or lentils, or any combination of the three, plus herbs, most conspicuously fresh mint and dill. This recipe is from Barbara Chernetz, who grew up in Rochester, New York, next door to a Greek family.

One 8-ounce jar grape leaves

3 tablespoons extra virgin olive oil

1 cup finely chopped onions

2 garlic cloves, minced

⅓ cup uncooked long-grain white rice or basmati
  rice

½ teaspoon ground allspice

1 cinnamon stick

½ teaspoon kosher salt

2 tablespoons pignoli (pine nuts), toasted

2 tablespoons dried currants

1 tablespoon chopped mint

1 tablespoon chopped dill

1 tablespoon chopped Italian parsley

Freshly ground black pepper

2 tablespoons fresh lemon juice

Lemon wedges

1. Rinse the grape leaves under cold water; drain. Blot dry with paper towels. Use a sharp knife to cut the stems from the leaves. Reserve any torn or small leaves separately.

2. Heat 1 tablespoon of the oil in a medium saucepan. Add the onion; cook over medium-low heat, stirring, until tender, about 5 minutes. Add the garlic; cook for 1 minute. Add the rice, allspice, and cinnamon stick; cook, stirring, for 2 minutes. Add ⅔ cup water and the salt; heat to a boil. Reduce the heat to low and simmer, covered, until all the liquid is absorbed, about 15 minutes.

3. Remove the rice from the heat; discard the cinnamon stick. Stir in the pignoli, currants, mint, dill, and parsley. Add a grinding of black pepper.

4. Place one grape leaf smooth side down on a work surface. Place about 1 tablespoon of the rice mixture in the center of the leaf. Fold in the sides of the leaf

and firmly roll up the leaf to make an oval package. Repeat with the remaining ingredients until you have 24 stuffed grape leaves.

5. Line a large skillet with a tight-fitting lid with the remaining grape leaves (including the reserved torn or small ones). Place the stuffed grape leaves in a single layer, seam side down, in the skillet, lining them up side by side. Combine 2 tablespoons water, the remaining 2 tablespoons olive oil, and the lemon juice in a small bowl. Sprinkle over the grape leaves. Heat over medium-high heat until the liquid is simmering. Cover and cook over medium-low heat for 30 minutes; check occasionally to make sure the grape leaves are moist, and add more water, a few tablespoons at a time if needed. Let cool.

6. Serve at room temperature or cold, with lemon wedges.

Rice Balls Sushi-Style

**Makes about
36 rice balls:
6 to 8 servings**

These small balls of sushi rice are great party fare. I serve them to groups of friends and let them shape and stuff their own as we stand at the counter or sit and talk. First give everyone a hot towel to wipe their hands. Supply small bowls of cold water for rinsing and dampening hands as the sushi balls are formed. The rice can be made ahead and kept at room temperature until ready to shape. All of the stuffings and condiments can be measured out and placed in small bowls. It is difficult to give exact amounts since people will pick and choose their own combinations, but don't worry, leftovers will never go to waste. I took my leftovers and mixed them together with the leftover rice to make a luscious rice salad. Forming the balls takes a little practice. Have fun and enjoy. Serve cold beer, dry white wine, or sake with these.

2 cups uncooked medium-grain Japanese-style rice
   (Kokuho Rose, Botan, Nishiki, Tamaki, or Mogami)
½ cup unseasoned Japanese rice vinegar
2 tablespoons sugar
Kosher salt

Fish fillings (2 or 3 of the following)
3-ounce piece of sushi-quality fresh tuna, minced
3-ounce piece sushi-quality fresh salmon, minced
3 ounces cooked shrimp, minced
2 ounces smoked salmon, minced

Vegetable fillings (2 or 3 of the following)
¼ cup minced seedless cucumber
¼ cup minced scallion (white and green parts)

¼ cup diced (⅛-inch) avocado
2 tablespoons minced shiso leaf, optional

**Condiments (2 or 3 of the following: see Note,
  page 93)**
2 tablespoons minced pickled ginger
1 tablespoon wasabi paste
1 tablespoon red plum paste

Seasonings
¼ cup brown sesame seeds (see Note, page 30)
Soy sauce, preferably Japanese

1. Place the rice in a large bowl; cover with cold water and stir; drain. Repeat three or more times until the water is clear. (Rinsing the rice releases the excess starch and helps the rice absorb the vinegar.)

2. Place the rice in a large deep pot with straight sides and a tight-fitting lid. Add 2⅓ cups water and let stand for 10 minutes. Set the pot over high heat; heat to a boil. Reduce the heat to low, cover, and cook for 15 minutes. Remove from the heat and let stand, covered, for 5 minutes.

3. Meanwhile, combine the vinegar, sugar, and salt in a cup. Stir to dissolve the sugar. Set aside.

4. Use a wet wooden rice paddle or wooden spoon to scrape the rice out onto a large tray or platter, spreading it out with the paddle. With a fan or a piece of cardboard, immediately begin to fan the rice to cool it off while turning it with the paddle to expose the hot rice on the bottom. When there is no longer any steam rising from the rice, begin to sprinkle it with the vinegar mixture, turning the rice with the wet paddle to season evenly. Then keep fanning until the rice has a glossy sheen. Cover the rice with a dampened cloth to keep it moist. (Do not use aluminum foil or anything that will collect condensation; do not refrigerate.)

5. Just before you are ready to make the balls, place the ingredients for the fillings and coatings in small individual bowls. Have handy a small spoon or butter knife for each of the bowls.

6. Wetting your hands frequently to keep the rice from sticking, pinch off a small (about 2 tablespoons) portion of the rice. Place in the palm of your hand and squeeze to compress the grains. Then flatten slightly in your palm and make an indentation in the center with a finger of your other hand. Add a tiny pinch of each stuffing (usually a combination of 2 or 3) to the indentation. Carefully close your hand and squeeze to form the rice into a ball around the filling. Dip or roll balls in sesame seeds and/or scallions. Or sprinkle seeds and/or scallions over the tops. (Instead of stuffing the balls, you can simply make small balls of rice and roll in scallions or sesame seeds.) Arrange the rice balls on a platter and serve. Serve with small dishes of soy sauce for dipping. (Rice balls can be made a few hours ahead, arranged on a platter, covered with a wet cloth and set aside at room temperature until ready to serve.)

NOTE: These ingredients are available in Japanese markets or the Asian section of some supermarkets.

Popular combinations of ingredients: raw salmon or tuna, wasabi and pickled ginger; tuna, red plum paste, scallion or shiso; raw salmon or shrimp, pickled ginger and scallion; smoked salmon or shrimp, avocado and cucumber; red plum paste, cucumber and shiso; shrimp, cucumber, and pickled ginger; and so on.

Persian-Style Basmati Rice

Makes 6 to 8 servings

Persian rice is prepared by a unique technique, slowly cooking the rice in a heavy pan over very low heat until a crust forms on the bottom. Here, the rice is partially cooked on top of the stove and then finished in the oven. That, and using a well-seasoned or non-stick skillet, ensures that the crust will be golden and will slip out of the pan intact when inverted, to make a spectacular presentation. This recipe has become a reliable friend as I have served it repeatedly, always to accompany a grilled leg of lamb. Don't skimp on the clarified butter; it is essential to the success of the dish. (Clarified butter is preferred in this recipe, because the solids or milk proteins in butter burn when subjected to high temperatures.) For another version of Persian-style basmati rice, see Lamb Kebabs on Persian-Style Golden Rice (page 203).

12 tablespoons (1½ sticks) cold unsalted butter, cut into ¼-inch pieces
2 cups uncooked basmati rice (see Note)
2 teaspoons salt
1 cinnamon stick

3 whole cloves
3 black peppercorns
3 whole cardamom pods
1 cup thinly sliced onions
¼ teaspoon crushed saffron threads

1. Melt the butter in a small saucepan over low heat; do not brown. Remove from the heat and let stand until the solids settle to the bottom of the pan. Skim the foam from the top and spoon the clear liquid (the clarified butter) into a measuring cup; there should be ½ cup. Discard the solids on the bottom of the pan.

2. Heat 8 cups water to a boil in a large saucepan. Add the rice, salt, cinnamon stick, cloves, peppercorns, and cardamom; cook, stirring occasionally, until the rice is almost tender, 10 to 12 minutes. Drain immediately; let stand in the sieve until ready to use. (Leave the spices and peppercorns in the rice.)

3. Preheat the oven to 350°F.

4. Add 2 tablespoons of the clarified butter to a 10-inch heavy ovenproof skillet or wide saucepan, preferably nonstick. Add the onions; cook, stirring, until golden. Add the saffron threads; cook, stirring, for 1 minute.

5. Spread the onions evenly over the bottom of the pan. Spoon the rice on top. Drizzle with the remaining clarified butter; smooth the top and press down with a spatula. Cover with a double thickness of foil, pressing down on the foil to compact the rice. Bake until the bottom is crisp and golden, 55 to 60 minutes. Let stand, covered, for 10 minutes.

6. Uncover the pan, place a large platter over it, and carefully invert the rice onto the platter.

NOTE: For this dish I prefer to use imported basmati rice, because it elongates more than the American basmati hybrids. I do not soak it, because the recipe calls for it to be cooked in plenty of boiling water (a technique preferred by many chefs), but I do rinse it, especially if it looks as if it contains dust or bits of chaff. To rinse, place in a bowl, fill with water, stir, and spoon off any debris that comes to the top; drain.

Baked Rice and Cheese

Makes 6 to 8 servings

Like macaroni and cheese, but this homey version is made with cooked rice instead of elbow macaroni. Perfect food for cold weather.

2 tablespoons unsalted butter

2 tablespoons all-purpose flour

3 cups milk, warmed

1 teaspoon kosher salt, or to taste

Dash of Tabasco sauce

2 cups coarsely shredded Cheddar

3 to 4 cups cooked medium- or long-grain white rice

1 cup coarsely shredded mozzarella

1. Preheat the oven to 350°F. Lightly butter a shallow 2-quart baking dish, about 8 inches square or 11 × 7 inches.

2. Melt the butter in a large saucepan. Add the flour and cook, stirring, over low heat for 5 minutes. Gradually stir in the milk; cook, stirring, until the milk boils and the sauce is slightly thickened. Remove from the heat. Add the salt and Tabasco sauce. Stir in the Cheddar. Taste and add more salt if needed.

3. Spread the rice in the baking dish. Pour the cheese sauce over the top. Sprinkle with the mozzarella. Bake until the top is browned and bubbly, about 45 minutes. Let stand for 10 minutes before cutting into squares and serving.

MUSHROOM-AND-BACON BAKED RICE AND CHEESE. Omit the Tabasco. Heat 1 tablespoon olive oil in a large skillet. Add 1 slice bacon, diced, and cook, stirring, until lightly browned. Add 2 cups sliced cremini or white button mushrooms and ½ cup chopped onion. Cook, stirring, until golden brown, about 10 minutes. Season with salt and pepper. To assemble the casserole, spread half of the rice in the baking dish. Spoon the mushroom filling evenly over the top. Add the remaining rice in an even layer. Pour the cheese sauce on top. Sprinkle with the mozzarella and bake as directed.

Fried Rice

It wasn't until my friend Ken Lee reheated a fried rice recipe that I was testing (and had run over to his house for him to critique) that I realized what was wrong with my fried rice dishes. Being a man of action, Ken immediately set my pan over a high flame and got to work. Rather than gently stirring the rice, as I had done, he pressed it down hard along the bottom and sides of the pan. Then he scraped up the rice, flipped it over, and hacked (a technique it had never occurred to me to use) at the rice, separating the grains. Each one emerged coated with the seasonings and hot from its contact with the pan. As I watched, I realized it was my technique (or lack of technique), not the recipe ingredients, that had been wrong. I also realized what a profound difference it makes to learn by watching. Since we all can't go to Ken's house, here is a list of the tips I learned from him.

- The rice should be cold and dry.

- Use cooked medium- or short-grain sushi rice, medium-grain white rice, medium-grain brown rice, or red rice. Cold leftover rice is best. Or cook the rice and let cool, then spread on a baking sheet and let stand at room temperature, or refrigerate, uncovered, to dry.

- Three cups cold or room-temperature cooked dry rice is enough for 4 side-dish servings. Use 4 cups for 4 main-dish servings.

- Have all ingredients prepped and measured. Fried rice cooks quickly, about 5 minutes from start to finish. Once you begin, there is no time to unscrew the top from the soy sauce bottle, or reach for a measuring spoon.

- A wok is fine, but not necessary. You can use a large heavy skillet. I use a skillet shaped like a wok with a nonstick coating.

- A big wooden spoon with a flat edge, a short wide wooden spatula, or a wooden rice paddle is best for stirring fried rice.

- Heat the pan first, then add the oil. Peanut oil is preferable, but any vegetable oil can be used.

- Tender vegetables like snow peas, bell peppers, bok choy, and zucchini will cook in minutes right in the hot rice. Firm vegetables like broccoli or cauliflower take longer; they should be parboiled first in boiling salted water for 1 to 2 minutes.

- When the oil is hot enough to sizzle a pinch of the prepared vegetables, add the vegetables to the skillet. Ken learned from his Chinese father to begin his stir-fry with chopped onion, cooked until golden. Then add the minced ginger, garlic, and chile pepper, if using, after adding the other vegetables.

- Add the rice all at once, sprinkle with soy sauce and sesame oil, if using, and spread it over the bottom and up the sides of the pan. Press the rice against the surface of the hot pan. After a few seconds, lift the rice, turn, and press again; repeat several times. As the rice is cooking, make hacking motions, straight down and into the rice, with the side of the spoon, spatula, or paddle. This separates the rice grains and coasts then with the seasonings.

- When the rice is well mixed with the other ingredients, push it to one side of the pan, or spread it around the sides of the pan, clearing a spot. Add the egg to the cleared spot and cook until partially set. Chop it up with the edge of your stirring utensil and stir it into the rice, using quick hard strokes, or the hacking motion you used to stir the rice and vegetables. In 30 seconds, your fried rice is ready.

Fried Rice with Oyster Mushrooms, Snow Peas, and Black Sesame Seeds

Makes 6 to 8 servings

Oyster mushrooms, also called pleurotes, are a delicate lacy-capped mushroom the color of alabaster. If snow peas aren't available, substitute thawed frozen green peas. If your market doesn't stock black sesame seeds (available where Asian products are sold), substitute white sesame seeds, lightly toasted, or natural brown sesame seeds.

2 large eggs

Toasted sesame oil

Tamari or soy sauce

3 tablespoons peanut or other vegetable oil

¼ cup thinly sliced white part of scallions, plus
   ¼ cup thinly sliced scallion greens

1 tablespoon minced fresh ginger

1 tablespoon minced garlic

8 ounces snow peas, strings removed, tips trimmed
   on the diagonal

8 ounces oyster mushrooms, trimmed, halved
   if large

3 to 4 cups cold cooked sushi rice or medium-grain
   white rice

1 teaspoon black sesame seeds

1. Break the eggs into a small bowl; add ½ teaspoon each sesame oil and tamari. Beat gently with a fork or chopstick just to combine. Set aside.

2. Heat a wok or large skillet, preferably nonstick, over high heat until hot enough to sizzle a drop of water upon contact. Add the peanut oil and a pinch of the scallion whites. When the scallions sizzle, add the remaining scallion whites; fry for 20 seconds, stirring with a flat wooden spatula or spoon. Add the ginger and the garlic; stir-fry for 10 seconds. Stir in the snow peas; cook for 20 seconds. Stir in the mushrooms; cook for 20 seconds.

3. Add the rice; break up any clumps with the edge of the spatula mixing in the other ingredients. Press the rice against the bottom and up the sides of the pan. Sprinkle with 1 tablespoon tamari and 1 teaspoon sesame oil. Continue heating the rice, lifting up sections with the spatula, and turning, pressing, and hacking

at it with the side of the spatula, until all the ingredients are evenly mixed and coated with the seasonings, about 1 minute.

4. Push the rice to one side or up the sides of the pan to make an open space. Add the eggs and fry until partially set, about 30 seconds. Stir into the rice until blended.

5. Sprinkle the fried rice with the scallion greens and sesame seeds. Spoon into a serving dish and serve at once. Let each person season the rice with extra tamari and sesame oil to taste.

Fried Red Rice with Shiitakes and Bok Choy

Makes 4 servings

Red rice from Bhutan, a sticky medium-grain rice with a distinctive earthy taste and chewy texture, makes delicious fried rice. I like to mix it with an equal amount of brown rice. If preferred, make this versatile recipe with all red rice or brown rice, or white rice, or a combination.

1 large egg

Toasted sesame oil

Tamari or soy sauce

3 tablespoons peanut or other vegetable oil

½ cup chopped onion

4 ounces shiitakes, stems discarded, caps wiped clean and cut into ¼-inch slices

½ cup diced cooked smoked ham, optional

2 teaspoons minced fresh ginger

2 teaspoons minced garlic

1 teaspoon minced jalapeño

4 ounces baby bok choy (4 or 5 heads), trimmed and cut crosswise into ½-inch slices (about 2 cups)

2 cups cold cooked Bhutanese red rice

2 cups cold cooked medium-grain brown rice

1. Break the egg into a small bowl; add ¼ teaspoon each sesame oil and tamari. Beat gently with a fork or chopstick just to combine. Set aside.

2. Heat a wok or large skillet, preferably nonstick, over high heat until hot enough to sizzle a drop of water upon contact. Add the peanut oil and a pinch of the onion. When the onions sizzle, add the remaining onions; fry, stirring with a flat wooden spatula or spoon, about 30 seconds. Add the shiitakes; stir-fry, until golden, about 1 minute. Add the ham, if using, ginger, garlic, and jalapeño; stir-fry for 10 seconds. Stir in the bok choy; cook for 20 seconds.

3. Add the rice; break up any clumps with the edge of the spatula, mixing in the other ingredients in the wok. Press the rice against the bottom and up the sides of the pan. Sprinkle with 1 tablespoon tamari and 1 teaspoon sesame oil. Continue heating the rice, lifting up sections with the spatula, and turning, pressing, and hacking at it with the side of the spatula until all the ingredients are evenly mixed and coated with the seasonings, about 1 minute.

4. Push the rice to one side or up the sides of the pan to make an open space. Add the egg and fry until partially set, about 30 seconds. Stir into the rice until blended.

5. Spoon the rice into a serving dish and serve at once. Let each person season the rice with extra tamari and sesame oil to taste.

Orange-Vegetable Fried Rice

Makes 4 servings

Orange zest adds a fresh clean taste to this easy-to-make fried rice dish. To make quick work of the zesting, peel the orange with a vegetable peeler. Stack the strips of peel and cut into fine slivers, then cut into 1-inch lengths. You will need the zest from about half an orange. This fried rice is excellent with shreds of cooked chicken or chopped cooked shrimp or as a side dish with fish or chicken.

3 cups small broccoli and cauliflower florets (1-inch pieces)
2 large eggs
Toasted sesame oil
Tamari or soy sauce
3 tablespoons peanut or extra virgin olive oil
1 medium red bell pepper, stemmed, seeded, quartered, and cut crosswise into ⅛-inch pieces

1 tablespoon slivered orange zest (see headnote)
¼ cup thinly sliced white part of scallion, plus ¼ cup thinly sliced scallion greens
2 teaspoons minced fresh ginger
2 teaspoons minced garlic
3 to 4 cups cooked white (or half white and half medium-grain brown) rice
½ teaspoon chile oil, or to taste

1. Heat a saucepan of water to a boil. Add the broccoli and cauliflower; cook, stirring several times, for 2 minutes. Drain; rinse with cold water. Spread on a double thickness of paper towels to dry.

2. Break the eggs into a small bowl; add ½ teaspoon each sesame oil and tamari. Beat gently with a fork or chopstick just to combine. Set aside.

3. Heat a wok or large skillet, preferably nonstick, over high heat until hot enough to sizzle a drop of water upon contact. Add the peanut oil and a sliver of the red pepper. When the red pepper sizzles, add the remaining peppers; fry, stirring with a flat wooden spatula or spoon, until wilted, about 30 seconds. Add the orange zest, scallion whites, ginger, and garlic; stir-fry for 10 seconds. Stir in the broccoli and cauliflower; cook for 20 seconds.

4. Add the rice; break up any clumps with the edge of the spatula, mixing in the other ingredients in the wok. Press the rice against the bottom and up the sides of the pan. Sprinkle with 1 tablespoon tamari, 1 teaspoon sesame oil, and the chile oil. Continue heating the rice, lifting up sections with the spatula, and

turning, pressing and hacking at it with the side of the spatula, until all the ingredients are evenly mixed and coated with the seasonings, about 1 minute.

5. Push the rice to one side or up around the sides of the pan to make an open space. Add the eggs and fry until partially set, about 30 seconds. Stir into the rice until blended.

6. Spoon the rice into a serving dish; sprinkle with the scallion greens. Serve at once. Let each person season the rice with extra tamari and sesame oil to taste.

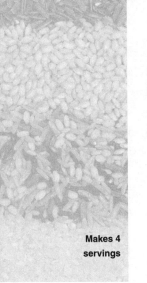

Spicy Fried Rice with Broccoli Rabe and Golden Garlic Threads

Makes 4 servings

Broccoli rabe, a leafy green with small clusters of florets, has a slightly bitter taste that helps to balance the sweetness of the rice. If unavailable, regular bunch broccoli can be substituted. Use all white or half brown and half white rice in this simple dish.

1 bunch (about 1 pound) broccoli rabe, thick stems trimmed

3 tablespoons canola or other vegetable oil

1 tablespoon slivered garlic

¼ cup finely chopped onion

¼ cup finely chopped carrot

⅛ teaspoon red pepper flakes

2 tablespoons soy sauce

1 teaspoon toasted sesame oil

3 cups cold cooked medium-grain white or brown rice (or a combination)

2 large eggs, slightly beaten

1. Heat a large saucepan of water to a boil. Add the broccoli rabe and cook for 4 minutes; drain. Cool. Chop into ½-inch pieces; wrap in a kitchen towel and press out excess moisture.

2. Heat the oil and garlic in a wok or large skillet over medium-low heat until the garlic begins to sizzle. Stir constantly until the garlic begins to turn a pale yellow, about 30 seconds. Immediately skim the garlic from the oil with a perforated spoon or spatula; drain on absorbent paper. Set aside.

3. Add the onion, carrot, and red pepper flakes to the oil; fry, stirring with a flat wooden spatula or wooden spoon, for 2 minutes. Add the broccoli rabe; stir-fry over medium heat, until well blended, about 2 minutes. Add the soy sauce and sesame oil; stir to blend.

4. Add the rice; break up any clumps with the edge of the spatula, mixing in the other ingredients in the wok. Press the rice against the bottom and up the sides of the pan. Continue heating the rice, lifting up sections with the spatula, and

turning, pressing, and hacking at it with the side of the spatula until all the ingredients are evenly mixed and coated with the seasonings, about 1 minute.

5. Push the rice to one side or up around the sides of the pan to make an open space. Add the eggs and fry until partially set, about 30 seconds. Stir into the rice until blended.

6. Spoon the rice onto a serving platter and sprinkle with the golden garlic threads.

Wild Rice with Mushrooms and Prosciutto

Makes 4 to 6 servings

The flavors of wild rice and mushrooms complement each other. Make this dish with just one or up to three different types of mushrooms. They shrink when cooked, so use a ratio of at least 4 cups raw mushrooms to 3 cups cooked wild rice. Prosciutto is easier to snip with scissors than to cut with a knife. Do not trim the fat, as it is very flavorful and part of the delicacy of the ham. I also serve this as a main course with cooked greens like broccoli rabe, escarole, or Swiss chard.

1 cup uncooked wild rice, rinsed with warm water and drained
Kosher salt
2 tablespoons extra virgin olive oil
¼ cup diced (¼-inch) onion (about 2 ounces)
¼ cup snipped (¼-inch pieces) prosciutto
6 ounces cremini mushrooms, trimmed and cut into ½-inch pieces (about 2 cups)
4 ounces shiitakes, stems removed, caps wiped clean and cut into ¼-inch dice (about 2 cups)

1 garlic clove, minced
4 ounces chanterelle or oyster mushrooms, cut into ½-inch pieces (about 1½ cups)
Freshly ground black pepper
½ cup dry white wine
2 tablespoons finely chopped Italian parsley
½ teaspoon fresh thyme leaves or a pinch of dried thyme, optional
2 tablespoons chopped toasted peeled hazelnuts or pignoli (pine nuts), optional

1. Heat 3 cups water in a large saucepan; stir in the rice and 1 teaspoon salt. Cover and cook over low heat until the rice is tender, 35 to 55 minutes, depending on the rice. Uncover and cook over low heat until any excess liquid is evaporated.

2. Heat the olive oil in a large heavy skillet; add the onion and prosciutto; cook for 2 minutes. Add the cremini and shiitakes; cook, stirring, over medium heat until the mushrooms begin to brown, about 5 minutes. Add the garlic; cook for 1 minute. Stir in the chanterelles; cook until tender, about 2 minutes. Add salt and pepper to taste. Add the wild rice, wine, parsley, and thyme; cook, stirring, until the wine boils away, about 5 minutes.

3. Correct the seasoning. Spoon into a serving dish and sprinkle with the toasted nuts, if using.

Stuffed Vegetables

Some vegetables—scooped-out roasted eggplant, winter squash, tomatoes, artichokes, and, of course, mushrooms—seem to beg for a filling, especially leftover cooked rice. You can use any combination of rice you have on hand. The same goes for the vegetables used in the filling.

The variations for rice-stuffed vegetables are endless and versatile. For aromatics use finely chopped leeks, onions, or shallots. For moisture add chopped mushrooms, tomatoes, or spinach. Fresh or dried herbs add flavor and cheese helps to bind the filling together. Nuts add crunch while dried fruits will add sweetness.

All of the following stuffed vegetable recipes are meant to be served as side dishes, but bits of cooked shrimp or fish, chicken, sausage, ground meats, bacon, or ham will make them hearty enough for a main course. For a vegetarian main course double the non-meat or fish version.

Rice-Stuffed Artichokes with Lemon, Dill, and Toasted Pignoli

Makes 4 to 8 servings

Once the fuzzy center and inner leaves (the choke) are scooped from a halved artichoke, a nice little crevice is perfect for a filling. Serve as a first course or as a side dish with lamb chops or grilled fish.

5 large artichokes

Kosher salt and freshly ground black pepper

2 tablespoons fresh lemon juice

2 tablespoons extra virgin olive oil

½ cup chopped onion

1 garlic clove, minced

2 cups cooked long-grain white rice or Arborio, Baldo, or other medium-grain white rice (see Notes)

2 tablespoons diced, seeded plum tomato

1 tablespoon pignoli (pine nuts), toasted and coarsely chopped

1 tablespoon minced dill

1 tablespoon minced Italian parsley

1 teaspoon minced fresh oregano or ½ teaspoon dried oregano (see Notes)

¼ teaspoon ground cinnamon

¼ cup freshly grated Parmigiano-Reggiano

½ cup dry white wine

1. Pull off the two or three outer layers of large mature leaves from each artichoke, leaving the more tender, paler green leaves. (Discard the large leaves, or steam and reserve for a snack.) Lay the artichoke on its side and cut ½ inch off the top. Leave the stem attached. With a small knife, trim the tough outer skin off the stem, and trim around the base of the artichoke until smooth.

2. Heat 1 to 2 inches of water in a large deep saucepan or vegetable steamer. Place the artichokes on the steamer rack. Cover and steam until tender when pierced with a skewer, 20 to 30 minutes. Let cool slightly.

3. Halve the artichokes lengthwise. With a teaspoon, scoop out the center thorn-tipped leaves and fuzzy choke. Arrange 8 artichoke halves cut side up in a large baking dish. Dice the remaining 2 halves into ⅛-inch pieces, discarding stringy

leaves. (There should be 1 to 1½ cups diced artichoke.) Season each of the artichoke halves with salt and pepper and a few drops of lemon juice.

4. Heat the oil in a large skillet. Add the onion; cook, stirring, over medium-low heat until golden, about 5 minutes. Stir in the garlic; cook for 1 minute. Add the rice, diced artichoke, tomato, pignoli, dill, parsley, oregano, and cinnamon; stir to blend. Add the remaining lemon juice. Season to taste with salt and pepper. Let cool to room temperature.

5. Preheat the oven to 400°F.

6. Stuff each artichoke with about ¼ cup of the stuffing. Sprinkle the top of each with ½ tablespoon grated cheese. Pour the wine and ½ cup water into the baking pan.

7. Bake until the tops are golden, 20 to 25 minutes. Serve at once.

NOTES: Basmati rice isn't as successful in this recipe because it isn't sticky enough to hold the rice filling together.

If using dried oregano, chop it together with the dill and parsley. The moisture from the fresh herbs will help to rehydrate the dried oregano and freshen the flavor.

Rice, Tomato, and Black Olive–Stuffed Roasted Eggplant with Feta

Makes 4 servings

Fillings for stuffing vegetables are endless. In the following recipe, fresh red bell pepper can be substituted for the roasted pepper, capers used in place of the black olives, and grated Parmesan or provolone cheese can stand in for feta. Almost any rice, white, brown, or red, can be used as well.

2 small eggplants, about 8 ounces each, halved lengthwise (do not trim)

2 tablespoons extra virgin olive oil, plus extra for brushing

½ cup chopped onion

2 plum tomatoes, halved, seeds and pulp removed, and diced (about ½ cup)

Kosher salt and freshly ground black pepper

1½ cups cooked long- or medium-grain white or brown rice

2 tablespoons chopped Italian parsley

1 teaspoon dried oregano

½ cup crumbled mild feta cheese

¼ cup diced (¼-inch) rinsed jarred roasted red pepper

8 Kalamata olives, pitted and chopped

1. Preheat the oven to 400°F.

2. Brush the cut side of each eggplant half with olive oil. Place cut side down on a baking sheet. Roast until the eggplant is soft and the cut sides are golden, about 20 minutes. Let cool. Reduce the oven temperature to 350°F.

3. Meanwhile, heat the 2 tablespoons olive oil in a large skillet. Add the onion; cook, stirring, over medium-low heat until golden, about 5 minutes. Stir in the tomatoes; cook, stirring, until soft, about 5 minutes. Sprinkle lightly with salt and a grinding of black pepper. Add the rice and stir until blended. Remove from the heat.

4. Using a tablespoon, carefully scoop the tender flesh from the eggplant skins, leaving the skins intact. Chop the flesh. Measure out ½ cup and add to the rice;

reserve the remaining eggplant for another use. Finely chop the parsley and oregano together. Add the parsley mixture, feta cheese, roasted pepper, and olives to the rice mixture; stir to blend. Add salt and pepper to taste.

5. Arrange the eggplant shells in a baking dish. Carefully fill with the rice mixture, pressing it down lightly. If there is any extra filling, spoon it around the eggplant.

6. Roast until the filling is heated through and the top is golden, about 25 minutes. Serve hot or at room temperature.

Rice, Anchovy, and Caper Tomatoes with Garlic Crumb Topping

The perfect summer food when tomatoes are lush and ripe. Add a mixture of fresh vegetables—corn, diced scallions, red bell pepper. Add shredded mozzarella or grated Parmesan too, if you'd like.

4 large moderately ripe tomatoes

Extra virgin olive oil

Kosher salt and freshly ground black pepper

2 cups cooked long- or medium-grain white rice or
   Arborio or Baldo rice

½ cup diced (¼-inch) red onion

1 tablespoon drained rinsed capers

1 tablespoon rinsed, drained, and minced anchovy
   fillets

1 tablespoon finely chopped Italian parsley

1 tablespoon finely chopped basil

Garlic Crumbs

1 cup coarse crumbs from day-old Italian bread

1 tablespoon olive oil

1 teaspoon minced garlic

1. Preheat the oven to 350°F. Lightly oil a shallow baking dish just large enough to hold the tomatoes.

2. Cut ½ inch off the tops of the tomatoes. Using a teaspoon, scoop out the pulp and seeds, leaving the tomato shells intact. Chop ½ cup of the pulp and set aside; reserve the remaining pulp for another use. Sprinkle the inside of the tomatoes with salt and pepper, rub the outside lightly with olive oil. Arrange in the prepared baking dish.

3. Combine the rice, red onion, chopped tomato pulp, capers, anchovies, parsley, and basil in a large bowl. Add 1 tablespoon olive oil; toss to blend. Carefully stuff into the tomatoes, distributing the filling evenly.

4. *For the crumbs:* Combine the bread crumbs, olive oil, and garlic in a small bowl; toss to blend. Sprinkle on top of the tomatoes.

5. Bake until the crumbs are golden and the tomatoes are heated through, 20 to 25 minutes. Serve warm or at room temperature.

Rice, Mushroom, and Spinach–Stuffed Roasted Red Peppers

Makes 4 servings

Roasting the peppers first before filling is the secret to avoiding that soggy stuffed pepper taste. What is lost in height (the peppers won't stand up as rigidly) will be gained in flavor. The stuffing calls for a small amount of diced red pepper, so pick up an extra pepper (a smaller one will do just fine) when shopping. Yellow peppers, or a combination of red and yellow, can be used.

2 large red bell peppers (about 12 ounces each)

3 tablespoons extra virgin olive oil, plus extra for roasting the peppers

2 teaspoons thyme leaves

2 garlic cloves, finely chopped

Kosher salt and freshly ground black pepper

½ cup chopped onion

1 cup coarsely chopped white button mushrooms

½ cup diced (¼-inch) red bell pepper

1 tablespoon chopped Italian parsley

2 cups packed coarsely chopped spinach leaves (about 4 ounces)

2 cups cooked long-grain white rice or jasmine or basmati rice (or 1 cup each brown and white rice)

¼ cup freshly grated Parmigiano-Reggiano

½ cup shredded mozzarella, Monterey Jack, or other flavorful cheese

1. Preheat the oven to 400°F.

2. Cut the peppers lengthwise in half, leaving the stems intact if possible. Remove the seeds and ribs with a small sharp knife. Rub a baking dish with a thin film of olive oil. Arrange the peppers cut side up in the baking dish. Sprinkle 1 teaspoon of the thyme, half of the chopped garlic, and salt and pepper to taste, into the cavities of the peppers. Roast, turning once, until the peppers begin to char, about 30 minutes.

3. Meanwhile, heat the 3 tablespoons oil in a large skillet. Add the onion; cook, over low heat, stirring, until softened, about 5 minutes. Add the mushrooms and diced red pepper; cook over medium heat, stirring, until the vegetables begin to brown, about 5 minutes. Add the parsley, the remaining 1 teaspoon thyme leaves, and the remaining chopped garlic; cook for 1 minute. Stir in the spinach until well blended. Cover; cook over low heat until the spinach is wilted, about 3 minutes. Add the rice and Parmesan cheese; stir until blended. Season to taste with salt and pepper. Remove from the heat.

4. Carefully spoon the stuffing into the roasted pepper halves, packing the mixture and lifting up the sides of the peppers as they are filled. Sprinkle the tops with the shredded cheese.

5. Bake until the tops are browned, about 25 minutes. Serve warm or at room temperature.

Quick Hits with Rice

Plain cooked rice provides a tempting blank canvas for the creative cook. In addition to a variety of rices available, the cook need only have on hand a few basics—a palette of ingredients—from which to choose. It is exciting to see how easily a handful of raisins, a sautéed onion, or a spoonful of spice will transform a pot of plain rice. It all depends on the cook's resources and imagination. Add the following to 3 cups hot cooked rice, and fluff with a fork to blend.

Green Rice

1 cup packed cilantro leaves

¼ cup low-sodium chicken or vegetable broth

1 garlic clove

1 tablespoon coarsely chopped fresh ginger, pureed together in a food processer

Carrot and Ginger Rice

1 medium carrot, coarsely shredded

1 teaspoon grated fresh ginger

1 tablespoon Japanese rice vinegar

Toasted Coconut Rice

1 cup dried unsweetened flaked coconut, toasted in a skillet over medium-low heat

Parmesan and Toasted Walnut Rice

½ cup broken walnuts, toasted in 2 tablespoons unsalted butter

¼ cup freshly grated Parmigiano-Reggiano

Sesame Rice with Scallions

1 tablespoon brown sesame seeds

1 teaspoon toasted sesame oil

2 tablespoons thinly sliced scallion greens

Lemon Rice with Peas and Mint

1 cup cooked frozen petite peas or fresh peas

1 tablespoon unsalted butter

1 teaspoon grated lemon zest

1 tablespoon finely chopped mint

Crispy Chickpeas and Garlic Rice

1 cup chickpeas, heated in 2 tablespoons olive oil until crispy

1 teaspoon minced garlic, sautéed

Fresh Corn, Butter, and Basil Rice

1 cup corn kernels (from 1 to 2 ears), heated in 1 tablespoon unsalted butter

1 tablespoon torn basil leaves

Hazelnut and Mushroom Rice

1 cup chopped white button mushrooms and ½ cup chopped peeled toasted hazelnuts (see box, page 76), sautéed in 2 tablespoons unsalted butter until golden

Scrambled Egg and Ham Rice

3 large eggs, beaten

½ cup minced ham, cooked in 1 tablespoon olive oil

Risotto

Risotto (*riso* is the Italian word for rice; *risotto* means "big rice") is unique in the world of rice dishes. Like no other rice dish the rice in risotto is stirred constantly during the entire cooking time. The friction of the stirring releases the starch and combines with the gradually added hot broth to make a creamy "sauce" that surrounds each tender grain. What is distinctive about risotto is the contrast in textures. When you bite into perfectly cooked risotto, the rice feels creamy until you reach the centers of the grains, where there will be a pleasant resistance. At first you may not recognize when risotto is properly cooked, but with practice, you will.

The rice used to make risotto must be a medium-grain rice with a higher percentage of amylopectin (the sticky starch) than amylose (the dry starch). Three popular varieties of Italian risotto rice are Carnaroli, Vialone Nano, and Arborio. If you examine the raw grains, you see a large oval grain with a clearly visible white core (sometimes called the pearl) surrounded by a translucent border. It is this core that gives the rice its unique texture, or bite. Baldo, another Italian rice, now grown in the United States, as well and other medium-grain rices grown in California make a creamy risotto, but the grains are smaller and the core less distinct.

As in all cooking, choosing the right pot for making risotto is important. Use a shallow 8- or 10-quart heavy-bottomed pot or a deep (about 3 inches) 12-inch heavy-bottomed skillet or sauté pan. The wide pot allows the rice to spread out and cook evenly and provides ample room for stirring constantly throughout the cooking process. If you use a tall narrow saucepan, the ingredients will be too crowded, making it difficult to cook—and stir—the rice evenly.

How do you know when risotto is done? The time it takes to cook depends on an assortment of variables, many of which cannot be controlled by the cook. Generally, risotto takes between 20 and 30 minutes (longer at higher altitudes) to cook. But the age (older rice is drier and needs more time; younger rice is moister and cooks a little faster) and the variety (large grains cook more slowly than small) are two important factors. The rice will take slightly longer to cook if you add acidic ingredients such as tomatoes or wine. When I add the first half cup of broth, I set my timer for 15 minutes. When the 15 minutes is up, I begin to taste the risotto every few minutes to check the consistency of the rice as the cooking continues over the next 5 to 10 minutes. Look for a creamy sauce surrounding the grains of rice and rice that is tender on the outside with a very slight resistance when you bite

---

Risotto Troubleshooting

- Never rinse the rice for risotto; that would wash away the starch essential for its creamy consistency.

- Stir with a long-handled, flat-edged wooden spoon that can reach the edges of the pot and sweep across the bottom in just a couple of strokes.

- Add the rice all at once to the hot olive oil or butter, stirring until each grain of rice is coated and heated through.

- Use good-quality broth, either homemade or store-bought.

- For measuring the broth easily, use a 4-ounce ladle. The amount of broth called for is approximate because of the many other variables involved, like the moisture content of the rice, the weight and size of the pan, and the intensity of the heat. Keep a kettle of water simmering; if you run out of broth, add boiling water as necessary.

- Adjust the heat as necessary to maintain a gentle boil or steady simmer.

- Never cover the risotto.

- When the risotto is cooked, add the cheese and butter, stirring vigorously to loosen the starch, making the risotto thicker and creamier.

- Let finished risotto stand, off the heat, for a few minutes before serving.

---

through the grain. The rice should not be gummy or chalky. You, and the rice, not the clock, are the best judges.

Risotto, like pasta, is a canvas for any number of flavor additions. The basic formula (butter or olive oil, onion, rice, chicken broth, and cheese) is straightforward and simple, but it can become complex with the addition of wine, fish broth, dried mushrooms, meats, and/or vegetables. Stir fresh or thawed frozen peas, crisp-cooked diced vegetables (carrot, zucchini, yellow squash, red bell pepper), sautéed mushrooms, or cooked sausage, meat, or fish into the risotto during the last 5 minutes of cooking. Just before serving, stir in a chunk of butter and cheese to taste. A mild-flavored hard grating cheese like Parmigiano-Reggiano is most often used, but Asiago, Fontina, and even Gruyère are good. Add them sparingly at first and taste before adding more. To preserve their color and fresh flavor, fresh herbs, such as slivered basil, rosemary and thyme leaves, or chopped parsley, are added just before serving.

In Italy, risotto is served as the *primi piatti*, or first course—except for *risotto alla milanese*, which is served as a side dish with osso buco. The American palate, accustomed to a main course of pasta, also enjoys risotto as a main course. One cup of rice makes enough risotto to serve two as a main course or four as a first course.

Serve risotto in warmed shallow soup dishes, mounding it in the center of the bowls. Risotto is always eaten with a fork. Serve extra cheese on the side if you like, but I usually add plenty of cheese during the finishing step.

A Basic Risotto

Makes 4 one-cup servings

Called *risotto bianco*, or "white risotto," this is a classic risotto made with rice, broth, and cheese. Top it with curls of cheese cut from a wedge of Parmigiano-Reggiano with a cheese plane or sturdy vegetable peeler. Substitute red wine for the white and beef for the chicken broth.

6 to 8 cups reduced-sodium chicken broth
   (or half broth and half water)
3 tablespoons unsalted butter
⅓ cup finely chopped onion
½ cup dry white wine

1½ cups Carnaroli, Vialone Nano, or Arborio rice
⅓ cup freshly grated Parmigiano-Reggiano, plus
   Parmigiano-Reggiano curls
Kosher salt

1. Heat the broth to a simmer in a saucepan; keep at a gentle simmer.

2. Melt 2 tablespoons of the butter in a large wide saucepan or deep skillet. Add the onion; cook over low heat, stirring, until golden, about 10 minutes. Do not brown. Stir in the rice until coated, about 2 minutes. Add the wine; cook over medium-high heat, stirring constantly, until absorbed.

3. Add ½ cup of the hot chicken broth; cook, stirring constantly, over medium heat until the broth is almost all absorbed. Add the remaining broth ½ cup at a time, stirring constantly, until the risotto is creamy and the rice is plump and tender with a slight resistance to the bite, 20 to 25 minutes. (If you run out of broth, finish the risotto with a little boiling water.)

4. Add the remaining 1 tablespoon butter and the grated cheese; stir vigorously until the risotto is creamy, about 30 seconds. Taste and add salt if needed. Let stand off the heat for a few minutes before serving.

5. Spoon the risotto into shallow soup dishes. Top with Parmesan curls and serve at once.

Risotto with Asparagus, Peas, and Saffron

Makes 4 one-cup servings

In early spring, slender green asparagus and bunches of bright yellow daffodils first appear in the market, announcing the change in the seasons. This risotto is my culinary bridge from the dullness of winter to the anticipation of spring. The rice tinted yellow by the saffron reminds me of daffodils.

¼ teaspoon crushed saffron threads

½ cup dry white wine

12 ounces asparagus, trimmed, stems peeled, and soaked in cold water

6 to 8 cups reduced-sodium chicken broth (or half broth and half water)

3 tablespoons unsalted butter

¼ cup finely diced peeled carrot

¼ cup diced shallots

1½ cups Carnaroli, Vialone Nano, or Arborio rice

½ teaspoon finely shredded lemon zest

1 tablespoon fresh lemon juice

¼ cup freshly grated Parmigiano-Reggiano

Kosher salt

1. Sprinkle the saffron into a small dry skillet; heat over low heat for 30 seconds. Add the wine; heat to a simmer. Remove from the heat, let stand, covered, for 15 minutes.

2. Drain the asparagus. Cut the stalks into ¼-inch diagonal slices up to the tips; leave the tips whole. Set aside.

3. Heat the broth to a simmer in a saucepan; keep at a gentle simmer.

4. Melt 2 tablespoons of the butter in a large wide saucepan or deep skillet. Add the carrot and shallots; cook over low heat, stirring, until tender, about 5 minutes. Do not brown. Stir in the rice until coated, about 2 minutes. Add the wine and saffron mixture; cook over medium-high heat, stirring constantly, until the wine is absorbed.

5. Add ½ cup of the hot chicken broth. Cook, stirring constantly, over medium heat until the broth is almost all absorbed. Add the remaining broth ½ cup at a time, stirring constantly, until the risotto is creamy and the rice is plump and tender with a slight resistance to the bite, 20 to 25 minutes. During the last 5 minutes of cooking, stir in the asparagus, lemon zest, and lemon juice. (If you run out of broth, finish the risotto with a little boiling water.)

6. Add the remaining 1 tablespoon butter and the cheese. Stir vigorously until the risotto is creamy, about 30 seconds. Taste and add salt if needed. Let stand off the heat for a few minutes before serving.

7. Spoon the risotto into shallow soup dishes and serve at once.

Roasted Carrot and Leek Risotto with Lemon and Thyme

Makes 4 one-cup servings

Roasting vegetables intensifies their flavor. The roasted carrots lend a pretty golden color to this risotto and both the carrots and the leeks add richness and a hint of sweetness.

4 medium carrots, halved lengthwise

2 garlic cloves, bruised with the side of a knife

4 thin lemon slices

2 tablespoons extra virgin olive oil

Kosher salt and freshly ground black pepper

6 to 8 cups reduced-sodium chicken broth (or half broth and half water)

3 tablespoons unsalted butter

1 large leek, trimmed, washed, and cut into ¼-inch dice (about 1 cup)

1½ cups Carnaroli, Vialone Nano, or Arborio rice

½ cup dry white wine

1 teaspoon grated lemon zest

½ cup freshly grated Parmigiano-Reggiano

Kosher salt

1 tablespoon thyme leaves

1. Preheat the oven to 400°F.

2. Combine the carrots, lemon slices, garlic, and oil in a 13 × 9-inch baking dish. Sprinkle with salt and pepper. Roast, stirring occasionally, until the carrots are tender and lightly browned, 45 to 55 minutes. Let cool. Discard the lemons and garlic. Cut the carrots into ¼-inch dice; set aside.

3. Heat the chicken broth to a simmer in a saucepan; keep at a gentle simmer.

4. Melt 2 tablespoons of the butter in a large wide saucepan or deep skillet. Add the leek; cook over low heat, stirring, until tender, about 10 minutes. Do not brown. Stir in the rice until coated, about 2 minutes. Add the wine; cook over medium-high heat, stirring constantly, until absorbed.

5. Add ½ cup of the hot chicken broth. Cook, stirring constantly, over medium heat until the broth is almost all absorbed. Add the remaining broth ½ cup at a time, stirring constantly, until the risotto is creamy and the rice is plump and tender with a slight resistance to the bite, 20 to 25 minutes. During the last 5 minutes of cooking, stir in the carrots and lemon zest. (If you run out of broth, finish the risotto with a little boiling water.)

6. Add the remaining 1 tablespoon butter and the cheese. Stir vigorously until the risotto is creamy, about 30 seconds. Taste and add salt if needed. Let stand off the heat for a few minutes before serving.

7. Spoon the risotto into shallow soup dishes. Sprinkle with the thyme. Serve at once.

Green Risotto with Dried Tomatoes and Pecorino Romano

Makes 4 one-cup servings

Spinach gives this risotto a green-flecked appearance. The sharpness of the pecorino Romano, an Italian sheep's milk cheese, is mellowed and softened by the richness of the rice. If preferred, use half Parmigiano-Reggiano and half pecorino.

6 to 8 cups reduced-sodium chicken broth
  (or half broth and half water)
3 tablespoons unsalted butter
½ cup finely chopped onion
1½ cups Carnaroli, Vialone Nano, or Arborio rice
⅓ cup dry white wine

12 ounces spinach, trimmed, washed, and coarsely
  chopped (4 cups lightly packed)
4 halves sun-dried tomatoes in oil, rinsed, drained,
  and cut into ¼-inch pieces
¼ cup freshly grated pecorino Romano
Kosher salt and freshly ground black pepper

1. Heat the broth to a simmer in a saucepan; keep at a gentle simmer. Melt 2 tablespoons of the butter in a large deep skillet. Add the onion; cook over low heat, stirring, until golden, about 10 minutes. Do not brown. Stir in the rice until coated, about 2 minutes. Add the wine; cook over medium-high heat, stirring constantly, until absorbed.

2. Add ½ cup of the hot chicken broth. Cook, stirring constantly, over medium heat until the broth is almost all absorbed. Add the remaining broth ½ cup at a time, stirring constantly, until the risotto is creamy and the rice is plump and tender with a slight resistance to the bite, 20 to 25 minutes. During the last 5 minutes of cooking, add the spinach and dried tomatoes. (If you run out of broth, finish the risotto with a little boiling water.)

3. Add the remaining 1 tablespoon butter and the cheese. Stir vigorously until the risotto is creamy, about 30 seconds. Taste and add salt if needed. Let stand off the heat for a few minutes before serving.

4. Spoon the risotto into shallow soup dishes. Add a grinding of black pepper to each bowl. Serve at once.

Tomato Risotto with Asiago, Mozzarella, and Basil

Makes 4 one-cup servings

Make this risotto when fresh tomatoes are in season. A variety of cheeses can be successfully paired in this risotto—try a tangy cheese such as Asiago or ricotta salata with a creamy cheese such as mozzarella or fresh goat cheese. But if none is available, freshly grated Parmigiano-Reggiano works just fine.

2 cups seeded and diced (¼-inch) ripe plum
   tomatoes (about 8 tomatoes)
1 tablespoon chopped basil, plus 4 large basil
   leaves, tightly curled together and cut into
   paper-thin slivers or chiffonade
1 garlic clove, crushed through a press
½ teaspoon kosher salt
4 to 6 cups reduced-sodium chicken broth
   (or half broth and half water)

3 tablespoons unsalted butter
½ cup finely chopped onion
1½ cups Carnaroli, Vialone Nano, or Arborio rice
½ cup dry white wine
½ cup diced mozzarella, preferably fresh
¼ cup freshly grated Asiago

1. Combine the tomatoes, 1 tablespoon of the chopped basil, the garlic, and salt in a small bowl. Stir; set aside at room temperature.

2. Heat the broth to a simmer in a saucepan; keep at a gentle simmer.

3. Melt 2 tablespoons butter in a large wide saucepan or deep skillet. Add the onion; cook over low heat, stirring, until golden, about 10 minutes. Stir in the rice until coated, about 2 minutes. Add the wine; cook over medium-high heat, stirring constantly, until absorbed.

4. Add ½ cup of the hot chicken broth. Cook, stirring constantly, over medium heat until the broth is almost all absorbed. Add the remaining broth ½ cup at a time, stirring constantly, until the risotto is creamy and the rice is plump and tender with a slight resistance to the bite, 20 to 25 minutes. About 5 minutes before the risotto is cooked, add 1½ cups of the tomatoes. (If you run out of broth, finish the risotto with a little boiling water.)

5. Add the remaining 1 tablespoon butter, the mozzarella, and Asiago. Stir vigorously until the risotto is creamy, about 30 seconds. Taste and add salt if needed. Let stand off the heat for a few minutes before serving.

6. Spoon the risotto into shallow soup dishes. Garnish with the remaining tomatoes and the basil chiffonade.

Shrimp and Fresh Corn Risotto

Makes 4 one-cup servings

Cheese and seafood are rarely served together in Italian cooking, but this shrimp and corn risotto is an exception. Shell the shrimp and make the shrimp broth for the risotto up to one day before preparing the risotto.

2 tablespoons olive oil

1 pound medium shrimp, shelled and deveined (shells reserved)

1 garlic clove, chopped

½ cup dry white wine

1 bay leaf

1 onion slice

1 leafy celery top

Kosher salt

3 tablespoons unsalted butter

½ cup thinly sliced white part of scallions

1½ cups Carnaroli, Vialone Nano, or Arborio rice

1 cup corn kernels (from 2 ears)

1 teaspoon grated lemon zest

2 tablespoons freshly grated Parmigiano-Reggiano, plus more for serving

1 tablespoon fresh lemon juice

2 tablespoons chopped basil

1. **For the shrimp broth:** Heat the oil in a large wide saucepan over medium heat until hot enough to sizzle a shrimp shell. Add the shrimp shells; cook, stirring, until they change color, about 5 minutes. Add the garlic; cook for 1 minute. Add the wine; boil until reduced by half. Add 10 cups water, the bay leaf, onion slice, and celery top; heat to a boil. Reduce the heat; simmer, uncovered, until reduced to 6 to 8 cups, about 1 hour. Strain; discard the solids.

2. Transfer the shrimp broth to a saucepan; add salt to taste. Keep at a simmer over low heat.

3. Melt 2 tablespoons of the butter in a large wide saucepan or deep skillet. Add the scallions; cook over low heat, stirring, until tender, about 5 minutes. Do not brown. Stir in the rice until coated, about 2 minutes.

4. Add ½ cup of the hot shrimp broth. Cook, stirring constantly, over medium heat until the broth is almost all absorbed. Add the remaining broth ½ cup at a time, stirring constantly, until the risotto is creamy and the rice is plump and tender with a slight resistance to the bite, 20 to 25 minutes. About 5 minutes before the

risotto is cooked, add the shrimp, corn, and lemon zest. (If you run out of broth, finish the risotto with a little boiling water.)

5. Add the remaining 1 tablespoon butter and the cheese. Stir vigorously until the risotto is creamy, about 30 seconds. Add the lemon juice and basil. Taste and add salt if needed. Let stand off the heat for a few minutes before serving.

6. Spoon the risotto into shallow soup dishes. Serve at once, with additional cheese on the side.

Roasted Beet Risotto with Dill and Beet Greens

Makes 4 one-cup servings

Oven-roasted beets, with their intense sweet flavor and their stunning deep pink color, make a festive dish. Select beets with tender leafy green tops, and cook the tops to use as a garnish.

4 medium beets, tops and roots trimmed (reserve tender leafy tops)
1 teaspoon minced rosemary, plus 4 rosemary sprigs, about 1 inch long
6 to 8 cups reduced-sodium chicken broth (or half broth and half water)
3 to 4 tablespoons unsalted butter

½ cup finely chopped onion
1½ cups Carnaroli, Vialone Nano, or Arborio rice
⅓ cup dry red wine
1 teaspoon grated orange zest
Kosher salt and freshly ground black pepper
⅓ cup freshly grated Parmigiano-Reggiano

1. Preheat the oven to 350°F.

2. Cut four pieces, each about 10 inches square, of aluminum foil. Set a beet in the center of each; top with a little minced rosemary. Wrap the beets in the foil, crimping the edges to keep in the juices. Place directly on an oven rack and roast until the beets are tender when pieced with a fork, about 1½ hours. Let cool.

3. Unwrap the beets, reserving the juices. Rub off the beet skins. Cut the beets into ¼-inch slices; stack and cut into ¼-inch strips, then dice. Set aside in a bowl with the beet juices. (This can be done up to 2 days ahead.)

4. If the beet tops are tender and unblemished, rinse well and trim the long stems. Cut into 1-inch pieces. Blanch in boiling salted water for 5 minutes; drain. Reserve.

5. Heat the broth to a simmer in a saucepan; keep at a gentle simmer.

6. Melt 2 tablespoons of the butter in a large wide saucepan or deep skillet. Add the onion; cook over low heat, stirring, until golden, about 10 minutes. Stir in the

rice until coated, about 2 minutes. Add the wine; cook over medium-high heat, stirring constantly, until absorbed.

7. Add ½ cup of the hot chicken broth. Cook, stirring constantly, over medium heat until the broth is almost all absorbed. Add the remaining broth ½ cup at a time, stirring constantly, until the risotto is creamy and the rice is plump and tender with a slight resistance to the bite, 20 to 25 minutes. About 5 minutes before the risotto is cooked, stir in the beets with their juices and the orange zest. (If you run out of broth, finish the risotto with a little boiling water.)

8. Meanwhile, if using beet greens, melt 1 tablespoon of the butter in a small skillet over low heat. Add the beet greens; heat, stirring, about 2 minutes. Season with salt and pepper; keep warm over very low heat.

9. Add the remaining 1 tablespoon butter and the cheese to the risotto. Stir vigorously until the risotto is creamy, about 30 seconds. Taste and add salt if needed. Let stand off the heat for a few minutes before serving.

10. Spoon the risotto into shallow soup dishes. If using beet greens, tuck a small portion of beet greens into the center of each mound of risotto. Garnish with the rosemary sprigs. Serve at once.

Roasted Red Pepper and Italian Sausage Risotto

Makes 4 one-cup servings

Make this with the most flavorful sweet Italian sausage you can find, preferably with fennel seeds. Ideally the bell peppers should be freshly roasted and peeled, but in a pinch, use store-bought roasted peppers. Rinse jarred peppers well with cold water before using.

2 red bell peppers
8 ounces sweet Italian sausage, casings removed
6 to 8 cups reduced-sodium chicken broth (or half broth and half water)
2 tablespoons olive oil
½ cup finely chopped onion

1 small garlic clove, minced
1½ cups Carnaroli, Vialone Nano, or Arborio rice
2 tablespoons unsalted butter
¼ cup freshly grated Parmigiano-Reggiano
Kosher salt and freshly ground black pepper

1. Preheat the broiler. Lay a sheet of aluminum foil just large enough to enclose the peppers on the broiler pan; place the peppers on top. Broil about 2 inches from the heat source, turning frequently, until evenly charred. Remove from the broiler. Wrap the foil around the peppers and let stand until cool enough to handle.

2. Working over the foil to catch the juices, remove the stems, seeds, membranes, and skin from the peppers. Cut into ¼-inch dice; place in a small bowl. Set a strainer over the bowl; drain the juices in the foil over the peppers. (This can be done up to 1 day ahead.)

3. Heat a large heavy skillet over medium heat. Add the sausage; cook, breaking it into pieces with the side of a fork, until lightly browned, about 10 minutes. Drain off the fat. Reserve the sausage.

4. Heat the broth to a simmer in a saucepan; keep at a gentle simmer.

5. Heat the olive oil in a large wide saucepan or deep skillet over low heat. Add the onion; cook, stirring, until golden, about 10 minutes. Add the garlic; cook for 1 minute. Stir in the rice until coated, about 2 minutes.

6. Add ½ cup of the hot chicken broth. Cook, stirring constantly, over medium heat until the broth is almost all absorbed. Add the remaining broth ½ cup at a time, stirring constantly, until the risotto is creamy and the rice is plump and tender with a slight resistance to the bite, 20 to 25 minutes. About 5 minutes before the risotto is cooked, add the roasted peppers with their juices and half of the sausage. (If you run out of broth, finish the risotto with a little boiling water.)

7. Add the butter and cheese. Stir vigorously until the risotto is creamy, about 30 seconds. Taste and add salt if needed. Let stand off the heat for a few minutes before serving. Meanwhile, reheat the remaining sausage.

8. Spoon the risotto into shallow soup dishes. Place a few pieces of sausage on each mound of risotto. Add a grinding of black pepper to each bowl. Serve at once.

Artichokes and Pancetta Risotto with Rosemary and Lemon

Makes 4 one-cup servings

Artichokes so fresh you could almost hear them gasp when you snapped off the leaves, the lemon tree in our garden heavy with fruit, and fresh new growth on our rosemary hedge convinced me that it was time to make risotto with artichoke hearts. I like to use pancetta, unsmoked Italian-style bacon, in the risotto, as the smokiness of regular bacon detracts from the sweetness of the artichokes. If pancetta is unavailable, use slivers of prosciutto.

4 medium artichokes

1 bay leaf

1 garlic clove, bruised with the side of a knife

Kosher salt

3 tablespoons extra virgin olive oil

1 teaspoon sherry vinegar or aged red wine vinegar

2 teaspoons minced rosemary, plus 4 small sprigs (about 1 inch)

Freshly ground black pepper

6 to 8 cups reduced-sodium chicken broth (or half broth and half water)

1 slice (¼-inch) pancetta, minced

⅓ cup finely chopped carrot

⅓ cup finely chopped onion

1½ cups Carnaroli, Vialone Nano, or Arborio rice

½ cup dry white wine

1 teaspoon grated lemon zest

2 tablespoons unsalted butter

¼ cup freshly grated Parmigiano-Reggiano, plus Parmigiano-Reggiano curls for garnish

1 tablespoon fresh lemon juice

1. Pull off the tough outer layers of artichoke leaves and discard. Trim the ends of the stems. Lay the artichokes on their sides and cut 1 inch off the top. Place in a large pot; add water to cover. Add the bay leaf, garlic, and 2 teaspoons salt. Place a plate small enough to fit inside the pot on top of the artichokes to keep them submerged (they are floaters!). Heat to a boil. Reduce the heat, cover, and boil gently until the artichokes are tender when pierced with a skewer, 20 to 25 minutes. Drain. Let cool.

2. Pull off the outer artichoke leaves, set aside. Discard the small inside leaves with the thorny tips. Using the tip of a teaspoon, scoop out and discard the fuzzy chokes. Dice the hearts and tender stems into ¼-inch pieces. (There should be about 2 cups.) Reserve half the outer artichoke leaves for garnish. Reserve the remaining leaves for another use.

3. In a small bowl, combine 1 tablespoon of the olive oil, the vinegar, 1 teaspoon of the minced rosemary, a pinch of salt, and a grinding of black pepper; whisk to blend. Add the reserved artichoke leaves; toss to coat. Set aside.

4. Heat the broth to a simmer in a saucepan; keep at a gentle simmer.

5. Heat the remaining 2 tablespoons olive oil in a large wide saucepan or deep skillet over medium-low heat. Add the pancetta; cook, stirring, until lightly browned, about 5 minutes. Add the carrot and onion; cook until the onion is tender, about 5 minutes. Do not brown. Stir in the rice until coated, about 2 minutes. Add the white wine, cook, stirring, over medium-high heat until absorbed.

6. Add ½ cup of the hot chicken broth. Cook, stirring constantly, over medium heat until the broth is almost all absorbed. Add the remaining broth ½ cup at a time, stirring constantly, until the risotto is creamy and the rice is plump and tender with a slight resistance to the bite, 20 to 25 minutes. About 5 minutes before the risotto is cooked, add the diced artichoke hearts and the lemon zest. (If you run out of broth, finish the risotto with a little boiling water.)

7. Add the butter and cheese. Stir vigorously until the risotto is creamy, about 30 seconds. Stir in the lemon juice. Taste and add salt if needed. Let stand off the heat for a few minutes before serving.

8. Spoon the risotto into shallow soup dishes. Sprinkle each dish with a pinch of the remaining rosemary. Top with a few curls of cheese. Arrange the artichoke leaves in a sunburst pattern around each serving of risotto. Place a rosemary sprig in the center. Serve at once.

Fresh Fig Risotto with Rosemary Butter–Glazed Walnuts

Makes 4 one-cup servings

I moved to California from New York kicking and screaming, but I became a California convert on a sunny Saturday morning while standing before a pile—yes, a pile—of fresh figs. I picked one up and held it in my hand. It was warm and heavy. When I turned it over, there was a teardrop of sugary fig syrup dripping from its blossom end. I almost wept with joy. I had never seen so many figs in one place. People were filling bags and buying them by the pound. I had come a very long way indeed from New York City, where figs by the piece cost what I paid that morning for an entire pound. Talk about fig heaven. The practical cook in me quickly snapped out of my reverie as I began to plan my menu for the evening. This fig risotto was the result.

½ cup walnut pieces (halves or quarters)
3 tablespoons unsalted butter
1 teaspoon chopped rosemary
6 to 8 cups reduced-sodium chicken broth
  (or half broth and half water)
¼ cup minced shallots
1½ cups Carnaroli, Vialone Nano, or Arborio rice

½ cup dry white wine
1 pound ripe green figs (Calimyrna, Kadota, or
  Adriatic) rinsed, stems trimmed, and cut into
  ½-inch cubes
½ cup coarsely slivered Parmigiano-Reggiano
Kosher salt

1. Sprinkle the walnuts into a small skillet and toast over medium-low heat until golden. Add 1 tablespoon of the butter and the rosemary; stir until the butter is melted. Remove from the heat; set aside.

2. Heat the broth to a simmer in a saucepan; keep at a gentle simmer.

3. Melt the remaining 2 tablespoons butter in a large wide saucepan or deep skillet over medium-low heat. Add the shallots; sauté until tender, about 5 minutes. Stir in the rice until coated, about 2 minutes. Add the wine; cook, stirring, over medium-high heat, until absorbed.

4. Add ½ cup of the hot chicken broth. Cook, stirring constantly, over medium heat until the broth is almost all absorbed. Add the remaining broth ½ cup at a time, stirring constantly, until the risotto is creamy and the rice is plump and tender with a slight resistance to the bite, 20 to 25 minutes. Halfway through the cooking, add half of the diced figs. (If you run out of broth, finish the risotto with a little boiling water.)

5. Add the remaining figs, half of the walnut butter mixture, and half of the cheese; stir to blend. Taste and add salt if needed. Let stand off the heat for a few minutes before serving.

6. Spoon the risotto into shallow soup dishes. Spoon the few remaining walnuts and rosemary butter over each. Top with the remaining cheese. Serve at once.

Winter Squash Risotto with Nutmeg and Sage

Makes 4 one-cup servings

Almost any winter squash can be used in this risotto, but for a rich flavor I prefer the round Japanese squash called Kabocha.

One 1½-pound Kabocha or other winter squash, peeled and cut into ¼-inch dice (about 2 cups)

6 to 8 cups reduced-sodium chicken broth (or half broth and half water)

3 tablespoons unsalted butter

½ cup finely chopped onion

½ cup dry white wine

1½ cups Carnaroli, Vialone Nano, or Arborio rice

¼ cup freshly grated Parmigiano-Reggiano, plus more for serving

Freshly grated nutmeg

Kosher salt

1 tablespoon torn sage leaves

1. Heat the chicken broth to a simmer in a saucepan; keep at a gentle simmer. Melt 2 tablespoons of the butter in a large wide saucepan or deep skillet. Add the onion; cook over low heat, stirring, until golden, about 10 minutes. Stir in the rice until coated, about 2 minutes. Add the wine; cook over medium-high heat, stirring constantly, until absorbed.

2. Add ½ cup of the hot chicken broth. Cook, stirring constantly, over medium heat until the broth is almost all absorbed. Add the remaining broth ½ cup at a time, stirring constantly, until the risotto is creamy and the rice is plump and tender with a slight resistance to the bite, 20 to 25 minutes. Ten minutes before the risotto is done, stir in the squash. (If you run out of broth, finish the risotto with a little boiling water.)

3. Add the remaining 1 tablespoon butter, the cheese, and a generous grinding of nutmeg. Stir vigorously until the risotto is creamy, about 30 seconds. Taste and add salt if needed. Let stand off the heat for a few minutes before serving.

4. Spoon the risotto into shallow soup dishes. Sprinkle the top of each with a few gratings of nutmeg and a pinch of sage leaves. Serve at once, with additional Parmesan on the side.

Fennel and Leek Risotto with Orange

**Makes 4
one-cup
servings**

It wasn't until I was an adult that I discovered the sweet mellow taste of cooked fennel. As a child growing up in an Italian family, the only fennel I knew (and adored) was raw. With its distinctive licorice taste, we were a family divided into fennel lovers and fennel haters. Today slowly cooked fennel is one of my favorite vegetables. Here it is paired with leeks in a delicate creamy risotto.

1 fennel bulb (about 12 ounces), stalks trimmed and feathery tops reserved, bulb trimmed, any blemishes removed, and cut into quarters

6 to 8 cups reduced-sodium chicken broth (or half broth and half water)

3 tablespoons unsalted butter

1 medium leek, trimmed, washed, and finely chopped (about 1 cup)

1½ cups Carnaroli, Vialone Nano, or Arborio rice

½ cup dry white wine

1 teaspoon grated orange zest, plus three strips 2 × ½-inch orange zest, cut into thin lengthwise slivers

¼ cup freshly grated Parmigiano-Reggiano, plus additional for serving

Kosher salt

1 tablespoon extra virgin olive oil

1. Soak the fennel in ice water for 20 minutes; drain well. Dry and chop as uniformly as possible into ¼-inch pieces; set aside. (There should be about 1½ cups.) Finely chop enough of the reserved fennel tops to make ¼ cup; set aside.

2. Heat the chicken broth to a simmer in a saucepan; keep at a gentle simmer.

3. Melt 2 tablespoons of the butter in a large wide saucepan or deep skillet. Add the leek; cook over low heat, stirring, until tender, about 10 minutes. Do not brown. Stir in the rice until coated, about 2 minutes. Stir in the chopped fennel. Add the wine; cook over medium-high heat, stirring constantly, until absorbed.

4. Add ½ cup of the hot chicken broth. Cook, stirring constantly, over medium heat until the broth is almost all absorbed. Add the remaining broth ½ cup at a time, stirring constantly, until the risotto is creamy and the rice is plump and ten-

der with a slight resistance to the bite, 20 to 25 minutes. (If you run out of broth, finish the risotto with a little boiling water.)

5. Add the grated orange zest, the remaining 1 tablespoon butter, the cheese, and half of the fennel tops. Stir vigorously until the risotto is creamy, about 30 seconds. Taste and add salt if needed. Let stand off the heat for a few minutes before serving.

6. Meanwhile, heat the olive oil and strips of orange zest in a small skillet over medium heat, stirring until the edges of the zest begin to turn golden, about 3 minutes. Remove from the heat.

7. Spoon the risotto into shallow soup dishes. Sprinkle with the remaining fennel tops and the strips of orange zest. Serve at once, with additional Parmesan on the side.

Leftover Risotto

Risotto Pancakes

Use leftover risotto to make little pancakes. Combine cold risotto with a little beaten egg, shape it into small pancakes, and brown in melted butter or hot olive oil in a skillet over medium heat. See the recipe for Risotto al Salto on page 86.

Risotto Baked in Roasted Portobello Mushrooms

Makes 2 or 4 servings   Use leftover Basic Risotto (page 120) or Green Risotto with Dried Tomatoes and Pecorino Romano (page 125) or prepare risotto to use as the filling if there are no leftovers. This makes an excellent first course or side dish with beef or chicken.

2 or 4 medium (about 4 inches in diameter) portobello mushrooms, stems removed
4 teaspoons extra virgin olive oil

Kosher salt and freshly ground black pepper
1 to 2 cups leftover cooked risotto
Freshly grated Parmigiano-Reggiano

1. Preheat the oven to 400°F.

2. Arrange the portobello mushrooms smooth side down in a roasting pan. Drizzle each with 1 teaspoon olive oil and sprinkle with salt and pepper. Roast for 15 minutes. Turn over and roast smooth side up for 10 minutes. Remove the pan from the oven.

3. Turn the portobellos smooth side down and spoon the risotto onto the mushrooms, mounding it slightly in the center. Sprinkle the tops with a little grated cheese. Roast until the cheese is melted and the risotto is heated through, about 10 minutes longer.

Risotto Baked in Roasted Acorn Squash Halves

Makes 2 to 4 servings Use leftover Winter Squash Risotto (page 138) or Basic Risotto (page 120). Serve as a first course or as a side dish with pork, lamb, or chicken.

1 or 2 small acorn squash (about 1 pound each)
Kosher salt and freshly ground black pepper

1 to 2 cups leftover cooked risotto
Freshly grated Parmigiano-Reggiano or Gruyère

1. Preheat the oven to 400°F.

2. Break off the stem(s), if still attached, from the squash. Place the squash on its side and, with a large heavy knife, cut in half across the "equator." Scoop out the seeds and membranes. Cut a small slice from the pointed ends so the halves will stand straight. Sprinkle the insides with salt and pepper.

3. Place the squash cut side down in a baking pan. Add about ½ inch hot water to the pan. Cover and roast 30 minutes. Remove the pan from the oven. Turn the squash over.

4. Spoon the risotto into the scooped-out section of each squash half, mounding it slightly in the center. Sprinkle with cheese. Roast for 15 minutes longer, or until the risotto is lightly browned and the cheese is melted.

Pilaf

Pilaf, risotto, and paella are similar yet a world apart. Each uses a different rice and a different technique, and each is native to a specific geographic area. Of the three dishes, pilaf is, indisputably, the simplest and most easily adaptable.

Pilaf is made with long-grain rice that cooks into dry, separate grains. Traditionally, the rice is rinsed and soaked, then it is sautéed in butter or oil. Sometimes onions, garlic, and other vegetables, or bits of meat, are added. Then the entire mixture is cooked in simmering broth.

Each time I uncover a pot of cooked pilaf, I am thrilled at the sight. The rice has exploded into hundreds of long, long grains, and although they have obviously cooked side by side, they appear not to be touching, as if they are suspended by invisible threads. How can this be?

Basmati rice is traditionally used to make pilaf, since it contains more amylose (the drier starch) than amylopectin (the stickier starch). As the grains cook, they expand in length rather than girth. The result is cooked grains of rice that are tender yet dry, separate, and fluffy.

To make things interesting, there are always exceptions. On a trip to Istanbul, I was introduced to a pilaf made with shorter, plumper grains of rice similar to Arborio. This type of rice, higher in amylopectin, results in a creamy pilaf, with a consistency similar to risotto.

For a perfect pilaf, use a pan with a concave lid that will not collect condensation. When the pilaf is done, there will be tiny indentations on the surface of the rice, indicating that all the liquid has been absorbed. Traditionally pilaf is cooked with a dry cloth placed between the lid and the pot to collect the condensation from the lid and prevent it from dripping into the pilaf. If not using a cloth, quickly invert the lid when you remove it to catch the condensation.

The recipes in this chapter begin with the most basic pilaf, perfect as a side dish to any weeknight meal, and move all the way up to very elaborate pilafs appropriate for grander occasions. Like so many other classic rice dishes, pilaf needs only the whim of the cook, or the necessity of what is at hand, to become a totally new dish.

To substitute brown rice for white rice in any of the following recipes, increase the liquid by ¾ cup and the cooking time to about 45 minutes.

Pilaf Techniques

In India and throughout the Middle East, the rice for pilaf is always rinsed and soaked. Rinsing cleans it of debris and soaking removes excess starch. The technique is to rinse the rice in two or three changes of cold water; soak it in clean water for 30 minutes or longer; and drain well. American grown basmati-type rice is very clean and does not need to be rinsed. But it also doesn't elongate quite as much as imported basmati rice when it is cooked.

As an experiment I cooked two pilafs side by side. For both pilafs I used imported basmati rice. For one pilaf I rinsed and soaked the rice in the traditional way and in the other I didn't rinse or soak it. In both pilafs the cooked rice was beautifully elongated, each grain dry and separate. But the rinsed and soaked rice had a lighter, less starchy texture and taste than the rice that had not been soaked.

Basic Pilaf

In this recipe, there are two methods for the final cooking. Select the method that suits you, or experiment to see which one you like best.

2 tablespoons unsalted butter or olive oil
½ cup minced onion
2 cups uncooked imported or domestic basmati rice
  (see Pilaf Techniques, page 143)

3½ cups reduced-sodium chicken broth (or half
  broth and half water)
1 cinnamon stick, optional
Kosher salt

1. Melt the butter in a large wide saucepan or deep skillet. Add the onion; cook, stirring, over low heat until golden, about 5 minutes. Add the rice and cook, stirring, until it is coated with butter and looks tweedy, about 3 minutes. Add the broth, cinnamon stick, if using, and salt to taste; heat to a boil. Stir once.

2. *Cooking method #1:* Reduce the heat; simmer, uncovered, until almost all of the water is absorbed, about 5 minutes. Cover and cook over very low heat for 15 minutes. Do not uncover. Let stand off the heat covered for 15 minutes before serving.

3. *Cooking method #2:* Cover and cook over low heat until all of the water is absorbed and small holes appear all over the surface of the rice, about 15 minutes. This indicates that all the water has been absorbed. Do not stir the rice. Let stand, covered, off the heat for 10 minutes before serving.

Variations for Basic Pilaf

- Sauté ¼ cup diced carrot or parsnip with the onion.
  Substitute ½ cup chopped leeks or ¼ cup chopped shallots or white part of scallions for the onion.

- Add with the rice: ½ cup dark or golden raisins or dried currants, ½ cup diced dried apricots, 1 cinnamon stick, 2 whole cloves, 2 whole cardamom pods and/or 2 whole allspice berries, 1 slice (about ¼ inch thick) fresh ginger, 1 garlic clove, minced, 1 to 2 teaspoons curry powder, ½ to 1 teaspoon ground cumin, ¼ teaspoon crushed saffron threads (can be heated first in part of the liquid), and ½ to 1 cup green beans, chickpeas, cannellini beans or other white beans, diced peeled sweet potato or winter squash, or thawed frozen lima beans.

- Use as part of the liquid: ½ to 1 cup chopped fresh or canned tomatoes, vegetable broth, or beef broth.

- Add during the last 5 minutes: ½ to 1 cup thawed frozen (or fresh) peas and/or corn, diced zucchini, or diced yellow summer squash.

- Top cooked pilaf with: toasted sliced or chopped natural (skin-on) almonds; chopped walnuts, pecans, pistachios, toasted and peeled hazelnuts, dry-roasted peanuts, or cashews; sunflower seeds; chopped fresh herbs (dill, mint, parsley, cilantro, or basil); or fresh lemon juice.

Oven-Baked Rice Pilaf

Makes 4 servings

Typically pilaf is cooked on top of the stove, but in this version, after the onion and rice are sautéed in butter, hot broth is added and the pilaf is baked. Add ½ cup chopped mushrooms, diced carrots, or celery to the onion as you wish. Top the pilaf with toasted walnuts or almonds, or finely chopped parsley, chives, or dill.

1 tablespoon unsalted butter or olive oil
½ cup chopped onion
1 cup uncooked long-grain white or basmati rice

2 cups reduced-sodium chicken broth (or half broth and half water), heated to a boil
½ teaspoon kosher salt, optional

1. Preheat the oven to 400°F.

2. Select a flameproof baking dish with a cover. Melt the butter over low heat. Add the onion; cook, stirring, until golden, about 10 minutes. Add the rice; stir to coat with the butter. Add the broth and salt, if needed. Stir to distribute the rice evenly.

3. Cover and transfer to the oven. Bake until the liquid is absorbed and the rice is tender, 18 to 20 minutes. Remove from the oven and let stand, covered, for 5 minutes before serving.

Oven-Baked Brown Rice and Mushroom Pilaf

Makes 4 servings

The nutty taste of brown rice goes well with the richness of mushrooms. For variety, substitute shiitakes (stems discarded and caps diced) for the white button (or cremini) mushrooms. This is delicious topped with grated Parmesan cheese.

3 tablespoons extra virgin olive oil

1 cup coarsely chopped white button or cremini mushrooms

1 garlic clove, finely chopped

Freshly ground black pepper

1 cup uncooked medium- or long-grain brown rice

2½ cups reduced-sodium chicken or vegetable broth (or half broth and half water), heated to a boil

½ teaspoon kosher salt, optional

1. Preheat the oven to 350°F.

2. Select a flameproof baking dish with a cover. Heat the olive oil over medium-low heat. Add the mushrooms and onion; cook, stirring, until lightly browned, about 10 minutes.

3. Stir in the garlic; cook for 1 minute. Add a grinding of black pepper. Add the rice and stir to combine. Add the broth and salt, if needed. Stir to distribute the rice evenly.

4. Cover and transfer to the oven. Bake until the liquid is absorbed and the rice is tender, about 45 minutes. Remove from the oven and let stand, covered, for 5 to 10 minutes before serving.

Armenian-Style Pilaf

The secret of this pilaf is the vermicelli—thin strings of pasta that have been broken into small pieces and cooked in a generous knob of butter until toasted to a rich golden brown. Only then are the rice and currants added, and the whole thing cooked in simmering chicken broth. Perfect as a background for steamed or stir-fried vegetables or with grilled meats or fish.

¾ cup uncooked long-grain white rice
3 tablespoons unsalted butter
½ cup broken pieces (about ½-inch lengths) vermicelli or thin spaghetti

2 cups reduced-sodium chicken broth
2 tablespoons dried currants
Kosher salt

1. Place the rice in a large bowl and add cold water to cover. Swish the rice around; drain. Repeat two more times or until the water is clear. Drain in a strainer and let stand until ready to cook.

2. Melt the butter in a large wide saucepan or deep skillet over medium-low heat. Add the vermicelli; cook, stirring, until the pasta is golden brown, about 10 minutes.

3. Meanwhile, bring the broth to a simmer in a medium saucepan.

4. Add the rice and currants to the pasta; stir to blend. Add the hot broth and salt to taste. Heat to a boil; stir once. Cover and cook over medium-low heat until the broth is absorbed and the rice is tender, 15 minutes. Let stand, covered, off the heat for 10 minutes before serving.

Golden Rice Pilaf

Makes 4 servings

Brightly colored turmeric gives this pilaf its yellow color. I like the monochromatic yellows in this dish—yellow rice, golden raisins, toasted almonds. The sweet-tart golden raisins balance the heat and spice in the pilaf, but dark raisins will be just as dramatic visually.

2 tablespoons unsalted butter
½ cup chopped onion
1 to 2 teaspoons Madras curry powder
1 teaspoon ground turmeric
1 cup uncooked basmati rice

½ cup golden raisins
1 cinnamon stick
1¾ cups reduced-sodium chicken broth
Kosher salt
2 tablespoons sliced natural (skin-on) almonds

1. Melt the butter in a large wide saucepan or deep skillet over medium heat. Add the onion; cook, stirring, over low heat, until golden, about 10 minutes.

2. Stir in the curry, turmeric, rice, and raisins; cook, stirring, for 2 minutes. Add the chicken broth and cinnamon; heat to a boil. Stir once. Add ½ teaspoon salt, or more if needed. Cook, covered, over low heat until the broth is absorbed and the rice is tender, about 15 minutes. Let stand, covered, off the heat, for 10 minutes before serving.

3. Meanwhile, toast the almonds in a small dry skillet over low heat, stirring, until lightly browned, about 2 minutes.

4. Sprinkle the almonds over the pilaf just before serving.

Orzo and Rice Pilaf with Pignoli

Makes 4 servings

Orzo is an oval pasta shape that looks just like grains of rice; its name translates from Italian as "barley." This side dish quickly becomes a main dish with the addition of shredded cooked chicken and a topping of stir-fried broccoli.

2 tablespoons unsalted butter or extra virgin
   olive oil
¼ cup chopped onion
1 garlic clove, minced
¾ cup uncooked basmati rice

½ cup orzo
1 teaspoon kosher salt
2 tablespoons pignoli (pine nuts)
Freshly grated Parmigiano-Reggiano, optional

1. Melt the butter in a large wide saucepan over medium-low heat. Add the onion; cook, stirring, until golden, about 5 minutes. Stir in the garlic; cook for 1 minute.

2. Add the rice and orzo; cook, stirring, for 2 minutes. Add 2 cups water and the salt; heat to a boil. Stir, cover, and cook over medium-low heat for 15 minutes, or until the liquid is absorbed. Let stand off the heat, covered, for 10 minutes before serving.

3. Meanwhile, toast the pignoli in a small dry skillet over low heat, stirring constantly, until golden, about 2 minutes.

4. Add the pignoli to the cooked pilaf and toss to blend. Serve sprinkled with grated cheese, if desired.

Baby Basmati Rice Pilaf, Indian-Style

Makes 8 servings

Make this recipe with regular basmati rice or use the basmati with tiny grains called *Kali-jira* or *gobindavog* available in Middle Eastern groceries and some specialty food shops.

¼ teaspoon crushed saffron threads

3 tablespoons whole milk or heavy cream

3 tablespoons unsalted butter

½ cup chopped onion

2 garlic cloves, minced

1 teaspoon grated fresh ginger

1 cup uncooked baby basmati (see headnote) or regular basmati rice

⅓ cup golden raisins

1 cinnamon stick

2 cups reduced-sodium chicken broth

Kosher salt, optional

¼ cup coarsely chopped, natural (skin-on) almonds

¼ cup coarsely chopped, unsalted raw cashews

2 tablespoons minced cilantro

1. Toast the saffron in a small dry skillet over low heat for 20 seconds. Stir in the milk. Set aside, covered, until ready to use.

2. Melt 2 tablespoons of the butter in a large wide saucepan or deep skillet over low heat. Add the onion; cook, stirring, until golden, about 10 minutes. Add the garlic and ginger; cook for 1 minute. Add the rice, raisins, and cinnamon stick; cook, stirring constantly, for about 2 minutes.

3. Add the chicken broth; heat to a boil. Taste and add salt if necessary. Stir once; cook, covered, over low heat, until the rice has absorbed the liquid, about 15 minutes. Let stand off the heat, covered, for 10 minutes before serving.

4. Melt the remaining 1 tablespoon butter in a medium skillet. Add the almonds and cashews; cook, stirring, over medium-low heat, until golden, about 5 minutes.

5. Spoon the rice onto a serving platter. Sprinkle with the saffron and milk mixture; stir gently (the mixture should be unevenly distributed.) Top with the nuts and cilantro. Serve at once.

Red Rice Pilaf with Orange and Ginger

Makes 4 servings

The subtle orange and ginger flavors of this pilaf go well with grilled or pan-seared soy-marinated jumbo shrimp. If red rice is unavailable, substitute basmati rice and reduce the amount of cooking liquid by ½ cup.

2 tablespoons extra virgin olive oil
¼ cup finely chopped onion
Three 2 × ½-inch strips orange zest, minced
2 teaspoons finely chopped fresh ginger
1 teaspoon minced garlic

⅛ teaspoon red pepper flakes
1 cup uncooked Bhutanese red rice or other
　red-bran rice
1 teaspoon kosher salt
1 tablespoon chopped dill

1. Heat the oil in a large wide saucepan or deep skillet over medium-low heat. Add the onion; cook, stirring, over low heat, until golden, about 10 minutes. Add the orange zest, ginger, garlic, and red pepper flakes; cook for 2 minutes. Add the rice; cook, stirring, over medium heat until coated with the seasonings, about 2 minutes.

2. Add 2¼ cups water and the salt; heat to a boil. Stir once. Cook, covered, over low heat until the water is absorbed and the rice is tender, about 20 minutes. Let stand, covered, off the heat, for 10 minutes before serving.

3. Sprinkle the pilaf with the dill and serve.

Bulgur and Rice Pilaf with Walnuts and Dates

Makes 4 servings

Bulgur, a nutritious grain with a nutty flavor, goes well when combined with rice, dates, and sautéed walnuts. Bulgur (not to be confused with cracked wheat) is wheat berries that have been cooked, dried, and then cut up. It's available in different sizes; use medium-sized bulgur here. Serve this pilaf with vegetables as part of a vegetarian menu, or with grilled chicken or lamb.

2 tablespoons unsalted butter or olive oil
¼ cup thinly sliced scallions (white and green parts)
1 cup medium bulgur
1 cup uncooked basmati rice
2 cups reduced-sodium vegetable, beef, or chicken broth

Kosher salt
½ cup broken walnuts
1 garlic clove, minced
¼ cup diced (⅛-inch) moist dates

1. Melt 1 tablespoon of the butter in a large wide saucepan or deep skillet. Add the scallions; cook, stirring, over low heat until tender, about 3 minutes. Add the bulgur and rice; cook, stirring, until coated with butter, about 2 minutes.

2. Add the broth; heat to a boil. Add ½ teaspoon salt, or more if needed; stir well. Cook, covered, over medium-low heat until the liquid is absorbed and grains are tender, about 15 minutes. Let stand, covered, off the heat, for 10 minutes before serving.

3. Meanwhile, melt the remaining 1 tablespoon butter in a small skillet. Stir in the walnuts and garlic; cook, stirring constantly, until the walnuts are golden and fragrant, about 3 minutes. Stir in the dates.

4. Spoon the pilaf into a serving dish and sprinkle with the walnut mixture.

Wehani and Wild Rice Pilaf

Makes 6 servings

Wehani is an aromatic long-grain brown rice with a dark russet bran, a rich taste, and a chewy texture. Its flavor goes well with wild rice and, conveniently, it cooks in about the same amount of time. Add a stir-fry of shiitakes and scallions to the pilaf, and for an extra-special touch, make Tamari Walnuts and sprinkle on top. Serve with vegetables as part of a vegetarian menu, or with pork, chicken, or beef. This pilaf can also be made with either all Wehani or all wild rice.

¼ cup extra virgin olive oil, plus more if needed
½ cup chopped white part of scallions, plus ½ cup thinly sliced scallion greens
1 tablespoon plus 1 teaspoon finely chopped fresh ginger
1 tablespoon plus 1 teaspoon finely chopped garlic
1 cup uncooked wild rice, rinsed well with warm water

2 teaspoons kosher salt
1 cup uncooked Wehani rice
12 ounces shiitakes, stems discarded, caps wiped clean and cut into thin slices (about 3 cups)
2 tablespoons tamari or soy sauce
Tamari Walnuts (page 53), optional

1. Heat 2 tablespoons of the oil in a large wide saucepan or deep skillet over low heat. Add the scallions whites and 1 tablespoon each of the ginger and garlic; cook, stirring, for 2 minutes. Add the wild rice; cook, stirring to coat, about 1 minute.

2. Add 5 cups water and the salt; heat to a boil. Cover and cook over medium-low heat for 15 minutes. Add the Wehani and continue cooking, covered, until the liquid is absorbed and the rices are tender, about 45 minutes. Uncover and cook over medium-high heat to boil off any excess liquid if necessary.

3. Combine the remaining 2 tablespoons oil and 1 teaspoon each garlic and ginger in a large skillet; heat over medium-low heat until sizzling, about 1 minute. Add the mushrooms; stir-fry until they turn golden, about 5 minutes. Add more oil if the pan gets dry. Add the soy sauce; stir-fry until it is almost all absorbed, about 1 minute. Add ¼ cup of the scallion greens and remove from the heat.

4. Add the mushrooms to the cooked rice; stir to blend. Add soy sauce to taste. Sprinkle with the remaining 2 tablespoons scallions greens and the walnuts, if using. Serve at once.

Cooking Wild Rice

The cooking times of wild rice can range from as little as 35 minutes to as long as 55 minutes or longer, depending on how the rice was cured, no matter what the directions on the package say. You just have to be flexible. If the rice isn't done, cook it longer, adding more liquid if necessary. If it cooks very quickly and there is too much liquid left in the pan, drain it off, then put the pan back over medium-high heat for a few minutes to allow excess moisture still in the rice to evaporate. I prefer wild rice when it has burst, exposing the soft inside but leaving the outside chewy.

Artichoke, Tomato, Dill, and Lemon Pilaf, Istanbul-Style

Makes 4 servings

Buy the less expensive medium-sized artichokes for this pilaf, since most of the leaves are discarded. Serve with lamb, fish, or chicken, or as a main course for a simple supper.

Juice of 1 lemon, plus 1 tablespoon
4 medium artichokes
¼ cup extra virgin olive oil
1 cup diced (¼-inch) red onion
1 garlic clove, minced
Kosher salt and freshly ground black pepper
1 cup diced, peeled, seeded tomatoes (use firm canned tomatoes if fresh aren't available)

¼ cup chopped fresh dill
1 teaspoon grated lemon zest
1½ cups uncooked Baldo, Arborio, or other medium-grain white rice
3 cups water or reduced-sodium chicken broth (or half broth and half water)
2 tablespoons chopped mint

1. Fill a bowl with cold water and add the juice of 1 lemon. Trim the tough outer leaves from each artichoke (reserve for another use or discard). Peel off the tough outer layer of the stem. Quarter the artichoke. Using the tip of a paring knife,

---

Pilaf Istanbul-Style

A visit to Istanbul was a revelation, and it wasn't the Turkish baths or the silhouette of the minarets against the fiery sunset. No, it was the pilaf. Rather than the long, slender grains of basmati rice that I'd associated with this favorite dish, the pilaf in Istanbul was made with a medium-grain rice similar to Arborio. I discovered that most chefs were using an Italian rice variety called Baldo. It cooks up creamy, like Arborio, but without the firm core. Some chefs were using Arborio. But none I encountered in Istanbul used basmati. If you can find Baldo (now grown in Missouri—and exported to Turkey!), it makes a lovely soft pilaf. Otherwise, use Arborio or another medium-grain white rice.

Any of the Istanbul-style pilaf recipes can be made with basmati rice. Just reduce the liquid by ¼ cup for each cup of rice used. The result will be just as good, but the rice will be dry and separate, not moist and creamy.

---

cut out and discard the center leaves with sharp tips and the fuzzy choke. Place the trimmed artichokes in lemon water as you work.

2. Heat the oil in a large wide saucepan or deep skillet over medium-low heat. Drain the artichokes; pat dry. Add the artichokes and red onion; cook, stirring, until lightly browned, about 10 minutes. Add the garlic; cook, stirring, for 1 minute. Sprinkle with salt and pepper.

3. Add the tomatoes, half of the dill, and the lemon zest; stir until heated through, about 2 minutes. Add the rice; stir to blend. Add the liquid. Taste and add salt if needed. Heat to a boil; stir once. Cook, covered, over medium-low heat until the water is absorbed and the rice is tender, about 25 minutes.

4. Sprinkle the pilaf with the remaining 1 tablespoon lemon juice, the remaining dill, and the mint. Spoon into a serving dish and serve at once.

Lamb and Rice Pilaf with Dried Apricots and Walnuts, Istanbul-Style

Makes 4 main-course or 6 side-dish servings

For this moist pilaf, the rice is cooked in lamb-flavored broth, with bits of the meat flecking the pilaf. Serve with roasted vegetables and a cooked leafy green vegetable.

3 tablespoons extra virgin olive oil

1 pound bone-in lamb sirloin, fat trimmed

Kosher salt and freshly ground black pepper

1 carrot, halved lengthwise

1 small onion, halved, plus ½ cup chopped onion

1 bay leaf

1 medium tomato, cored and cut into wedges

1½ cups uncooked Baldo, Arborio, or other medium-grain white rice

4 ounces Italian romano beans or regular green beans, trimmed and cut into ½-inch lengths (about 1 cup)

1 garlic clove, minced

¼ cup diced dried apricots

½ cup walnuts, toasted

1. Heat 1 tablespoon of the oil in a large wide saucepan. Sprinkle the lamb with salt and pepper. Brown the lamb, carrot, and halved onion in the hot oil, turning once, about 10 minutes. Add 8 cups water, the bay leaf, and tomato. Heat to a boil over medium-high heat. Reduce the heat to medium-low; boil gently, uncovered, until the liquid is reduced by half, about 1 hour. Pour the broth through a strainer (there should be about 3½ cups broth). Reserve the solids; set the pan aside.

2. When it is cool enough to handle, dice the lamb; discard the bone and gristle. Remove the tomato skins and dice the flesh, if it hasn't dissolved. Discard the remaining solids. Skim the fat from the surface of the broth. Taste and add salt if needed.

3. Wipe out the pan. Add the remaining 2 tablespoons oil and the chopped onion to the pan; cook over low heat, stirring, until the onion is tender and golden, about 10 minutes. Stir in the rice, green beans, garlic, and apricots; cook for 1 minute, stirring to coat the rice.

4. Add the reserved lamb broth, diced lamb, and the tomato. Heat to a boil; stir once. Cook, covered, over low heat until the broth is almost all absorbed and the rice is tender, about 18 minutes. Spoon onto a deep platter or shallow bowl; sprinkle with the walnuts and serve.

Chicken and Rice Pilaf with Toasted Almonds and Golden Raisins, Istanbul-Style

Makes 4 servings

Chicken thighs instead of chicken breasts guarantee tender, juicy morsels of meat. I prefer golden raisins in this pilaf because they are plumper and a little less sweet than dark ones, although either can be used. (Both are made from Thompson seedless grapes, but they are dehydrated by a difference process.) Or, if preferred, substitute diced dried apricots. With steamed green beans or broccoli, this pilaf is hearty enough to be a main dish.

3 tablespoons extra virgin olive oil

1 medium onion, cup into ¼-inch wedges

1 pound boneless, skinless chicken thighs (about 6), cut into ½-inch pieces

1 garlic clove, minced

4 cups reduced-sodium chicken broth

2 teaspoons Madras-style curry powder

Kosher salt and freshly ground black pepper

1½ cups uncooked Baldo, Arborio, or other medium-grain white rice

½ cup golden raisins

1 cinnamon stick

½ cup sliced natural (skin-on) almonds, toasted

1. Heat the oil in a large wide saucepan or deep skillet. Add the onion; cook, stirring, over medium-low heat, until golden, about 10 minutes. Add the chicken and garlic. Sauté until the chicken is no longer pink, about 5 minutes.

2. Meanwhile, heat the chicken broth almost to a boil.

3. Sprinkle the chicken with the curry powder and salt and pepper; cook, stirring, for 1 minute. Stir in the rice, raisins, and cinnamon stick until blended. Add the hot chicken broth. Heat to a boil; stir once. Cook, covered, until almost all the liquid is absorbed, about 15 minutes.

4. Sprinkle the pilaf with the toasted almonds and serve.

Roasted Tomato Pilaf with Chickpeas and Dill

Makes 4 to 6 servings

The broth for this pilaf is made with roasted tomatoes and onions. The roasted juices from the vegetables have a depth of flavor similar to roasted meats. Ideal for vegetarians, served with cooked escarole or broccoli rabe seasoned with browned garlic and hot pepper flakes.

2 pounds ripe plum tomatoes, cored and quartered
1 large onion, cut into ¼-inch wedges
3 tablespoons extra virgin olive oil
Kosher salt and freshly ground black pepper
One 15-ounce can chickpeas, well drained
4 garlic cloves, bruised with the side of a knife
1 sprig dill, plus 2 tablespoons chopped dill

1 sprig thyme
1 sprig Italian parsley, plus 2 tablespoons chopped parsley
1½ cups uncooked Baldo, Arborio, or other medium-grain white rice
1 tablespoon fresh lemon juice

1. Preheat the oven to 400°F.

2. Spread the tomatoes and onion in a large roasting pan. Drizzle with the oil and sprinkle with salt and pepper. Roast for 30 minutes, stirring once or twice. Add the chickpeas, garlic, dill, thyme, and parsley sprigs. Roast, stirring once or twice, until the tomatoes begin to brown and the onions are golden, about 25 minutes more. Cover the pan with foil and let cool. The tomato skins will loosen.

3. Pull the skins from the tomatoes, and return the tomatoes to the roasting pan. Add 3 cups water and stir, scraping up any browned bits from the bottom of the pan. Taste the broth; add salt as needed.

4. Transfer the roasted tomatoes and broth to a large wide saucepan; heat to a boil. Cover and cook over low heat for 10 minutes. Remove the herb sprigs and discard. Stir in the rice until blended. Cover and cook over low heat until the liquid is absorbed, 20 to 25 minutes; the rice will be al dente. Let stand off the heat, covered, for 10 minutes, or until the rice is tender.

5. Transfer to a large bowl and sprinkle with the dill, parsley, and lemon juice. Serve at once.

Red Rice Summer Vegetable Pilaf

Makes 4 to 6 servings

Pilaf is the most versatile of dishes, easily adapting to the seasons, like this one inspired by a bounty of late summer vegetables found at my farmers' market. Use red rice from Bhutan if you have it, but brown rice or Wehani rice work as well. Because brown and Wehani rices are covered with a thick layer of bran, they will need a longer cooking time and more liquid: use 2¼ cups liquid for each cup of rice (for the 2 cups of rice, double the broth here) and cook for 45 to 55 minutes.

Stir-fry the vegetables and toss into the pilaf just before serving. Top with salted sunflower seeds.

¼ cup extra virgin olive oil

2 cups diced (¼-inch) onions

3 garlic cloves, finely chopped

2 cups uncooked Bhutanese red rice

4½ cups reduced-sodium vegetable or
   chicken broth (or half broth and half water)

1 cup diced (½-inch) red bell pepper

2 cups cubed (½-inch) zucchini (2 medium)

1 pound firm but ripe plum tomatoes (6 to 8),
   cored and cut into ½-inch pieces

1 cup corn kernels (from 2 large ears)

½ cup torn basil leaves

Kosher salt and freshly ground black pepper

¼ cup toasted unsalted sunflower seeds

1. Heat 2 tablespoons of the oil in a large wide saucepan or deep skillet. Add the onion; cook, stirring, over medium-low heat until golden, about 10 minutes. Add two-thirds of the garlic; cook for 1 minute.

2. Add the rice; stir to coat with oil. Add the broth; heat to a boil. Stir once. Cover and cook until the broth is absorbed and the rice is tender, 20 minutes. Uncover and let stand over low heat for 5 minutes, or until the excess moisture has evaporated. Do not stir.

3. Meanwhile, for the vegetables, heat the 2 remaining tablespoons olive oil in a large skillet over medium heat. Add the red bell pepper; cook, stirring, until the edges begin to brown, about 10 minutes. Add the zucchini; cook for 1 minute. Add the tomatoes; cook for 1 minute. Add the corn, the remaining garlic, and

the basil. Cook, tossing, until heated through, about 2 minutes. Season with salt and pepper. Spoon the vegetables onto the pilaf in the pot.

4. Spoon (do not stir) the rice and topping into a shallow bowl. Sprinkle with the sunflower seeds, and serve.

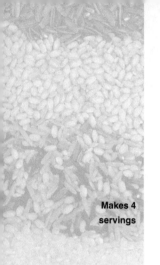

Curried Tomato, Eggplant, and Toasted Walnut Pilaf

Makes 4 servings

The combination of curry and tomato, although unusual, is extraordinarily good when paired in a pilaf fragrant with ginger and garlic. I prefer Madras-style curry powder, a sweeter and spicier blend, available in gold-colored tins in most supermarkets. This dish is good served with grilled lamb.

1 medium eggplant (about 1 pound), trimmed, peeled, and cut into ¼-inch slices
Kosher salt
Extra virgin olive oil
1 cup diced onions
1 teaspoon minced ginger
1 teaspoon minced garlic
1½ cups uncooked basmati rice

2 teaspoons Madras-style curry powder
1 large tomato (8 ounces), cored and cut into ½-inch chunks (about 1 cup)
2 tablespoons chopped basil
2 tablespoons chopped mint
Freshly ground black pepper
½ cup broken walnuts, toasted

1. Arrange the eggplant slices in layers in a colander, sprinkling each layer lightly with salt. Place a small plate on top of the eggplant and weight it with something heavy (a 28-ounce can of tomatoes works well). Place a soup dish under the colander and let stand for at least 2 hours.

2. Blot the eggplant dry with paper towels. Stack the slices and cut them in ¼-inch-wide strips.

3. Heat 1 tablespoon oil in a large wide saucepan or deep skillet over medium-low heat. Add the onions; cook, stirring, until golden, about 10 minutes. Add the ginger and garlic; cook for 2 minutes. Stir in the rice and curry powder; cook, stirring to coat the rice, about 1 minute.

4. Add 1¾ cups water, the tomato, and 1 teaspoon salt; heat to a boil. Cook, covered, over low heat until the broth is absorbed and the rice is tender, about 15 minutes. Let stand off the heat, covered, for 10 minutes before serving.

5. While the rice is cooking, heat ½ inch of olive oil in a large skillet until hot enough to sizzle a piece of eggplant upon contact. Fry the eggplant in two batches, stirring to keep the strips separate, until dark golden brown, about 10 minutes. Remove from the oil with a slotted spoon; drain on a double thickness of paper towels.

6. Add the eggplant, basil, mint, and a grinding of black pepper to the pilaf. Spoon into a serving bowl; sprinkle with the walnuts, and serve at once.

Golden Chickpea and Curried Lamb Pilaf

Makes 4 servings

Ground lamb, beef, or turkey can be used in this pilaf. Ground meat allows the pilaf to cook more quickly, but the meaty taste, enhanced by the addition of curry and cumin, is still distinctive. Caramelized tomatoes are spooned over the pilaf. All this dish needs to round out the menu is a big green salad.

6 tablespoons extra virgin olive oil

1 pound lean ground lamb

One 15-ounce can chickpeas, drained, liquid reserved

½ cup diced (¼-inch) onion

1 medium carrot, diced (about ½ cup)

1 teaspoon minced garlic

1½ cups uncooked Baldo, Arborio, or other medium-grain white rice

¼ cup dried currants

2 teaspoons Madras-style curry powder

1 teaspoon ground cumin

Kosher salt

1½ pounds plum tomatoes, cored and halved lengthwise

Freshly ground black pepper

Cilantro leaves

1. Heat 2 tablespoons of the olive oil in a large deep skillet or sauté pan over medium-high heat. Add the meat, stirring to break it up. Add the chickpeas. Cook, stirring occasionally, until the chickpeas are browned and beginning to pop, about 10 minutes.

2. Add the onion, carrot, and garlic; reduce the heat to medium-low and cook, stirring, just until the onion is softened but not browned, about 5 minutes. Add the rice, currants, curry powder, and cumin; stir to blend.

3. Add enough water to the reserved chickpea liquid to equal 3 cups. Stir the liquid and ¾ teaspoon salt into the rice; heat to a boil. Stir once. Cover and cook over medium-low heat until the liquid is absorbed and the rice is tender, about 20 minutes.

4. Meanwhile, heat the remaining ¼ cup olive oil in a 9-inch cast-iron or heavy nonstick skillet. Arrange the tomatoes, cut side up in the pan and adjust the heat

to maintain a steady sizzle. Sprinkle the tomatoes with salt and a grinding of black pepper. Cook, without stirring, until the tomato skins are blackened and blistered, 10 to 15 minutes. Carefully turn the tomatoes and sprinkle with salt and pepper. Cook, without stirring, adjusting the heat if necessary to maintain a steady sizzle, until the cut sides are browned, about 10 minutes. Set aside.

5. Spoon the pilaf onto a deep serving platter and spoon the tomatoes around the edges. Garnish with cilantro leaves, and serve.

Paella

Paella is said to have originated in Valencia, in the southeast coastal region of Spain, where the Moors introduced and grew rice from the East more than a thousand years ago.

The word *paella* comes from *patella*, the Latin word for "pan." Today paella is the name of the special pan used as well as the name of the dish. Originally paella was a midday meal cooked by the rice reapers over an open fire on a wide flat pan, made with ingredients on hand: frogs, eel, and snails, wild rabbit and birds, and, of course, rice.

Today paella in Valencia might be a simple mixture of rice, beans, snails, duck, and rabbit, or one extravagant with shellfish, saffron, sausage, and artichokes. Shellfish paella was only made along the coast of Spain where the Moors first planted rice and the sea offered its bounty. Experts assert that the ingredients in paella should complement, rather than overpower, each other. Sausage isn't combined with seafood in paella; seafood would never be found in paella made with poultry. This is not, however, a hard-and-fast rule, as there are exceptions everywhere. Nevertheless, paella is at its best when it contains a few distinctive ingredients, allowing the rice to remain the focal point.

Several different varieties of rice are grown in Valencia, but only a few of these are available in the United States. I can buy a quite expensive rice called Bomba. Classified as a short-grain rice, it resembles Arborio and other rices used to make risotto. Bomba becomes large and plump as it cooks, and it has the ability to absorb almost twice as much liquid as regular rice without losing its shape or semi-firm center. The absorption is important in paella, as all the flavors of the meats, seafood, vegetables, and broth infuse the rice. Calasparra is another Spanish rice traditionally used for paella. If you can't get or afford Spanish rice, substitute Italian or domestically grown Arborio or Baldo. Both have the ability to absorb flavors yet retain their plump shape. Other medium-grain rices, like the ones grown in California, also make acceptable paella. Because the rice is cooked uncovered and never stirred, the grains cook separate, unlike risotto.

Paella Pan

A paella pan is shallow and round. In Spain they are gauged according to the number of portions, and portions are quite generous. My pan is supposed to serve four but it feeds six to eight easily. Paella is traditionally cooked on an open fire so that the aroma can permeate the rice, which is why the pan is shallow, just 1½ to 2½ inches deep. My pan (13½ inches from rim to rim) sits on two burners on top of my stove; I occasionally turn the pan so that the rice will cook evenly. Allow the rice on the bottom of the pan to cook to a rich golden crust. Called the *socorrat*, it is considered a delicacy.

Paella Ingredients

Saffron
Although not essential, saffron is a traditional paella ingredient. Called *zafaran* for its yellow color, it is made from the stigmas of the purple crocus. Each flower produces just three stigmas, and the work of harvesting them is painstaking, making it the most expensive spice in the world. Added to dishes, the crushed threads release a haunting, almost medicinal flavor and aroma. They turn the rice in paella a pale golden color.

Always buy threads, not powdered saffron. Crush the threads in a mortar and pestle and heat briefly in a small dry skillet over low heat, or steep in boiling water or broth. The measurement in my recipes is for ¼ teaspoon crushed threads, equivalent to a generous pinch of whole threads.

Paprika

Another traditional paella ingredient is Spanish paprika, made from dried pulverized Spanish red peppers called *pimentón*. Although they are like no other peppers, you can substitute good-quality Hungarian paprika.

Broth

Use a full-flavored chicken or beef broth, either store-bought or homemade. While homemade is best, there are many good packaged broths now in the market. The ones packed in asceptic boxes seem to have a fresher taste than canned broths.

How much broth? I plan on 3 to 4 cups broth per cup of rice, depending on the type of rice. High-quality Spanish rices require more broth than domestic medium-grain rices. Because the broth is added in two installments, you can judge by how dry the rice is after the first 15 minutes. If you run out of broth, use boiling water.

Paella with Shrimp and Chicken

Makes 6 to 8 servings

Simple because it uses fewer ingredients than the recipes that follow, but all the essential flavors are here.

Kosher salt and freshly ground black pepper

8 boneless, skinless chicken thighs, fat trimmed and halved

1 pork tenderloin (about 12 ounces), cut into ½-inch slices

12 large shrimp, shelled (reserve the shells) and deveined

5 tablespoons extra virgin olive oil

2 teaspoons fresh rosemary leaves, chopped, or 1 teaspoon dried rosemary

2 garlic cloves, bruised with the side of a knife, plus 2 teaspoons minced garlic

2 strips orange zest, cut into thin slivers

One 14½-ounce can diced tomatoes, well drained, juices reserved

4 cups reduced-sodium chicken broth

½ cup dry white wine

¼ teaspoon crushed saffron threads

2 chorizo sausages (about 6 ounces), casings removed and diced (¼-inch)

1 cup chopped onions

½ cup chopped red bell pepper

1 teaspoon sweet Spanish paprika

2 cups uncooked Bomba, Arborio, or other medium-grain white rice

4 ounces Italian romano beans or regular green beans, trimmed and cut into ½-inch lengths (about 1 cup)

1 cup frozen petite green peas, thawed

Rosemary sprigs

1. *For the marinade:* Salt and pepper the chicken and pork on both sides. Place in a large bowl. Add the shrimp, 2 tablespoons of the olive oil, the rosemary, bruised garlic, and orange zest. Stir to blend. Cover and marinate in the refrigerator for at least 2 hours, or as long as overnight.

2. Place the reserved tomato juices in a large measuring cup and add enough water to measure 2 cups. Combine with the chicken broth in a saucepan and heat to a boil.

3. Meanwhile, heat 1 tablespoon oil in a medium skillet. Add the shrimp shells; cook, stirring, over medium heat, until dark red, about 2 minutes. Add 1 tea-

spoon of the minced garlic; cook for 1 minute. Add the wine; heat to a boil. Boil for 1 minute. Add to the simmering chicken broth. Cook, covered, for 15 minutes. Strain into another saucepan; discard the shells. Keep the broth warm over low heat.

4. Crumble the saffron into a small skillet or saucepan and heat gently over low heat for about 20 seconds. Add about ½ cup hot broth to the skillet; let stand, covered, off the heat, until ready to use.

5. Remove the chicken and pork from the marinade. Return the shrimp, still in the marinade, to the refrigerator. Heat 1 tablespoon oil in a paella pan or a large skillet with an ovenproof handle over medium-high heat. When hot enough to sizzle a piece of meat, gradually add the chicken and pork and quickly sear in batches just long enough to lightly brown; about 2 minutes per side; do not cook through. Transfer to a side dish. (If preferred, the meats can be seared on a hot grill.)

6. Add the remaining 1 tablespoon olive oil to the pan; heat over medium heat. Add the chorizo and cook, stirring, until golden, about 5 minutes. Stir in the onions and red bell pepper; cook, stirring, until golden, about 5 minutes. Add the remaining 1 teaspoon minced garlic; cook, stirring, until softened, about 1 minute. Add the paprika; stir to blend. Stir in the tomatoes until blended. (Paella can be prepared one or two hours ahead up to this point.)

7. Meanwhile, preheat the oven to 450°F.

8. Add the rice to the tomato mixture; cook, stirring, until heated through, about 3 minutes. Pour the saffron mixture over the rice. Taste the broth and add salt if needed. Add 3 cups of the hot broth and stir just to blend. Use the back of a spoon to spread the rice in an even layer. Add more broth, if needed, to cover the rice. Cook, uncovered, until most of the broth has been absorbed and the rice is almost tender, about 15 minutes. Pour the remaining hot broth over the rice. Tuck the chicken into the simmering broth around the edges of the pan. Add the pork and shrimp to the center. Top with the beans and peas. Press the ingredients into the rice, making sure they are all covered with broth; do not stir. Add boiling water to cover the ingredients if necessary.

9. Place the pan in the oven and bake for 10 minutes. Remove from the oven and cover with a large piece of heavy-duty aluminum foil. Let stand for 10 minutes, or until the liquid is absorbed and the rice is tender.

10. To serve, spoon onto a large platter or serve from the paella pan. Garnish the paella with rosemary sprigs.

Seafood Paella

Makes 6 to 8 servings

The more elaborate the paella, the more labor-intensive the preparation. But shelling the shrimp, cleaning the squid, and chopping the vegetables can be done ahead, and the ingredients wrapped in plastic and refrigerated until it is time to cook. Here the rice simmers in a tomato, shrimp, and chicken broth. While the recipe calls for scallops, shrimp, squid, clams, and mussels, simply increase one of the others if any one is unavailable. Wide flat pale green Italian beans, also called romano, are available in the fall and early winter. If necessary, use frozen Italian beans, or substitute fresh green beans.

8 ounces bay scallops, halved if large

8 ounces cleaned small squid, bodies cut into ½-inch rings, tentacles left whole

12 large shrimp, preferably with heads, shells removed, leaving the heads and tails on, and shells reserved

¼ cup extra virgin olive oil

2 garlic cloves, bruised with the side of a knife, plus 2 teaspoons minced garlic

2 strips lemon zest, cut into thin slivers

1 teaspoon thyme leaves, plus a few sprigs for garnish

Kosher salt and freshly ground black pepper

One 14½-ounce can diced tomatoes, well drained, juices reserved

4 cups reduced-sodium chicken broth

½ cup dry white wine

¼ teaspoon crushed saffron threads

Two ¼-inch-thick slices pancetta or thick slices bacon, cut into ¼-inch dice

1 cup chopped onions

½ cup diced (¼-inch) red bell pepper

½ cup diced (¼-inch) green bell pepper

1 teaspoon sweet Spanish paprika

2 cups uncooked Bomba, Arborio, or other medium-grain white rice

4 ounces romano (Italian) beans, trimmed and cut into ½-inch lengths (about 1 cup; see headnote)

1 cup frozen baby lima beans, thawed

12 small clams (preferably Manila), scrubbed and rinsed

12 small mussels, beards pulled off, scrubbed, and rinsed

Thyme sprigs

1. **For the marinade:** In a large bowl, combine the scallops, squid, shrimp, 2 tablespoons of the olive oil, the bruised garlic, lemon zest, thyme leaves, a pinch of salt, and a grinding of black pepper. Stir to blend. Cover and marinate, refrigerated, for 1 to 2 hours.

2. Place the reserved tomato juices in a large measuring cup and add enough water to measure 2 cups. Combine with the chicken broth in a saucepan; heat to a boil.

3. Meanwhile, heat 1 tablespoon oil in a medium skillet. Add the shrimp shells; cook, stirring, over medium heat, until dark red, about 2 minutes. Add 1 teaspoon of the minced garlic; cook for 1 minute. Add the wine; heat to a boil. Boil for 1 minute. Add to the simmering chicken broth. Cook, covered, for 15 minutes. Strain into another saucepan; discard the shells. Keep the broth warm over low heat.

4. Crumble the saffron into a small skillet or saucepan; heat gently over low heat, about 20 seconds. Add about ½ cup hot broth to the skillet; let stand, covered, off the heat, until ready to use.

5. Heat the remaining 1 tablespoon oil in a large paella pan or large shallow skillet with an ovenproof handle. Add the pancetta; cook over medium heat, stirring, until lightly browned, about 5 minutes. Spoon off and discard all but 2 tablespoons of the fat.

6. Add the onions and bell peppers to the pan; cook over medium-low heat, stirring, until the onions are golden, about 10 minutes. Add the remaining 1 teaspoon minced garlic; cook for 1 minute. Stir in the paprika; cook for 1 minute. Add the tomatoes; stir to blend. (Paella can be prepared one or two hours ahead up to this point.)

7. Meanwhile, preheat the oven to 450°F.

8. Add the rice to the tomato mixture; cook, stirring, until heated through, about 3 minutes. Pour the saffron mixture over the rice. Add the simmering broth; heat to boil. Taste the broth and add salt if needed. Stir once, and spread the rice in an even layer. Cook, uncovered, over medium heat until the rice is almost tender but still moist with broth, about 15 minutes. Do not stir.

9. Add the marinated seafood, green beans, and lima beans to the rice, pushing them down into the simmering rice in the center portion of the pan. Tuck the clams and mussels around the edges of the pan, with the hinged part of each shell deep in the rice.

10. Place in the oven and bake, uncovered, just until the clams and mussels open, about 10 minutes. Remove from the oven and cover with a large piece of heavy-duty aluminum foil. Let stand until the rice absorbs the seafood juices and softens slightly, 10 minutes.

11. To serve, spoon onto a large platter or serve right from the paella pan. Garnish the paella with thyme sprigs.

Paella with Rabbit, Artichoke Hearts, and Chorizo

Makes 6 to 8 servings

Paella was made as the midday meal outside over an open fire by field workers with what was on hand, including wild rabbit. This recipe, made with farmed rabbit, is an adaptation. Substitute chicken if rabbit is not available.

Marinade

1 tablespoon chopped lemon zest

1 tablespoon rosemary leaves, chopped

1 tablespoon minced garlic

2 teaspoons kosher salt

Freshly ground black pepper

1 rabbit (2¾ pounds), cut into 8 serving pieces

1 pork tenderloin (about 12 ounces), cut into 1-inch pieces

Braised Artichokes

Juice of 1 lemon

4 large artichokes or 1½ pounds baby artichokes

1 tablespoon extra virgin olive oil

1 teaspoon minced garlic

1 thin sliver onion

1 thyme sprig

1 bay leaf

1 teaspoon kosher salt

¼ cup extra virgin olive oil

4 cups reduced-sodium chicken broth

¼ teaspoon crushed saffron threads

2 links chorizo sausage (about 8 ounces), casings removed and cut into ¼-inch slices

½ cup chopped red bell pepper

½ cup chopped scallions (white and green parts)

1 teaspoon minced garlic

One 14½-ounce can diced tomatoes, well drained

1 teaspoon sweet Spanish paprika

2 cups uncooked Bomba, Arborio, or other medium-grain white rice

Kosher salt

4 ounces Italian romano beans or regular green beans, trimmed and cut into ½-inch lengths (about 1 cup)

1 cup frozen petite peas, thawed

Rosemary sprigs

1. **For the marinade:** Combine the lemon zest, rosemary, garlic, salt, and a generous grinding of black pepper in a small bowl; mash together with a fork. Arrange the rabbit and pork on a platter. Sprinkle with the marinade; rub it into the flesh. Cover and refrigerate for at least 1 hour.

2. **For the artichokes:** Half-fill a large bowl with water and add the lemon juice. If using large artichokes, cut off the stems and reserve. Trim off all the outer leaves from each artichoke (see Note) until only white leaves remain. Cut off the cone-

shaped white leaves. With the tip of a knife or a spoon, scoop out the fuzzy choke. Trim the outside from the artichoke bottom. Quarter the artichoke bottom and place it in the lemon water. Trim the green from the outside of the stems; cut into ½-inch lengths. Place in the lemon water. If using baby artichokes, trim the ends of the stems. Remove the outside dark green leaves from each artichoke until the cone of white leaves is exposed. Trim the dark green from the artichoke bottoms. Halve or quarter the artichokes. Place in the lemon water.

3. Drain the artichokes; discard the lemon. Heat the olive oil and minced garlic in a large deep skillet or wide shallow saucepan over medium-low heat just until sizzling. Add the artichoke hearts (and stems) and cook, stirring, until coated with oil, about 3 minutes. Add 2 cups water, the onion, the thyme sprig, bay leaf, and salt; heat to a boil. Cover and cook over medium heat until the artichokes are almost tender, about 15 minutes. Drain; reserve the liquid. Discard the bay leaf; taste and correct the seasoning. (The artichokes can be prepared up to 1 day ahead. Refrigerate the artichokes and liquid separately, covered, until ready to use.)

4. Heat the ¼-cup olive oil in a paella pan or a large (12 inches or more) deep skillet with an ovenproof handle. Add the rabbit pieces; cook over medium heat, turning occasionally, until lightly browned, about 10 minutes. Transfer to a side dish. Repeat with the pork, adjusting the heat as necessary to maintain a steady sizzle without overcooking the pork, about 3 minutes per side. Transfer to the dish with the rabbit. Set the pan aside.

5. Heat the chicken broth and artichoke liquid to a boil in a medium saucepan; keep hot. Crumble the saffron into a small skillet or saucepan and heat gently over low heat for about 20 seconds. Add about ½ cup hot broth to the skillet; let stand, covered, off the heat, until ready to use.

6. Add the chorizo to the pan you used for the rabbit; cook, stirring, until browned, about 5 minutes. Drain off and discard all but 1 tablespoon of the oil. Add the red bell pepper, scallions, and minced garlic; cook, stirring, over medium-low heat until golden, about 5 minutes. Add the tomatoes; cook for 2 minutes. Add the paprika; stir to blend. (Paella can be prepared one or two hours ahead up to this point.)

7. Meanwhile, preheat the oven to 450°F.

8. Add the rice to the tomato mixture, stirring until coated and heated through, about 3 minutes. Spread the rice in a flat layer. Pour the saffron liquid over the top. Add 4 cups of the hot broth; taste and add salt if needed. Stir once, making sure that the rice is covered with broth. Cook, uncovered, without stirring, over medium heat until most of the broth is absorbed, about 15 minutes.

9. Tuck the rabbit pieces around the edges of the pan. Place the pork, artichoke hearts, green beans, and peas in the center, pressing them down into the rice. Drizzle with any meat juices left in the dish. Ladle the remaining hot broth over the top.

10. Place in the oven and bake for 10 minutes. Remove from the oven and cover with a large piece of heavy-duty aluminum foil. Let stand for 10 minutes, or until the liquid is absorbed and the rice is tender.

11. To serve, spoon onto a large platter or serve right from the paella pan. (Garnish the edges of the platter with the reserved artichoke leaves, if using.) Garnish with rosemary sprigs.

NOTE: If using large artichokes, reserve some of the outside leaves and braise them along with the artichoke hearts in Step 3. Cover and keep warm to use as a garnish.

Other Main Courses

Rice is a staple like eggs, butter, and bread. It can bind meat loaf, transform a few eggs into a meal, or be the foundation for a hearty stew. And so this chapter is hefty with recipes—a handful are authentic traditional or ethnic dishes, but many more are eclectic, as I cook from my culinary soul, one that is heavily influenced by the places I travel, the food that I eat, and the cooks that I meet.

From New Delhi and Bangkok to Charleston and London, and places in between, the recipes in this chapter all have one thing in common: a cup or two, or maybe three, of rice.

Baked Rice with Egg and Parmesan Crust

Makes 4 servings

I adapted this recipe for *Arròs amb Crosta* (Rice with Egg Crust) from Colman Andrews's book *Catalan Cuisine* when I wanted a simple dish to prepare in the evening after work. Serve this homey scaled down version of the original recipe from the cast-iron skillet in which it is baked. A salad of leafy greens completes the meal.

2 tablespoons extra virgin olive oil

½ cup chopped onion

1 pound plum tomatoes, cored, seeded, and diced (about 2 cups)

2 tablespoons finely chopped Italian parsley

1 teaspoon minced garlic

1 cup uncooked Arborio or other medium-grain white rice

2 cups reduced-sodium vegetable or chicken broth

Kosher salt

1 cup frozen petite peas, thawed, optional

5 large eggs

¼ cup freshly grated Parmigiano-Reggiano

Freshly ground black pepper

1. Preheat the oven to 350°F.

2. Heat the oil in a 10-inch cast-iron skillet or 4-quart Dutch oven (or other stovetop-to-oven pot) over medium heat. Add the onion; cook over medium-low heat, stirring, until golden, about 10 minutes. Add the tomatoes, parsley, and garlic: heat over high heat to a boil. Reduce the heat and cook until the tomatoes are softened and most of the liquid has evaporated about 10 minutes.

3. Stir the rice into the tomatoes until coated. Add the broth; heat to a boil. Taste the broth and add salt if necessary. Stir the rice well. Cover tightly with foil or a lid. Bake until the broth is absorbed and the rice is tender, about 15 minutes. Remove from the oven. Uncover the pan. Leave the oven on.

4. Spread the peas, if using, on the top of the rice. Whisk the eggs and cheese in a large bowl until blended; add black pepper. Pour evenly over the rice. Return to the oven and bake, uncovered, until the eggs are set and lightly browned, about 12 minutes. Let stand for a few minutes before serving directly from the pan.

Green Rice Frittata with Sautéed Tomatoes and Red Onions

Makes 4 servings

Serve this frittata plain, with a sauce of chopped raw tomato seasoned with a little olive oil and basil, or topped with the Sautéed Tomatoes with Red Onions. Round out the menu with a loaf of crusty bread and some tangy brine-cured black olives.

½ cup packed Italian parsley sprigs
1 scallion, trimmed and cut into ½-inch lengths
1 garlic clove, chopped
8 large eggs
2 tablespoons freshly grated Parmigiano-Reggiano
Freshly ground black pepper

1 tablespoon extra virgin olive oil
1½ cups cooked long- or medium-grain white rice
1 cup shredded mozzarella (about 4 ounces)
6 thin slices provolone (about 3 ounces)
Sautéed Tomatoes with Red Onions (recipe follows), optional

1. Finely chop the parsley, scallion, and garlic together with a large knife or in the food processor; set aside. Whisk the eggs, Parmesan, and a grinding of black pepper in a large bowl; set aside.

2. Heat the oil in a large heavy skillet, preferably nonstick, over medium heat. Add the rice and the parsley mixture; cook, stirring, until blended and hot, about 1 minute. Pour the egg mixture over the rice; sprinkle with the mozzarella. Cook over low heat, without stirring, just until the eggs begin to set, about 2 minutes. With a spatula, lift the edges of the frittata and tilt the pan so that the runny center flows to the edges. Cover and cook over medium-low heat, shaking the pan occasionally, until the eggs are set around the edges and almost set in the center, about 12 minutes.

3. Preheat the broiler, if using it to finish the frittata. Arrange the provolone slices on top of the frittata. If using the broiler, place the skillet about 3 inches from the heat and broil until the cheese is browned and bubbly, about 2 minutes. Or, cover the frittata and cook over very low heat until the cheese is melted, about 5 minutes.

4. Carefully loosen the sides and bottom of the frittata with a rubber spatula; slide onto a serving dish. Cut into wedges. Serve with the sautéed tomatoes, if desired.

Sautéed Tomatoes with Red Onions

Makes about 2 cups

Serve with the frittata or simply over a bowl of hot freshly cooked rice.

1 tablespoon extra virgin olive oil
½ medium red onion, cut into ¼-inch wedges
1 garlic clove, finely chopped
1 pound plum tomatoes, cored and cut into ¼-inch wedges

Kosher salt and freshly ground black pepper
Torn basil leaves

1. Heat the oil in a medium skillet over medium heat. Add the red onion; cook, stirring occasionally, until crisp-tender, about 3 minutes. Add the garlic; cook for 1 minute.

2. Add the tomatoes; stir to blend. Cover and cook over low heat until soft, about 5 minutes. Season with salt and pepper to taste. Add basil to taste. Serve hot.

Red Pepper, Fennel, and Rice Frittata

Makes 4 servings

A hearty frittata flavored with roasted peppers and fennel. Use freshly grated Parmigiano-Reggiano in the frittata itself and top with smoked or plain mozzarella.

2 tablespoons extra virgin olive oil

1 cup diced (¼-inch) fennel bulb (see Note), plus
 ¼ cup finely chopped feathery fennel tops

½ large sweet yellow onion, cut into ¼-inch
 lengthwise slices (about 1 cup)

½ cup slivered (1 × ⅛-inch strips) red bell pepper

1 cup cooked long- or medium-grain white rice

2 tablespoons chopped Italian parsley

Kosher salt and freshly ground black pepper

8 large eggs

2 tablespoons freshly grated Parmigiano-Reggiano

4 ounces plain or smoked mozzarella, thinly sliced

1. Heat the olive oil in a large heavy skillet, preferably nonstick. Add the diced fennel, onion, and red pepper; cook over medium-low heat, stirring occasionally, until golden brown, about 10 minutes. Stir in the rice, parsley, fennel fronds, and salt and pepper to taste.

2. Whisk the eggs and Parmesan cheese in a medium bowl. Pour over the rice mixture. Cook over low heat, without stirring, until the eggs begin to set, about 2 minutes. With a spatula, lift the edges of the frittata and tilt the pan so that the runny center flows to the edges. Cover and cook over medium-low heat, shaking the pan, until the eggs set around the edges and almost in the center, about 12 minutes.

3. Preheat the broiler, if using it to finish the frittata. Arrange the cheese on top of the frittata. If using the broiler, place the skillet about 3 inches from the heat and broil until the cheese is browned and bubbly, about 2 minutes. Or cover the frittata and cook over very low heat until the cheese is melted, about 5 minutes.

4. Loosen the edges and bottom of the frittata with a rubber spatula; slide onto a large round platter. Cut into wedges to serve.

NOTE: To ensure crispness and flavor, always soak trimmed fennel bulb in a bowl of ice water for about 20 minutes before using.

Persian-Style Omelet with Leeks and Peas

Makes 4 servings

In Persian cooking, an omelet, or *kuku*, is similar to an Italian frittata, but it contains a small amount of flour and baking powder, so the texture is more like an eggy pancake. I have no idea if a Persian cook would add rice to a *kuku*, but because rice is so popular in Persian cooking, I assume there would be some leftovers on hand. Authentic or not, the results are delicious.

¼ cup extra virgin olive oil

1 cup chopped leeks (white and pale green parts)

1 teaspoon minced garlic

1 cup cooked medium- or long-grain white rice

1 cup frozen petite green peas, thawed

¼ cup chopped dill

2 tablespoons chopped mint

5 large eggs

1 tablespoon all-purpose flour

½ teaspoon baking powder

½ teaspoon kosher salt

Freshly ground black pepper

1. Preheat the oven to 350°F.

2. Heat 2 tablespoons of the oil in 10-inch heavy ovenproof skillet, preferably non-stick. Add the leeks; cook, stirring, over low heat, until wilted, about 10 minutes. Stir in the garlic; cook for 1 minute. Add the rice, peas, dill, and mint; stir to blend. Remove from the heat.

3. In a large bowl, whisk the eggs, flour, baking powder, salt, and pepper to taste until well blended. Add the rice and leek mixture and stir to blend.

4. Add the remaining 2 tablespoons oil to the empty skillet; heat over medium heat until very hot. Pour in the egg mixture; smooth out the ingredients. Place in the oven and bake until the eggs are set, about 15 minutes.

5. With a spatula, slide the omelet onto a serving plate. Cut into wedges. Serve warm or at room temperature.

Scrambled Eggs with Rice and Tomato-Jalapeño Salsa

Makes 2 generous servings (recipe can be doubled)

Try these buttery cumin-flavored scrambled eggs and rice for brunch or supper. The accompaniments—salsa, sliced avocado, and cilantro—give the dish a Southwestern flavor. For a heartier entrée, add a cup or two of cooked black beans to the salsa.

Salsa

1 cup diced ripe tomatoes (including seeds and juices)

1 scallion, trimmed and thinly sliced

1 tablespoon chopped cilantro

1 jalapeño, or more to taste, seeded and minced

2 tablespoons extra virgin olive oil

2 teaspoons fresh lime juice

1 teaspoon minced mint, optional

Kosher salt

5 extra-large eggs

Pinch of kosher salt

Freshly ground black pepper

½ teaspoon ground cumin

1 tablespoon unsalted butter

1 cup cooked long- or medium-grain white rice

1 tablespoon thinly sliced scallion greens

Cilantro sprigs

2 tablespoons sour cream, optional

½ ripe avocado, peeled, pitted, and thinly sliced

1. ***For the salsa:*** Combine the tomatoes, scallion, cilantro, jalapeño, olive oil, lime juice, and mint in a small bowl; season with salt. Cover and set aside at room temperature.

2. Whisk the eggs and 2 tablespoons cold water in a large bowl until blended; add the salt and a grinding of black pepper. Set aside.

3. Sprinkle the cumin into a medium skillet; heat over medium-low heat, stirring gently, until fragrant, about 30 seconds. Transfer to a side dish. Melt the butter in the skillet. When the foam subsides, stir in the rice; cook, stirring, until coated with butter and heated through, about 2 minutes. Stir in the cumin and scallion greens.

4. Add the eggs all at once; cook, stirring gently with a heatproof rubber spatula, just until they begin to set. Immediately spoon onto serving plates or a platter. Top with cilantro sprigs and sour cream, if using. Garnish with the avocado slices. Serve with the salsa on the side.

Spicy Pork Fried Rice with Green Beans and Peanuts

Makes 4 servings

Chinese chile sauce gives this quick fried rice and pork entrée its spicy flavor. The sauce is a thick jam-like mixture of ground chiles, salt, and vinegar, cooked in oil. Have all the ingredients assembled and ready to go before heating up the pan. Once you start cooking, this dish is ready in a matter of minutes.

8 ounces green beans, trimmed and cut into 1-inch lengths
Kosher salt
1 large egg
2 tablespoons plus ½ teaspoon tamari or soy sauce, or more to taste
3 tablespoons peanut or other vegetable oil
½ cup chopped onion

1 tablespoon minced fresh ginger
1 teaspoon minced garlic
8 ounces lean ground pork
1 tablespoon Chinese chile sauce
½ cup unsalted dry-roasted peanuts
1 tablespoon minced seeded jalapeño
2 to 3 cups cold or freshly cooked and cooled long- or medium-grain white rice

1. Heat a saucepan of water to a boil. Add the beans and a pinch of salt; cook for 2 minutes. Drain; rinse with cold water. Spread on a double thickness of paper towels to dry.

2. Break the egg into a small bowl. Add ½ teaspoon of the tamari; stir with a fork or chopstick just to break up the yolk. Set aside.

3. Heat a wok or a large skillet, preferably nonstick, over high heat until hot enough to sizzle a drop of water upon contact. Add the oil and a pinch of the onion. When the onion sizzles, add the remaining onions. Cook, stirring, with a spatula or wooden spoon, until beginning to turn golden, about 30 seconds. Add the ginger and garlic; stir-fry for 10 seconds.

4. Add the ground pork. Stir-fry, breaking up the meat with the side of the spatula or spoon, until the pork loses its pink color. Add the chile sauce and 1 tablespoon tamari; stir to blend. Add the green beans, peanuts, and jalapeño; stir to blend.

5. Add the rice; break up any clumps with the edge of the spatula, mixing in the other ingredients. Press the rice against the bottom and the sides of the pan. Sprinkle with the remaining 1 tablespoon tamari. Continue heating the rice, lifting up sections with the spatula, and turning, pressing, and hacking at it with one side of the spatula, until all the ingredients are evenly mixed and coated with the seasonings, about 1 minute. Spoon onto a platter and serve at once.

Stir-fried Soy-Glazed Chicken, Rice, and Cashews

Makes 4 servings

I use a combination of white and brown rices in this dish, but any combination can be used. To ensure neat thin, even slices of chicken, wrap it in foil and partially freeze just until firm, 20 to 30 minutes, before slicing.

Marinade

1 teaspoon tamari or soy sauce
1 teaspoon toasted sesame oil
½ teaspoon grated fresh ginger
½ teaspoon sugar
12 ounces boneless, skinless chicken breasts, cut crosswise into thin slices

Egg Pancake

2 large eggs
¼ teaspoon toasted sesame oil
Pinch of kosher salt
Freshly ground black pepper
1 teaspoon peanut or other vegetable oil

Sauce

1 tablespoon oyster sauce
1 tablespoon water or chicken broth
1 tablespoon tamari or soy sauce
1 teaspoon toasted sesame oil
2 tablespoons peanut or other vegetable oil
½ cup coarsely chopped unsalted cashews
2 teaspoons minced fresh ginger
1 teaspoon minced garlic
½ cup slivered red bell pepper
3 scallions, trimmed and cut into thin diagonal slices
2 to 3 cups cold or freshly cooked and cooled long- or medium-grain brown or white rice (or a combination of the two)
Cilantro leaves, optional

1. *For the marinade:* Combine the tamari, sesame oil, ginger, and sugar in a medium bowl. Add the chicken; let stand at room temperature for 30 minutes, or refrigerate, covered, for 1 hour or more.

2. *For the egg pancake:* Whisk the eggs, sesame oil, salt, and pepper to taste in a medium bowl until frothy. Heat the oil in a wok or large skillet until hot. Add the eggs, tilting the pan to coat evenly with egg; cook until set, about 1 minute. Transfer to a plate; let cool. Cut the pancake into thin strips; reserve.

3. *For the sauce:* Combine the oyster sauce, water, soy sauce, and sesame oil in a small bowl; set aside.

4. Just before serving, heat 1 tablespoon of the oil in a wok or large heavy skillet, preferably nonstick, until very hot. Add the cashews; stir-fry for 30 seconds. With a slotted spoon, remove to a side dish. Add the remaining 1 tablespoon oil to the pan and heat. Add the ginger and garlic; stir-fry for 10 seconds. Add the chicken and stir-fry until lightly browned, about 1 minute. Add the red pepper and scallions; stir-fry for 1 minute.

5. Add the rice; break up any clumps with the edge of the spatula, mixing in the other ingredients. Press the rice against the bottom and the sides of the pan; pour the sauce over the top. Continue heating the rice, lifting up sections with the spatula, and turning, pressing, and hacking at it with the side of the spatula until all the ingredients are evenly mixed and coated with the seasonings, about 2 minutes. Serve at once, sprinkled with the cashews and cilantro, if using.

Stir-fried Fiery Shrimp, Orange Rice, and Spinach

Makes 4 servings

The flavor of orange, whether it is juice, zest, or pulp, seems to temper the assertive taste of seafood. Stir-frying the orange zest in peanut oil ensures that its flavor is evenly distributed, as the oil coats every grain of rice.

Marinade

2 teaspoons tamari or soy sauce

1 teaspoon peanut oil

1 garlic clove, crushed

1 teaspoon minced or grated fresh ginger

½ teaspoon Chinese chile oil

½ teaspoon red pepper flakes

¼ teaspoon freshly ground black pepper

1 pound medium shrimp, shelled and deveined

2 tablespoons peanut or other vegetable oil

2 strips (2 × ½-inches) orange zest, cut into very thin slivers

1 teaspoon minced fresh ginger

½ teaspoon minced garlic

3 scallions, trimmed and cut into thin diagonal slices

4 cups torn spinach leaves (about 5 ounces)

3 cups cold cooked long-grain white or brown rice

2 tablespoons tamari or soy sauce

1. *For the marinade:* Combine the soy sauce, peanut oil, garlic, ginger, chile oil, red pepper flakes, and black pepper in a large bowl. Add the shrimp; toss to coat. Cover and marinate for 30 minutes at room temperature, or 1 hour or longer in the refrigerator.

2. When ready to serve, heat a wok or large nonstick skillet, preferably nonstick, over medium-high heat until hot enough to evaporate a drop of water upon contact. Add 1 tablespoon of the peanut oil; heat until hot. Add the shrimp, a few at a time; stir-fry just until lightly browned on both sides. Transfer to a side dish as they are cooked. Scrape any pan drippings over the shrimp; wipe out the pan with paper towels.

3. Add the remaining 1 tablespoon oil to the pan; heat until hot enough to sizzle a piece of the orange zest. Add all the orange zest; stir-fry for 1 minute. Add the ginger and garlic; stir-fry for 30 seconds. Add the scallions; stir once. Add the spinach; stir to coat with the ingredients.

4. Add the rice and shrimp; break up any clumps of rice with the edge of the spatula mixing in the other ingredients. Press the rice against the bottom and the sides of the pan. Sprinkle with the soy sauce. Continue heating the rice, lifting up sections with the spatula until all the ingredients are evenly mixed and coated with the seasonings, about 2 minutes.

5. Spoon into a serving dish and serve at once.

Hoppin' John

Makes 4 to 6 servings

Certainly rice and dried peas were staples of the slaves in the South, but eating hoppin' John at the beginning of the New Year is symbolic of good luck for the year ahead for all the people of the South. There are several legends surrounding the origin of its name. Supposedly children hopped around the dining table on New Year's Day before sitting down to eat rice and peas—but who knows if the dish was named for the children's hopping, or if the children's hopping was named for the dish. Another more likely hypothesis is that the name is a corruption of *pois à pigeon*, French for "pigeon peas," a dish that is popular in the Caribbean. This is adapted from a recipe of a friend and culinary scholar John Martin Taylor and appears in a slightly different form in his book *Hoppin' John's Lowcountry Cooking.*

1 cup dried black-eyed peas, sorted and rinsed

1 dried chile pepper

1 smoked ham hock

¾ cup chopped onion

1 cup uncooked long-grain white rice

1. Combine the peas, chile pepper, ham hock, onion, and 6 cups water in a large wide saucepan. Heat to a boil. Reduce the heat to low; gently simmer, uncovered, until the peas are soft but not mushy, about 1½ hours. There should be about 2 cups liquid remaining; add water as necessary.

2. Add the rice and stir to distribute evenly. Cover and cook over low heat for 20 minutes; do not lift the lid. Let stand off the heat for 10 minutes. Fluff with a fork and serve.

Rice and Beans

Rice and beans are considered complementary proteins, which, in the simplest terms, means that rice, a fair source of protein, becomes a complete protein when combined with beans. More specifically, rice contains all eight amino acids but is low in the amino acid lysine, which is found in beans, making the classic combination a particularly healthful dish.

Golden Yellow Rice with Black Beans and Roasted Red Peppers

Makes 6 to 8 servings

The bold presentation of black beans against bright yellow rice makes this a stunning dish. Arrange the roasted red peppers between where the yellow rice meets the black beans and garnish the dish with cilantro sprigs. The variety of chiles and peppers cooked with the beans contributes to their complex flavor.

Beans

1 pound dried black beans, sorted, rinsed, and soaked overnight in cold water to cover generously

1 large green bell pepper, halved, stemmed, seeded, and cut into wedges, plus ½ cup chopped green bell pepper

1 bay leaf

4 garlic cloves, 1 bruised with the side of a knife, 3 chopped

2 tablespoons extra virgin olive oil

2 cups chopped onions

½ cup chopped red bell pepper

1 jalapeño, seeded and finely chopped

1 serrano chile, seeded and finely chopped

2 teaspoons ground cumin

Kosher salt and freshly ground black pepper

2 to 3 cups water or low-sodium vegetable or chicken broth

½ cup heavy cream, at room temperature

Yellow Rice

1¾ cups water or low-sodium vegetable or chicken broth

¼ teaspoon crushed saffron threads

1 tablespoon olive oil

1 cup uncooked long-grain white rice

1 garlic clove, minced

½ teaspoon ground turmeric

1 teaspoon kosher salt, or to taste

Garnish

1 cup (2 large peppers) roasted, peeled, and seeded red bell peppers (see Note), cut into quarters

Cilantro leaves

1. *For the beans:* Drain the beans and combine with 10 cups water, the bell pepper wedges, bay leaf, and bruised garlic clove in a large pot. Heat to boiling, reduce heat, and cook, stirring occasionally, over medium-low heat until the beans are tender enough to crush against the side of the pan with a spoon and most of the liquid is absorbed, about 2½ hours. Remove and discard the bay leaf and any visible green pepper skins. Set aside.

2. Heat the oil in a medium skillet over low heat. Add the chopped onions, green and red peppers, and garlic; cook, stirring, over medium-low heat until golden, about 15 minutes. Add the chiles and cumin; cook for 1 minute. Season to taste with salt and pepper.

3. Stir the vegetables into the beans; bring to a simmer and cook, stirring often, over low heat, until the flavors are blended, 1 to 1½ hours, adding as much of the water or broth as needed to keep a thick consistency, without sticking. Stir in the heavy cream. Taste and correct the seasoning.

4. *For the yellow rice:* Just before serving, heat ¼ cup of the water or broth to a boil in a small saucepan. Add the saffron threads; cover and let stand for 5 minutes.

5. Meanwhile, in a large wide saucepan or deep skillet, heat the olive oil over low heat. Add the rice and garlic. Cook, stirring, just until the rice is coated and the garlic is fragrant, about 2 minutes; do not brown the garlic. Stir in the turmeric. Stir in the remaining 1½ cups water or broth, the saffron and broth mixture, and the salt. Heat to a boil; stir once. Cook, covered, over low heat until the liquid is absorbed and the rice is tender, about 15 minutes. Let stand, covered, off the heat, for 10 minutes.

6. Spoon the rice into a large shallow serving bowl. Ladle the black beans on top. Garnish with the roasted peppers and a halo of cilantro leaves.

NOTE: If buying jarred roasted peppers, for the best flavor, look inside the jars for the peppers with the most charred surfaces. Drain the peppers and rinse off the juices. Quarter the peppers, place in a bowl, and drizzle with extra virgin olive oil. Add salt to taste and a grinding of black pepper. Sprinkle with about ½ teaspoon thyme leaves if desired.

Basmati Rice with Winter Squash, Chickpeas, and Crispy Garlic Threads

This eclectic dish came about simply because the main ingredients just happen to be among my favorites. Accompany by a green salad or steamed green beans or broccoli.

1 tablespoon canola or other flavorless vegetable oil
½ cup chopped onion
1 jalapeño, seeded and finely chopped
1 garlic clove, minced
2 teaspoons ground coriander
1 teaspoon ground cumin
1 cup uncooked basmati rice
2 cups diced (½-inch cubes) peeled butternut, acorn, or Kabocha squash

One 15- or 16-ounce can chickpeas, rinsed and drained
2 cups water or low-sodium vegetable or chicken broth
1 teaspoon kosher salt

Crispy Garlic Threads
2 tablespoons canola or other flavorless vegetable oil
1 tablespoon long thin garlic slivers

1. Heat the oil in a large wide saucepan. Add the onion and cook over low heat, stirring, until golden, about 10 minutes. Stir in the jalapeño and garlic; cook for 1 minute. Stir in the coriander and cumin; cook for 1 minute. Add the rice, squash, and chickpeas; stir to coat the rice with the seasonings, about 3 minutes.

2. Stir in water or broth and salt; heat to a boil. Stir well. Cover and cook over medium-low heat until the liquid is absorbed and the rice is tender, about 20 minutes. Let stand, uncovered, off the heat, for 5 minutes before serving.

3. *Meanwhile, for the crispy garlic threads:* Combine the oil and garlic in a small skillet; heat over low heat just until the garlic begins to sizzle. Cook, stirring, until the garlic turns golden, about 1 minute. Immediately lift the garlic from the oil with a slotted spoon. Drain on paper towels.

4. Sprinkle the garlic over the rice and serve at once.

Lentils and Basmati Rice with Green Chile Oil

Makes 6 main-course or 8 to 10 side-dish servings

Like the country, the flavors of India may overwhelm the senses at first, but gradually they grab—and then you are either hooked for life or never go back. I'm hooked for life. This particular dish is one of my favorites. Hearty and filling, it's the kind of food I enjoy when the weather is cold. Serve with cold beer, preferably Indian.

1½ cups brown lentils, sorted and rinsed
2 tablespoons canola or other flavorless vegetable oil
2 cups finely chopped onions
1 garlic clove, finely chopped
2 teaspoons ground cumin
½ teaspoon ground coriander
¼ teaspoon red pepper flakes, or more to taste
1½ cups uncooked basmati rice
1 slice (about ¼-inch) fresh ginger
1 cinnamon stick
2 whole cardamom pods

One 14½-ounce can diced tomatoes with their juices
1½ cups (approximately) water or low-sodium vegetable or chicken broth
1 teaspoon kosher salt

Chile Oil
⅓ cup canola or other flavorless vegetable oil
⅓ cup thinly sliced seeded moderately hot green chiles (such as jalapeño or serrano)
2 garlic cloves, minced

2 tablespoons torn cilantro leaves, optional

1. Combine the lentils and 8 cups water in a large saucepan; heat to a boil. Reduce the heat; simmer, uncovered, for 10 to 15 minutes, until the lentils are almost tender (they will continue cooking with the rice). Drain and set aside.

2. Heat the oil in a large wide saucepan. Add the onion and cook, stirring, over low heat, until golden, about 10 minutes. Stir in the garlic, cumin, coriander, and red pepper flakes; cook, stirring, for 2 minutes. Add the rice, ginger, cinnamon stick, and cardamom; cook, stirring, for about 2 minutes. Stir in the lentils.

3. Pour the tomatoes, with their juices, into a 4-cup measure; add enough water or broth to measure 3½ cups. Stir into the rice; add the salt. Heat to a full boil; stir once. Cover and cook over medium-low heat until the liquid is absorbed and the rice is tender, 20 to 25 minutes.

4. ***Meanwhile, for the green chile oil:*** Heat the oil in a small skillet until hot enough to sizzle a slice of chile. Add the chiles; cook, stirring, just until wilted, about 2 minutes. Add the garlic; saute for 30 seconds. Remove from the heat.

5. Spoon the rice and lentils into a large shallow bowl; pour the chile oil mixture over the top. Garnish with the cilantro leaves, if using. Serve at once.

Curried Coconut Rice with Cauliflower, Butternut Squash, Green Beans, and Cashews

Makes 4 main-course or 6 to 8 side-dish servings

Don't let the long list of ingredients deter you from making this sumptuous dish. It goes together very quickly once the vegetables are cut up and the spices measured. The dish cooks in 15 minutes, then should stand for 10 minutes, which gives you time to prepare the coconut cream. Serve as a vegetable main dish or a side dish with grilled chicken or fish.

2 tablespoons unsalted butter or canola oil or other flavorless vegetable oil

1 large onion, cut into 1-inch cubes

1 tablespoon finely chopped fresh ginger

2 garlic cloves, minced

1 tablespoon Madras-style curry powder

1 teaspoon ground cumin

1/2 teaspoon ground coriander

1/2 teaspoon ground cardamom

1/8 teaspoon red pepper flakes, or more to taste

1 cinnamon stick

1 cup uncooked basmati rice

2 cups cauliflower florets broken into 1-inch pieces (1/2 medium head)

2 cups cubed (1/2-inch) peeled butternut squash or sweet potato (8 ounces)

1 cup (1-inch lengths) green beans (about 4 ounces)

1 cup frozen lima beans, thawed

1 cup cubed (1/2-inch) carrots (about 2 carrots)

2 cups reduced-sodium chicken or vegetable broth

1/2 teaspoon kosher salt

Freshly ground black pepper

2/3 cup half-and-half or whole milk

1/4 cup unsweetened dried coconut

1/2 cup coarsely chopped unsalted roasted cashews

Chopped cilantro

1. Melt the butter in a large wide saucepan, or deep skillet. Add the onion; cook, stirring, over low heat until golden, about 15 minutes. Add the ginger and garlic; cook, stirring, for 2 minutes. Add the curry powder, cumin, coriander, cardamom, red pepper flakes, and cinnamon; cook, stirring, for 1 minute. Add the rice; stir to coat with the spices, about 1 minute.

2. Add the cauliflower, squash, green beans, lima beans, and carrots; stir to blend with the rice. Add the broth, salt, and a grinding of black pepper; heat to a boil over high heat. Stir thoroughly, making sure that all the rice is moistened. Cover and cook over low heat until the broth is absorbed and the rice is tender, about 15 minutes. Let stand, covered, off the heat, for 10 minutes before serving.

3. Meanwhile, combine the half-and-half or milk and coconut in a food processor. Process just until blended, about 30 seconds.

4. Heat the cashews in a small skillet over low heat, stirring, until toasted, about 3 minutes. Let cool, then coarsely chop.

5. Just before serving, pour the coconut milk over the rice and gently fold together. Spoon the rice into a serving bowl. Sprinkle with the cashews and cilantro, and serve.

Roasted Eggplant Stuffed with Lamb, Feta Cheese, and Rice

Makes 4 servings

The lamb, feta cheese, and mint make this a Greek-inspired dish, but experiment with ground beef, Parmesan cheese, and fresh basil instead for an Italian flavor. Use red, brown, or white rice, long- or medium-grain; all work perfectly. Vary the presentation by using an equal weight (2 pounds) of smaller eggplants and serving as a first course or side dish. Half of a medium eggplant makes a hearty supper dish served with a simple green salad. Make this ahead and reheat just before serving.

2 eggplants (about 1 pound each)

Kosher salt

3 tablespoons extra virgin olive oil

8 ounces ground lean lamb (or beef and lamb or all beef)

1 cup coarsely chopped onions

½ cup diced (about ¼-inch) green bell pepper

2 garlic cloves, minced

1 cup diced seeded fresh or canned tomatoes

2 tablespoons finely chopped Italian parsley

2 tablespoons finely chopped dill

2 tablespoons finely chopped mint

½ teaspoon ground cinnamon

Freshly ground black pepper

2 cups cooked red, brown, or white rice (medium- or long-grain)

1 cup crumbled feta (about 4 ounces)

1 cup shredded mozzarella (about 4 ounces)

1. Halve the eggplants lengthwise. Score the cut sides at ½-inch intervals with a paring knife. Sprinkle the surfaces with 1 teaspoon salt. Place the eggplants cut side down on a wire rack set on a tray. Let drain for at least 2 hours (see Note).

2. Preheat the oven to 400°F.

3. Carefully squeeze the excess water from the eggplants and blot dry with paper towels. Rub the cut sides of the eggplant with 1 tablespoon of the olive oil and place oiled side down in a 13 × 9-inch baking pan. Bake for 15 minutes, or until partially softened. Remove from the oven; turn the eggplant cut side up and let stand until cool enough to handle. Turn the oven down to 350°F.

4. Meanwhile, crumble the lamb into a large skillet; cook, stirring to break up the meat, until well browned, about 5 minutes. Transfer the lamb to a large bowl.

5. Heat the remaining 2 tablespoons olive oil in the skillet. Add the onions and green pepper; cook, stirring, over medium-low heat until golden, about 10 minutes. Add the garlic; cook for 1 minute.

6. Meanwhile, use a tablespoon to scoop out the cooked eggplant flesh, leaving about a ¼-inch-thick shell. Return the eggplant shells, scooped side up, to the baking pan. Coarsely chop the eggplant and add to the skillet with the onion. Cook the eggplant with the onion mixture, stirring occasionally, until the eggplant is tender, about 10 minutes. Stir in the tomatoes, parsley, dill, mint, cinnamon, and salt and pepper to taste. Transfer to the bowl with the cooked lamb.

7. Add the rice and feta; stir to blend. Taste and add more seasonings, if desired. Carefully spoon into the reserved eggplant shells, dividing the mixture evenly. Sprinkle the tops with the mozzarella.

8. Bake for 45 minutes, or until the cheese is well browned and bubbly. Serve warm or at room temperature.

NOTE: When I buy the squeaking-fresh eggplant at the farmers' market, I eliminate this step. Salting is intended to release excess moisture and, along with it, any bitterness, but the times I have chosen not to salt and drain it, the eggplant has tasted just fine.

Lamb Kebabs on Persian-Style Golden Rice

Makes 6 to 8 servings

Rice slowly cooked in the Persian style creates a golden layer of rice on the bottom of the pot called *tah-dig*. Traditionally the rice is cooked on top of the stove in a very heavy pot. To release the rice easily, the pot is immersed in a shallow pan of ice water, which causes the hot pan to contract and release the rice. Instead I use a heavy ovenproof skillet with a nonstick surface, first cooking the rice partially on top of the stove and then finishing it in the oven. This guarantees that the rice will be golden and not scorch on a too-hot flame. Marinate the lamb a day ahead. Just before serving, slide the lamb onto skewers and grill to desired doneness. Arrange the grilled lamb around the large circle of golden rice, then sprinkle the top with the roasted walnuts. This is a stunning dish for entertaining. Serve grilled or roasted red bell peppers, pattypan squash, and halved red onions as a vegetable side dish.

Marinade

½ cup whole-milk yogurt
2 tablespoons fresh lime juice
1 teaspoon grated fresh ginger
1 teaspoon minced garlic
1 teaspoon ground cumin
1 teaspoon ground coriander
¼ teaspoon ground turmeric

1½ to 2 pounds boneless lamb sirloin, cut into slices ½ inch thick, 1 inch wide, and 2 inches long

½ pound (2 sticks) unsalted butter
Kosher salt
2 cups uncooked basmati rice
2 whole cardamom pods
2 whole cloves
1 cinnamon stick
1 large (8 ounces) onion, halved and cut into thin slices
¼ teaspoon crushed saffron threads
½ cup dried sweet and sour cherries, optional
1 cup broken walnuts
2 tablespoons chopped dill

1. *For the marinade:* Combine the yogurt, lime juice, ginger, garlic, cumin, coriander, and turmeric in a large bowl; stir to blend. Add the lamb; stir to coat. Cover and marinate in the refrigerator for at least 4 hours, or overnight.

2. *To clarify the butter:* Melt the butter in the microwave or in a saucepan over low heat. Let stand until the solids separate. Spoon off the solids on top. Ladle

off the clear butter; discard the solids on the bottom. You should have about ¾ cup clarified butter. Cover tightly and refrigerate until ready to use. (This can be made several days ahead. Reheat to return the butter to a liquid consistency.)

3. Heat a large saucepan of water to a boil. Add 2 teaspoons salt. Stir in the rice, cardamom pods, cloves, and cinnamon stick. Cook for 8 minutes; drain well.

4. Heat ¼ cup of the clarified butter in a large skillet, preferably nonstick, over medium-low heat. Add the onion and cook over low heat, stirring, until wilted and golden, about 15 minutes. Stir in the saffron. Spread the onions evenly in the skillet. Spoon half of the rice, along with the whole spices and the dried cherries, on top of the onions, pressing down with the back of the spoon. Drizzle with half of the hot clarified butter.

5. Lift the meat from the marinade; scrape the marinade back into the bowl. Place the meat in another bowl, cover, and refrigerate. Pour the marinade onto the layer of rice, spreading it evenly. Spoon the remaining rice on top. Press down with the back of the spoon. Drizzle with all but about 1 tablespoon of the remaining clarified butter. (Reserve the 1 tablespoon butter for the roasted walnuts.)

6. Preheat the oven to 400°F.

7. Cover the skillet with a large piece of heavy-duty aluminum foil or a double layer of regular foil. Press down hard on the foil to compress the rice. Crimp the edges to seal. Cook the rice over medium-low heat for 10 minutes. Transfer to the bottom oven rack and bake for 1 hour. Remove from the oven. Reduce the oven temperature to 350°F. Let the rice stand, covered, until ready to serve.

8. Meanwhile, spread the walnuts in a small baking pan; drizzle with the reserved 1 tablespoon clarified butter and sprinkle with salt. Roast until golden, about 10 minutes.

9. Preheat a broiler or the grill. Thread the lamb onto skewers. Grill or broil, turning once, 5 to 8 minutes per side, for medium to medium-rare meat. Slide the lamb from the skewers onto a plate and sprinkle with the dill. Cover and keep warm.

10. To unmold the rice, loosen the edges with a flexible spatula; invert a large round platter over the skillet. Protecting your hands with mitts, quickly turn the skillet over onto the platter. Remove the skillet. If any rice or onions have stuck to the bottom of the skillet, scrape off and spoon onto the rice. Arrange the lamb around the edges. Sprinkle with the roasted walnuts. Serve at once.

NOTE: Dried cherries are available in bulk or small packages in many supermarkets, health-food stores, and Middle Eastern groceries.

Peruvian Duck with Green Rice

Makes 4 to 6 servings

I learned to make this dish while visiting friends Christina and Peter and their daughters, Frances and Andrea, in Lima, Peru. Each morning we shopped in the market and in the afternoon Christina taught me to make classic Peruvian dishes. This recipe involves many steps, but the duck can be marinated and roasted and the broth made several days ahead. The chile paste used in Peru, *aji amarillo*, or yellow chile paste, is hard to find in the United States. Substitute pureed or finely chopped canned green jalapeño chiles. Duck parts (leg-thigh quarters and breasts) are sold in many specialty meat markets or ask the butcher to cut up a whole duck. *Arroz verde con pato* is traditionally served with rounds of corn on the cob and baked sweet potatoes cut crosswise into thick slices.

Marinade

1 tablespoon ground cumin
1 tablespoon minced garlic
2 teaspoons grated orange zest
1 teaspoon kosher salt
½ teaspoon freshly ground black pepper
½ cup fresh orange juice

6 duck leg-thigh quarters or 1 whole duck, cut into serving pieces
2 tablespoons extra virgin olive oil
½ cup chopped onion
¼ cup chopped carrot
¼ cup chopped celery
1 cup dark or amber beer

2 cups reduced-sodium chicken broth, plus more as needed
1 bay leaf
1 sprig thyme
1 sprig parsley

Cilantro Sauce

1 bunch cilantro, leaves pulled from stems (3 cups lightly packed)
1 jalapeño, seeded and chopped, or more to taste
1 teaspoon chopped garlic
Kosher salt

1½ cups uncooked long-grain white rice
Kosher salt

1. *For the marinade:* Combine the cumin, garlic, orange zest, salt, and pepper in a small bowl and mash together with a fork. Rub over the surfaces of the duck, getting into all the crevices and under the skin. Place in a bowl or a heavy-duty self-sealing plastic bag. Add the orange juice; turn to coat. Marinate in the refrigerator for at least 4 hours, or overnight.

2. Preheat the oven to 400°F.

3. Place the duck on a roasting rack set in a large roasting pan. Roast, spooning off the fat from the pan every 15 minutes, until the duck is well browned and most of the fat has been rendered, 30 to 40 minutes. Remove from the oven.

4. Spoon 1 tablespoon of the rendered duck fat into a large Dutch oven or wide heavy saucepan. (Reserve 1 additional tablespoon of the duck fat for cooking the rice.) Add the onion, carrot, and celery; cook, stirring, until tender, about 10 minutes. Add the beer; heat to a boil. Boil until reduced by half. Add the broth, bay leaf, thyme, and parsley; heat to a boil. Return the duck pieces to the pot. Cover and cook over low heat until the duck is very tender, about 1½ hours.

5. Use a slotted spoon to carefully lift the duck to a side dish; cover and refrigerate. Set a strainer over a bowl and strain the broth; refrigerate until the broth is cold and the fat has congealed on top, about 2 hours or overnight. (This can be done up to 1 day before serving.)

6. Skim the fat from the broth. Measure out 3½ cups of the broth. You need ½ cup broth for the cilantro sauce; reserve the remaining 3 cups for the rice (if there isn't enough duck broth, use additional chicken broth). Wash the pot and reserve for Step 8.

7. *For the cilantro sauce:* Combine the cilantro, jalapeño, garlic, and ½ cup duck broth in a blender jar. Blend until pureed. Taste and add more jalapeño, if desired, and salt if needed. Set aside.

8. *For the rice:* Heat the reserved 1 tablespoon duck fat in the pan used to cook the duck in Step 4. Add the rice and cook, stirring, until coated. Add the duck and the reserved 3 cups broth; heat to a boil. Cover and cook over low heat until the broth is absorbed and the rice is tender, about 15 minutes. Transfer the duck to a side dish and cover with foil to keep warm.

9. Pour the cilantro sauce evenly over the rice and toss to combine. Taste and add more salt if needed. Spoon onto a warmed serving platter and arrange the duck on top. Serve at once.

Baked Lemon-Oregano Chicken and Rice with Tomato–Black Olive Salsa

Makes 4 servings

The chicken is marinated in a classic Greek mixture of fresh lemon juice, olive oil, garlic, and oregano for an hour before it is cooked with the rice, but the rice and chicken need just 20 minutes or so to cook. Boneless, skinless chicken thighs will stay moist and tender while chicken breasts tend to dry out.

8 boneless, skinless chicken thighs, rinsed and
   dried

Marinade

2 teaspoons finely chopped or grated lemon zest

2 tablespoons fresh lemon juice

2 tablespoons extra virgin olive oil

1 tablespoon snipped fresh oregano leaves or
   1 teaspoon dried oregano

1 garlic clove, finely chopped

Pinch of kosher salt

Freshly ground black pepper

1 tablespoon extra virgin olive oil

2 cups uncooked Arborio, Baldo, or other medium-
   grain white rice

½ cup dry white wine

1 teaspoon kosher salt

1 bay leaf

Salsa

1 pound ripe plum tomatoes, cored and cut into
   ¼-inch dice

1 tablespoon pitted chopped Kalamata olives

1 teaspoon chopped, rinsed, and drained capers

1 tablespoon chopped Italian parsley

1 tablespoon chopped mint

1 tablespoon chopped fresh oregano or
   ½ teaspoon chopped dried oregano

½ teaspoon minced garlic

Pinch of kosher salt

1. Combine the chicken with the lemon zest, lemon juice, olive oil, oregano, garlic, salt, and a grinding of black pepper in a large bowl; stir to coat. Cover and marinate, refrigerated, for about 1 hour.

2. Heat the olive oil in a large wide saucepan or deep skillet over medium heat. Add the rice, and stir until coated with oil. Add the wine and heat to a boil; boil until evaporated by half.

3. Add the chicken and all of the marinade, 4 cups water, the salt, and bay leaf. Heat to a boil over high heat. Stir once, making sure the rice is covered with water. Cook, covered, over low heat until the water is absorbed and the rice is tender, about 20 minutes. Remove from the heat and let stand, covered, for 10 minutes, before serving.

4. *Meanwhile, for the salsa:* Combine the tomatoes, olives, and capers in a bowl. Finely chop the parsley, mint, and oregano (fresh or dried) together. Add to the tomatoes, along with the garlic and salt. Stir to blend. Let stand at room temperature until ready to serve.

5. Spoon the rice and chicken onto a large platter. Spoon the salsa on top. Serve at once.

Chicken Biriyani

Makes 8 servings

Biriyani, an elaborate Moghul dish from northern India, is made with rice cooked with saffron and spices and layered with meat. It is traditionally prepared with lamb, the preferred meat of Muslims, who don't eat pork, and Hindus, who consider the cow a sacred beast. There are probably hundreds of versions of biriyani with everything from lamb to seafood, but this one is made with chicken.

Garlic-and-Chile-Pepper Rice

1 tablespoon unsalted butter
1 garlic clove, minced
1 cup uncooked brown or basmati rice
2½ cups reduced-sodium chicken broth (or half broth and half water)
1 tablespoon finely chopped jalapeño or other hot green chile

Saffron Rice

¼ teaspoon crushed saffron threads
1 tablespoon unsalted butter
1 cup uncooked basmati rice
2 whole cloves
1 teaspoon kosher salt
1 cinnamon stick
1 slice (about ¼-inch) ginger
½ teaspoon ground turmeric

Chicken

2 tablespoons unsalted butter
2 medium onions, cut into ½-inch chunks (about 2 cups)

2 to 3 carrots, cut into ½-inch chunks (about 1 cup)
1½ pounds boneless, skinless chicken breasts and/or thighs, fat trimmed, cut into 1- to 2-inch pieces
3 garlic cloves, coarsely chopped
1 tablespoon Madras-style curry powder
½ teaspoon ground cumin
½ teaspoon ground ginger
½ teaspoon kosher salt
¼ teaspoon cayenne, or more to taste (if you like it very hot)
⅛ teaspoon freshly ground black pepper
2 cups whole-milk yogurt
¼ cup golden raisins
½ cup reduced-sodium chicken broth

Toppings

2 tablespoons vegetable oil
1 cup thinly sliced onion rings
½ cup chopped salted dry-roasted cashews or peanuts
¼ cup coarsely chopped cilantro
¼ cup coarsely chopped mint
Mango chutney (store-bought)

1. *For the garlic-and-chile-pepper rice:* Melt the butter in a large wide saucepan or deep skillet. Add the garlic; cook over low heat, stirring, for 1 minute. Stir in the rice just to coat. Add the broth; heat to a boil. Cook, covered, over medium-low heat for about 40 minutes; the rice should be slightly undercooked. Set aside, uncovered. Just before using, add the jalepeño to the rice and toss with a fork to blend.

2. *Meanwhile, for the saffron rice:* Toast the saffron in a small dry skillet over low heat for 20 seconds. Add ½ cup boiling water; cover and let stand for 15 minutes.

3. Melt the butter in a large wide saucepan or deep skillet. Add the rice, cloves, salt, cinnamon, ginger, and turmeric; heat, stirring, until the rice is coated with spices. Add 1½ cups water and the saffron water; heat to a boil. Cover and cook over medium-low heat for 12 minutes; the rice should be slightly undercooked. Uncover and let stand, off the heat.

4. *For the chicken:* Heat the butter in a large heavy skillet until the foam subsides; add the onions and carrots; cook, stirring, over medium-low heat, until the edges are browned and the vegetables are tender, about 10 minutes.

5. Add the chicken; cook, stirring, over medium-high heat, until lightly browned, about 5 minutes. Add the garlic; cook for 1 minute. Add the curry, cumin, ginger, salt, cayenne, and black pepper; cook over low heat, stirring, for 2 minutes, just to release the flavors of the spices and coat the chicken and vegetables evenly. Off the heat, stir in the yogurt and raisins until blended.

6. Preheat the oven to 350°F.

7. Select a shallow baking/serving dish about 13 × 9 inches. Spread half of the chile pepper rice in a shallow layer in one side of the baking dish. Spread half of the saffron rice on the other side. Spoon the chicken and yogurt mixture in an even layer on top of the rice. Spoon the remaining rice, half of the chile rice down one side and the saffron down the other, on top of the chicken. Drizzle with the broth.

8. Cover the dish tightly with foil. Bake for 45 minutes, or until steaming hot.

9. *Meanwhile, for the onion rings:* Heat the vegetable oil in a medium skillet over medium heat until hot enough to sizzle a piece of the onion. Add the onions and fry until dark brown, about 6 minutes. Lift from the oil with a slotted spoon; drain on paper towels.

10. Sprinkle the top of the biriyani with the cashews, cilantro, mint, and onion rings. Serve the chutney on the side.

Saffron-Orange Rice with Roasted Chicken and Pistachios

Makes 4 to 6 servings

The surprise ingredient in this sweet and savory rice dish is sugar. This recipe was inspired by a similar dish served at a modest little Afghan restaurant called Caravan located in the theater district of New York City. My version approximates the flavor and appearance of their chef's *shireen palow*, as it is called on the menu. The chicken is flavored with saffron water and roasted on a bed of onions. Then the meat is pulled from the bone and the cooked rice is piled on top of it. A mixture of yogurt thinned with cream is drizzled on top and the dish is kept warm in the oven. Festive with bright green pistachios sprinkled on pale yellow rice dotted with flecks of dark orange zest, this is a good company dish because it can be assembled ahead and kept warm for up to 1 hour.

¼ teaspoon crushed saffron threads

3 tablespoons unsalted butter, plus 1 tablespoon butter, softened

½ large onion, cut into thin slices

1 garlic clove, minced

6 chicken thighs

6 chicken legs

Kosher salt and freshly ground black pepper

4 strips orange zest, slivered (about 1 tablespoon)

3 tablespoons sugar

1½ cups uncooked basmati rice

2 tablespoons golden raisins or dried currants

2 whole cardamom pods

2½ cups reduced-sodium chicken broth

½ cup whole-milk yogurt

2 tablespoons milk

2 tablespoons shelled unsalted pistachios

1. Toast the saffron in a small dry skillet over low heat for 20 seconds. Add ½ cup boiling water; cover and let stand for 10 minutes.

2. Preheat the oven to 400°F. Butter a shallow 13 × 9-inch baking dish suitable for serving with the 1 tablespoon softened butter.

3. Spread the onions in a single layer in the baking dish. Add the garlic. Sprinkle the chicken with salt and pepper and place on top of the onions. Spoon 2 tablespoons of the saffron water over the chicken; leave the saffron threads in the remaining water.

4. Cover the chicken with foil and bake for 35 minutes. Remove from the oven and let stand until cool enough to handle.

5. Meanwhile, melt the remaining 3 tablespoons butter in a large wide saucepan or deep skillet over low heat. Add the orange zest and sprinkle with the sugar. Cook, stirring, until the sugar dissolves, about 3 minutes. Stir in the rice, raisins, and cardamom pods; cook, stirring, until coated with the butter mixture, about 2 minutes. Add the broth, the remaining saffron water, and 1 teaspoon salt; heat to a boil. Stir once. Cook, covered, over medium-low heat until the liquid is absorbed and the rice is tender, 15 minutes. Remove from the heat and let sit, covered, for 10 minutes.

6. Meanwhile, pull the cooked chicken meat from the bones in large pieces. Discard the skin and bones. Arrange the pieces of chicken on top of the onions. Cover and set aside.

7. Turn the oven on to 250°F.

8. Spoon the rice over the chicken in the baking dish. In a small bowl, whisk the yogurt and milk until smooth; drizzle over the rice. Cover and set in the oven for 30 to 60 minutes.

9. Meanwhile, toast the pistachios in a small skillet over low heat, stirring, 2 minutes. Let cool; chop.

10. Sprinkle the pistachios over the rice before serving.

Spanish Rice with Chicken, Chorizo, and Peas

Makes 4 servings

Arroz con pollo, or rice with chicken, is a classic Spanish dish similar to, but much simpler than, paella. If chorizo, a spicy Spanish sausage, is unavailable, use hot Italian sausage and add a pinch of red pepper flakes. The saffron flavor is rich and pungent, but if preferred, substitute ½ teaspoon ground turmeric and 1 teaspoon ground cumin.

This version makes four generous portions; add another 4 pieces of chicken to make 6 servings.

1 tablespoon extra virgin olive oil

1 to 2 links chorizo (about 5 ounces), casings removed and cut into ⅛-inch dice

1 whole chicken breast, split, skin and excess fat trimmed, and each piece halved crosswise

4 chicken thighs, fat trimmed

Kosher salt and freshly ground black pepper

One 14½-ounce can diced tomatoes, well drained, juices reserved

2½ cups reduced-sodium chicken broth

¼ teaspoon crushed saffron threads

½ cup chopped onion

½ cup diced (¼-inch) green bell pepper

1 garlic clove, minced

1½ cups uncooked medium-grain white rice (such as Arborio or Bomba)

2 teaspoons thyme leaves

½ cup frozen petite green peas, thawed

2 tablespoons chopped pimiento-stuffed green olives

1. Heat the olive oil in a large deep skillet over medium-low heat. Add the sausage and cook, stirring, until it is browned and the fat is rendered, about 5 minutes. With a slotted spoon, transfer the sausage to a side dish. Discard all but 1 tablespoon of the fat from the pan.

2. Sprinkle the chicken on both sides with salt and pepper. Add the chicken to the hot skillet; increase heat to medium, and cook, turning once, until browned on both sides, about 10 minutes. Transfer to a side dish. Drain off and discard all but about 1 tablespoon of the fat from the skillet. Set the pan aside.

3. Combine the liquid from the tomatoes and the chicken broth in a 4-cup glass measuring cup. Add enough water to make 3¼ cups. Heat to a boil in a medium saucepan, cover and keep hot over low heat.

4. Toast the saffron in a small dry skillet over low heat for 20 seconds. Add ½ cup hot broth. Remove from the heat; cover and let stand until ready to use.

5. Add the onion and green pepper to the skillet you used for the chicken; cook, stirring, over medium heat until the edges are browned, about 5 minutes. Add the garlic; cook for 1 minute. Stir in the rice; cook, stirring, over low heat until the rice is thoroughly coated with the oil. Add the saffron, the hot broth, 1 teaspoon salt, and a grinding of black pepper; stir to combine.

6. Sprinkle the chorizo on top. Tuck the chicken into the rice mixture. Place the tomatoes and thyme on top. Cover and cook over medium heat for 15 minutes, or until most of the liquid has been absorbed. Add the peas; cover and cook 5 minutes more. Let stand, covered, off the heat, for 10 minutes.

7. Uncover the rice and cook over medium-high heat to cook off any excess moisture, about 1 minute. Sprinkle with the chopped olives and serve.

Chicken Jambalaya

Makes 8 to 10 servings

I have eaten jambalaya from Savannah to Houston, and points in between, and have yet to experience the same dish twice. Two main ingredients are found in the name—*jambon*, French for "ham," and *ya*, meaning "rice" in an African language. Jambalaya also often contains tomatoes, pork, ham (tasso, a highly seasoned Cajun smoked ham is popular) or seafood. This version, from friend and colleague Kristen O'Brien, uses boneless, skinless chicken and spiced beef sausage instead of pork. Kris says, "This is a great do-ahead dish; in fact the flavors are better if it's made a day ahead." It is perfect for feeding a crowd. The recipe can be halved.

1½ pounds smoked spiced beef sausage, cut into ¼-inch-thick slices

6 skinless, boneless chicken breast halves

8 skinless, boneless chicken thighs

Kosher salt and freshly ground black pepper

1 tablespoon vegetable oil, if necessary

4 cups chopped onions

2 cups chopped celery

2 cups chopped green bell peppers

3 garlic cloves, minced

4 cups uncooked converted or parboiled long-grain white rice

5 cups reduced-sodium chicken broth

½ teaspoon cayenne

1. Brown the sausage in a large Dutch oven over medium heat; transfer to a side dish. Salt and pepper the chicken. Working in batches, if necessary, add the chicken to the drippings in the pot and cook, turning once, until lightly browned on both sides, about 10 minutes. Transfer to a side dish.

2. Add about 1 tablespoon vegetable oil to the pan if necessary. Add the onions, celery, green peppers, and garlic; cook, stirring, over low heat until tender and just beginning to brown, about 15 minutes.

3. Meanwhile, preheat the oven to 325°F.

4. Add the rice, broth, salt if needed, and cayenne to the pot; heat to a boil. Add the chicken and sausage. Cover; bake for 30 minutes, or until the liquid is absorbed and the rice is tender, stirring once or twice. Let stand for 10 minutes, covered, before serving.

Meat Loaf with Rice, Spinach, and Dried Tomatoes

Makes 8 servings

Leftover rice, like bread crumbs, helps to bind ingredients together. For this meat loaf, balance sweet and salty ingredients: for the sweetness I use dried currants, and for the salty, chopped anchovy. If you suffer a fear of anchovy, as many do, don't skip this recipe. The anchovy simply lends a salty complexity, and none of the fishiness you might suspect. Serve this with thinly sliced crisp garlic-roasted potatoes.

3 tablespoons extra virgin olive oil
½ cup chopped onion
1 teaspoon minced garlic
2 anchovy fillets, rinsed, drained, and minced (about 1 tablespoon)
2 cups cooked long- or medium-grain white rice
1½ pounds meat loaf mixture (ground beef chuck, pork, and veal) or a combination of 1 pound ground chuck and ½ pound pork or veal

1 large egg
One 10-ounce package frozen chopped spinach, thawed, drained, and squeezed dry
¼ cup chopped sun-dried tomatoes in olive oil, drained and blotted dry, or 2 tablespoons tomato paste
2 tablespoons dried currants or chopped raisins
½ teaspoon ground cinnamon
½ teaspoon kosher salt
¼ teaspoon freshly ground black pepper

1. Heat the oil in a large skillet. Add the onion; cook, stirring, over low heat until soft and golden, about 10 minutes. Add the garlic; cook for 1 minute. Add the anchovies; cook, stirring and mashing with the back of a spoon, until they are dissolved. Stir in the rice until blended. Set aside.

2. Preheat the oven to 350°F.

3. In a large bowl, combine the meat loaf mixture, 1½ cups water, the egg, anchovy mixture, spinach, dried tomatoes, currants, cinnamon, salt, and pepper. Gently mix with your hands until thoroughly blended. Transfer a 9 × 5-inch loaf pan and smooth the top with a spatula.

4. Bake for 1 hour and 20 minutes, or until the juices run clear when the center is pierced with a skewer. Let stand for 15 minutes before lifting from the loaf pan (meat loaf will reabsorb some of the juices in the pan) and setting on a serving platter. To serve, cut into thick slices.

Rice and Seafood

Rice has a natural affinity for seafood—perhaps because they both grow in water. Consider just a handful of famous rice dishes: Spanish paella, Japanese sushi, jambalaya from the American South, and Italian seafood risottos (including the unique *risotto nero* made with cuttlefish or squid ink). Another—and perhaps—stronger rice and seafood link was revealed when my research uncovered a quaint, but intriguing, bit of rice lore. It seems the inhabitants of the northern Italian rice-growing regions and the rice farmers in Indonesia—two apparently disparate peoples—both eat frogs (and, in some instances, prawns) caught in the rice paddies in their local cuisine, including, naturally, combinations of rice and seafood. In fact, throughout Asia, it is not unusual for rice paddies to double as fish ponds between rice-growing seasons.

Roasted Marinated Shrimp and Rice with Salsa Verde

Makes 4 servings

More preparation than cooking time is necessary here. The shrimp are marinated and roasted in a hot oven. The rice, cooked separately, is stirred into the hot shrimp juices and seasoned with capers. The salsa verde, a puree of parsley, cilantro, scallions, olive oil, and lime juice, is used as a condiment on the roasted shrimp. This dish is Caribbean inspired, but as it's without any authentic lineage, I think of it more as a cook's fantasy.

Marinade
1 tablespoon extra virgin olive oil
½ teaspoon minced garlic
¼ teaspoon dried thyme
⅛ teaspoon red pepper flakes

16 jumbo or 24 extra-large shrimp, shelled and deveined

Salsa Verde
1 cup packed chopped curly leaf parsley
½ cup packed cilantro leaves
1 scallion, trimmed and coarsely chopped
¼ teaspoon minced garlic

½ teaspoon kosher salt
½ cup extra virgin olive oil
2 tablespoons fresh lime juice

Rice
1 tablespoon olive oil
2 tablespoons minced onion
1 cup uncooked long-grain white rice
1 teaspoon salt

1 tablespoon rinsed and drained capers
Parsley and/or cilantro sprigs
Lime wedges

1. **For the marinade:** Combine the olive oil, garlic, thyme, and red pepper flakes in a shallow dish. Butterfly each shrimp by cutting it three-quarters of the way open down the back. Place in the marinade, turning to coat. Cover and refrigerate for about 30 minutes.

2. **For the salsa verde:** Finely chop the parsley, cilantro, scallion, garlic, and salt in a food processor. With the motor running, slowly add the olive oil through the feed tube, stopping to scrape the sides once or twice, until the sauce is smooth. Add the lime juice; process until blended.

3. *For the rice:* Heat the oil in a large wide saucepan or deep skillet over low heat. Add the onion; cook, stirring, until tender, about 5 minutes. Stir in the rice until well coated with the oil. Add 1¾ cups water and the salt; heat to a boil. Stir well. Cover and cook over medium-low heat until the liquid is absorbed and the rice is tender, about 15 minutes. Set aside, covered, until ready to serve.

4. While the rice is cooking, preheat the oven to 450°F.

5. Arrange the shrimp, butterflied side down and tails up in the air, on an oven-proof platter or in an oven-to-table gratin or baking dish. Roast until the butterflied sides of the shrimp begin to brown, about 8 minutes for jumbo shrimp, 6 minutes for extra-large shrimp. Remove from the oven; transfer the shrimp to a side dish.

6. Stir the cooked rice into the shrimp juices on the platter or in the baking dish; sprinkle with the capers. Arrange the cooked shrimp (tails up) on the rice. Spoon a small amount of the salsa verde onto each shrimp. Garnish the dish with parsley and/or cilantro sprigs and lime wedges. Serve the remaining salsa verde on the side.

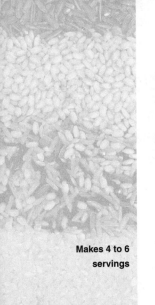

Roasted Manila Clams with Chorizo, Rice, and Lima Beans and Tomato-Cilantro Salsa

Makes 4 to 6 servings

The clam juices cook into the rice, imparting the complex flavors of the sea. The technique is similar to making paella, but less complicated. But use the same rice as you would in a paella recipe: a medium-grain rice with a creamy texture that will absorb the sweet clam juices. The cooked rice will be slightly sticky, as in paella. Top the dish with a fresh tomato, red onion, and cilantro salsa.

1 tablespoon extra virgin olive oil

1 to 2 links chorizo (4 ounces), casings removed and diced small

1½ cups uncooked Arborio, Baldo, or other medium-grain white rice

2 cups frozen lima beans, thawed

½ cup dry white wine, optional

1 teaspoon kosher salt

1½ to 2 pounds small Manila clams, scrubbed

Salsa

2 cups diced ripe plum tomatoes (about 1 pound)

½ cup finely chopped red onion

½ cup chopped cilantro leaves and tender stems

2 tablespoons extra virgin olive oil

1 tablespoon fresh lemon juice

½ teaspoon minced garlic

½ teaspoon kosher salt

Freshly ground black pepper

1. Preheat the oven to 450°F.

2. Heat 1 tablespoon of the oil in a large stovetop-to-oven baking dish, Dutch oven, or paella pan. Add the chorizo; cook, stirring, over medium heat until golden, about 5 minutes. Add the rice and lima beans; cook, stirring, until well blended. Add the wine, if using; boil until evaporated by half, about 2 minutes.

3. Add 3 cups water and the salt; heat to a boil. Flatten the rice with a spoon so that it is covered with water; do not stir. Cook, uncovered, over medium-low heat until half of the liquid is absorbed, about 10 minutes.

4. Tuck the clams, hinged side down, into the rice. Cover tightly with foil and transfer to the oven. Roast until the clams have opened and the rice has absorbed all of the liquid, about 10 minutes. Remove from the oven; let stand, covered, for 10 minutes before serving.

5. *Meanwhile, for the salsa:* Combine the tomatoes, onion, cilantro, olive oil, lemon juice, garlic, salt, and black pepper in a bowl; stir to blend.

6. To serve, spoon the rice and clams onto a platter, or serve directly from the pan. Spoon the salsa over the top.

Ratatouille over Rice with Gruyère

Makes 6 to 8 servings

This saucy ratatouille was inspired by the description in *Long Ago in France* written in 1929 by the late prolific writer on food and other subjects, M. F. K. Fisher. She wrote, "I learned to make ratatouille from a large strong woman, a refugee, not political, but economic, from an island off Spain." Fisher cooked her version slowly for five to six hours in a warm oven, probably more out of necessity than intent. I take a few shortcuts, thanks in part to the modern thermostat that allows an oven to heat up more or less accurately to any temperature one chooses. But my ratatouille, kept purposely sauce-like so it can be spooned over rice, does, like M. F. K. Fisher's, make a delicious and nourishing meal. It is especially good when the hot rice is first topped with a handful of shredded Gruyère cheese, as it is here.

1 eggplant, trimmed, peel alternating strips of skin and cut into ½-inch-thick slices

¼ cup extra virgin olive oil

1 large yellow onion, cut into ½-inch pieces

1 red bell pepper, stem and seeds removed, cut into ½-inch pieces

1 green bell pepper, stem and seeds removed, cut into ½-inch pieces

3 garlic cloves, coarsely chopped

1 zucchini, trimmed and cut into ½-inch pieces

1 yellow squash, trimmed and cut into ½-inch pieces

One 28-ounce can Italian plum tomatoes, with their juices

2 tablespoons coarsely chopped basil

1 teaspoon thyme leaves

Kosher salt and freshly ground black pepper

2 cups uncooked medium- or long-grain white rice

1 cup coarsely shredded Gruyère, or more as needed

1. Preheat the oven to 400°F.

2. Lightly brush both sides of the eggplant with half of the olive oil; arrange on a baking sheet. Bake until browned on the bottom, about 15 minutes. Turn and brown the other side, about 10 minutes. Cool slightly, then cut into 1-inch squares. Reduce the oven temperature to 300°F.

3. Combine the remaining 2 tablespoons oil, the onion, and peppers in a large wide ovenproof saucepan or deep skillet with a tight-fitting lid. Cook over medium-low heat, stirring, until the vegetables are golden, about 20 minutes. Add the garlic; cook, stirring, for 2 minutes. Add the eggplant, zucchini, yellow squash, tomatoes, with their juices, basil, thyme, ½ teaspoon salt, and a grinding of black pepper. Heat to a boil; cook, uncovered, over medium heat for 5 minutes.

4. Cover the pan and transfer to the oven. Bake for 1 to 1½ hours. Let stand, covered, while the rice cooks.

5. Heat 3¾ cups water to a boil in a wide shallow saucepan or deep skillet. Stir in the rice and 1 teaspoon salt. Cover and cook over low heat until the water is absorbed and the rice is tender, about 15 minutes. Let stand, covered, for 5 minutes.

6. Meanwhile, season the ratatouille with salt and pepper; reheat if necessary.

7. To serve, spoon mounds of rice onto dinner plates. Sprinkle half the cheese over the rice. Ladle the ratatouille on top. Top with more cheese. Serve at once.

Rice Pudding: Savory and Sweet

Rice puddings are enjoyed all over the world. In Thailand, a favorite is rice cooked in coconut milk served with luscious slices of ripe mango. A classic American rice pudding is rice slowly baked in custard with a sprinkling of ground cinnamon on top.

I have known and loved sweet rice pudding since childhood, but it was not until I was an adult that I first tried savory puddings. Inspired by a friend's recipe for noodle pudding made with mushrooms and onions, I adapted the idea with great success to rice. This ability to transform itself from a much-loved sweet dish eaten for breakfast or dessert to a savory side or main dish illustrates once again the outstanding versatility of rice.

Some of my favorite rice puddings (either sweet or savory) use precooked rice, a thrifty way to use up a cup of two of leftovers. Other puddings begin with uncooked rice. Almost any type of rice can be used in a pudding. Long-grain white rice makes a moderately creamy rice pudding. Medium- or short-grain white rice, like Arborio, Baldo, or sushi rice, make the creamiest puddings of all. One of my favorite puddings is made with medium-grain brown rice and sweetened with maple syrup (see page 244). Coconut milk rice pudding, a favorite in Thailand, is made with black or white rice. Both versions, when served with slices of ripe mango, are addictive. But then, I've never met a rice pudding that wasn't.

Savory Pudding Basics

- The ratio of rice to milk should be at least 1 cup cooked rice to 1 to 1½ cups whole or low-fat milk. For a richer version substitute cream for part of the milk.

- Feel free to improvise, but don't muddle the flavors by adding too many ingredients. Think in threes: mushrooms, onions, and Parmesan cheese *or* spinach, ham, and Gruyère cheese.

- Bake in a shallow baking dish and cut into squares for serving. Or bake in a deep casserole or soufflé dish and serve spooned out. Puddings can also be made in individual custard cups and turned out for serving; reduce baking time by 15 to 20 minutes.

- For a softer consistency bake the puddings in a water bath. They can be made ahead and kept warm in the water bath or reheated in a boiling water bath in a 350°F oven for 20 minutes.

- Serve as a main course, with salad, for a light meal. Or serve as an accompaniment to roasted meats or seafood, or with other vegetable dishes for a vegetarian meal.

Mushroom, Goat Cheese, and Roasted Red Pepper Rice Pudding

Makes 6 to 8 servings

Use all white button mushrooms or a combination, if you prefer (see the box following). A mixture of white button and the more flavorful cremini is nice. Or you might slice a few shiitake into the mix. (Remember the tough stems of shiitake mushrooms need to be discarded.) If preferred, substitute another relatively mild cheese like shredded Gruyère. Or for a totally different flavor, use grated Parmigiano-Reggiano or Sonoma Dry Jack.

3 tablespoons extra virgin olive oil
6 ounces white button or cremini mushrooms (or a combination), trimmed and cut into thin slices (about 2 cups)
½ cup chopped onion
⅓ cup chopped Italian parsley
1 teaspoon thyme leaves
1 teaspoon rosemary leaves
1 teaspoon minced garlic

½ cup diced (¼-inch) rinsed and patted dry jarred roasted red peppers
Kosher salt and freshly ground black pepper
2 cups cooked medium- or long-grain white or brown rice
4 ounces cold goat cheese, crumbled
2 large eggs
2 egg yolks
2 cups whole milk

1. Preheat the oven to 325°F. Set a shallow 8-inch square or 11 × 7-inch baking dish inside a 13 × 9-inch baking pan. Set a kettle of water on to heat.

2. Heat a large skillet over medium heat; add the oil. When it is hot enough to sizzle a mushroom, add all of the mushrooms; cook, stirring, for 5 minutes. Add the onions cook over medium-low heat until the onions are tender and the mushrooms are golden brown, about 5 minutes.

3. Meanwhile, finely chop the parsley, thyme, rosemary, and garlic together. Add to the mushrooms; cook for 1 minute. Stir in the roasted red peppers, 1 teaspoon salt, and a generous grinding of black pepper. Remove from the heat.

4. Add the rice, breaking up any clumps with the side of a spoon; stir to blend. Let cool slightly. Gently stir in half of the goat cheese; transfer to the baking dish. Sprinkle the remaining goat cheese on top.

5. Whisk the eggs and yolks in a large bowl until blended. Gradually whisk in the milk. Add 1 teaspoon salt and a grinding of black pepper. Carefully pour over the mushroom and rice mixture.

6. Place on the center oven rack. Carefully add enough very hot water to the baking pan to come halfway up the sides of the baking dish. Bake until the custard is almost set in the center and the tip of a knife inserted just off center comes out clean, about 1 hour and 15 minutes. Let the pudding stand in the hot-water bath for 15 minutes before serving. (The center will continue cooking and setting as the pudding stands.)

Mushrooms

Cremini mushrooms are related to the *agaricus*, or white button, mushroom. They are more mature and consequently have a more mushroomy taste. When selecting either white button or cremini mushrooms for this recipe, inspect the underside of the caps: select the ones with tightly closed caps and no gills exposed. Mushrooms with exposed dark brown gills, although flavorful, will darken light-colored foods like rice and custard.

Corn, Tomato, and Rice Pudding with Chipotle Chile–Cheddar Custard

Makes 6 to 8 servings

Tender fresh corn at the height of the season is my very first choice for this pudding. But if fresh corn is not available, canned white shoepeg corn kernels are an acceptable substitute. However, there is really no substitute for the warm smoky taste of chipotle chiles (see the box following). Small cans of these chiles are available in most large supermarkets, and they give the custard a distinctive flavor, not to mention a hint of heat.

2 cups whole milk
2 cups corn kernels (about 4 ears)
2 large eggs
2 egg yolks
3 tablespoons all-purpose flour
2 to 3 teaspoons pureed chipotle chile in adobo sauce (see box)
2 teaspoons kosher salt
Freshly ground black pepper

2 cups cooked medium- or long-grain white or brown rice
1 cup diced plum tomato flesh (seeds and pulp removed) (3 or 4 medium)
½ cup thinly sliced scallions (white and green parts)
2 teaspoons minced seeded jalapeño
2 cups shredded Cheddar (4 ounces)

1. Preheat the oven to 325°F. Set a shallow 8-inch square or 11 × 7-inch baking dish inside a 13 × 9-inch baking pan. Set a kettle of water on to heat.

2. Combine the milk and 1 cup of the corn kernels in a blender jar; blend until smooth.

3. Whisk the eggs and yolks in a large bowl until blended. Gradually whisk in the milk mixture and the flour. Whisk in the chipotle chile, salt, and pepper to taste.

4. Combine the rice, tomatoes, scallions, jalapeño, half of the cheese, and the remaining 1 cup corn in the baking dish; stir to blend. Spread into an even layer. Carefully pour the custard mixture over the rice mixture. Sprinkle the top with the remaining cheese.

RICE PUDDING: SAVORY AND SWEET   229

5. Place on the center oven rack. Carefully add enough very hot water to the baking pan to come halfway up the sides of the baking dish. Bake until the custard is almost set in the center and the tip of a knife inserted just off center comes out clean, about 1 hour and 15 minutes. Let the pudding stand in the hot-water bath for 15 minutes before serving. (The center will continue cooking and setting while the pudding stands.)

Corn Kernels

To cut corn kernels from the cob, husk the corn and break each ear in half. Set each cut end down in a shallow bowl or soup plate. Holding a small sharp knife at a 45-degree angle, cut from top to bottom in a straight line. Repeat, turning the ear as necessary, until all the kernels are removed. Then, scrape the dull side of the knife down the cob, pressing out any corn "milk" (there won't be much).

Chipotle Chiles

Chipotle chiles are smoked jalapeños. They can be found canned in adobo sauce in most markets. They are fiery and should be used sparingly. Since the tiny chiles are whole in the sauce, I suggest this simple procedure for using them: Place the contents of the can (it is usually 7 ounces) in a food processor and process until finely chopped into a coarse paste. Measure out level teaspoons of the paste and place the little mounds on a baking sheet. Place in the freezer. When the mounds are frozen, lift from the baking sheet with a small spatula and transfer to a plastic container. Cover tightly and store in the freezer. Stir into sauces, chili, salad dressings, mayonnaises, and savory rice pudding custard.

Three Rice, Three Cheese, and Three Mushroom Rice Pudding

Makes 6 to 8 servings

Use rice in any configuration you choose; try 1 cup each of brown, wild, and long-grain white as suggested here, or substitute Wehani, basmati, Italian medium-grain, or other rices. Select mild melting cheeses like mozzarella, Italian Fontina, or Gruyère. This is one of those dishes that improves upon standing, a fact that I rediscover each time there are leftovers. The recipe easily can be doubled if you want to serve a crowd or purposely create a generous amount of leftovers.

2 tablespoons extra virgin olive oil

5 ounces shiitakes, stems discarded, caps wiped clean and coarsely chopped (about 2 cups)

5 ounces cremini mushrooms, trimmed and coarsely chopped (about 2 cups)

5 ounces white button mushrooms, trimmed and coarsely chopped (about 2 cups)

½ cup chopped onion

1 garlic clove, minced

¼ cup finely chopped Italian parsley

1 teaspoon thyme leaves, optional

Kosher salt and freshly ground black pepper

1 cup cooked short-grain brown rice

1 cup cooked wild rice

1 cup cooked long-grain white rice

1 cup coarsely shredded mozzarella (about 4 ounces)

1 cup coarsely shredded Italian Fontina, Gruyère, or Jarlsberg (about 4 ounces)

½ cup freshly grated Parmigiano-Reggiano

2 cups whole milk

1. Preheat the oven to 350°F. Generously butter an 11 × 7-inch or other shallow (1½- to 2-quart) rectangular baking dish.

2. Heat the oil in a large skillet. Add the mushrooms and onion; cook, stirring, over medium-high heat until the mushrooms are browned, about 10 minutes. Stir in the garlic; cook for 1 minute. Add the parsley, thyme, and salt and pepper to taste. Add the rice, mozzarella, Fontina, and ¼ cup of the Parmigiano-Reggiano; stir to blend.

3. Spoon into the prepared baking dish and smooth the top. Pour the milk over the top. Sprinkle with the remaining ¼ cup Parmigiano-Reggiano.

4. Bake until the top is well browned and the cheese is bubbly, about 45 minutes. Let stand for at least 20 minutes to allow the pudding to firm up and set before serving. Serve warm or at room temperature. (This tastes even better when prepared a day ahead and reheated, covered with foil, in a 350°F oven for 15 minutes.)

Savory Spring Rice Custard with Goat Cheese

Makes 6 to 8 servings

This rice and vegetable pudding, like a quiche without the crust, is delicious served with baked ham or smoked meats.

2 tablespoons unsalted butter, plus butter for the baking dish

2 tablespoons fine dry bread crumbs

½ cup diced (¼-inch) carrots

½ cup thinly sliced (¼-inch) green beans

½ cup thinly sliced (¼-inch) asparagus

½ cup frozen petite peas, thawed

1 cup finely chopped leek (white and pale green parts)

1½ to 2 cups cooked medium-grain white rice

2 tablespoons minced dill

2 tablespoons minced mint

One 5-ounce package fresh goat cheese, very cold, cut into small pieces

2 large eggs

2 egg yolks

2 cups whole milk

1 teaspoon grated lemon zest

1 teaspoon kosher salt

Freshly ground black pepper

¼ cup freshly grated Parmigiano-Reggiano

1. Preheat the oven to 350°F. Lightly butter an 8-inch square or 11 × 7-inch baking dish. Sprinkle with the bread crumbs. Place in a 13 × 9-inch baking dish. Set a kettle of water on to heat.

2. Heat a medium saucepan of water to a boil. Add the carrots and green beans; cook for 2 minutes. Add the asparagus and peas; cook for 2 minutes longer. Immediately drain and rinse with cold water. Turn out onto a kitchen towel and blot dry.

3. Melt the 2 tablespoons butter in a large skillet. Add the leek; cook, stirring, over low heat until soft, about 5 minutes. Stir in the carrots, green beans, asparagus, and peas. Stir in the rice, dill, and mint. Transfer to the prepared baking dish; spread in even layer. Top with the goat cheese.

4. Whisk the eggs and yolks in a bowl. Whisk in the milk, lemon zest, salt, and pepper to taste. Pour evenly over the rice and vegetables. Sprinkle the top with the grated cheese.

5. Place on the center oven rack. Add enough very hot water to the pan to come halfway up the sides of the baking dish. Bake until the custard is set, about 45 minutes. Remove from the oven and let the custard cool in the hot-water bath. Cut into squares or spoon out to serve.

INDIVIDUAL CUSTARDS. Lightly butter eight 10- to 12-ounce custard cups. Fill each cup half-full with the rice mixture. Divide the milk and egg mixture evenly among the cups. Reduce the amount of goat cheese to 3 ounces; sprinkle the crumbled cheese evenly on top of the custards. Bake in a water bath as described above until the custards are set; 25 to 30 minutes. Cool in the water bath. To turn out, run the blade of a small knife around the edges and invert the custards onto serving plates or one large platter. Makes 8 servings.

Creamy Saucepan Rice Pudding for All Seasons

Makes 6 to 8 servings

I've never met a rice pudding I didn't like, but this one is one of my all-time favorites. The basic mixture of cooked rice, milk, and sugar can become the basis for many flavor combinations. In summer, I fold whipped cream into the rice and then gently fold sweetened berries into the mixture. In winter, I stew dried fruits and fold them into the rice and cream. Or use any of the imported spoon fruits or sauces now on the market.

1 cup uncooked medium- or long-grain white rice
2 teaspoons kosher salt
3 cups whole milk
¾ cup sugar

1 teaspoon pure vanilla extract
1 cup heavy cream, optional
Ground cinnamon

1. Combine the rice, 8 cups water, and salt in a large wide saucepan; heat to a boil, stirring frequently so the rice doesn't stick. Simmer, uncovered, until the grains are split and very soft, about 20 minutes; drain. Rinse out the pan.

2. Combine the cooked rice, milk, and sugar in the pan. Cook, stirring frequently, over medium-low heat until the mixture is creamy, about 20 minutes. Stir in the vanilla. Let cool to room temperature, about 30 minutes, stirring occasionally.

3. Serve plain, or whip the cream until stiff peaks form; fold into the rice. Spoon into dessert dishes and sprinkle lightly with cinnamon.

RICE PUDDING WITH SWEETENED BERRIES. Combine 2 cups berries (cut-up strawberries mixed with raspberries and blueberries, or any combination) with 2 tablespoons sugar in a bowl; stir to blend. Let stand until juicy. Fold into the plain rice pudding or the version lightened with whipped cream.

RICE PUDDING WITH STEWED DRIED APRICOTS. Flavor the rice pudding with ¼ teaspoon almond extract in addition to the vanilla. Combine 8 ounces dried apricots, 1½ cups water, and a cinnamon stick in a small saucepan. Heat to a simmer; cover and cook, stirring occasionally, over low heat for 15 minutes, or until the apricots are very soft and most of the liquid is absorbed. Let cool slightly. Remove the cinnamon stick. Stir the apricots to break them up into loose, rough pieces. Let cool. Fold the apricot compote into the plain rice pudding or the version lightened with whipped cream.

Sweet Pudding Basics

- Milk, sugar, and rice—the three main ingredients in pudding—scorch easily. Use a heavy saucepan and stir often over low heat.

- Sugar will interfere with the ability of the rice to absorb the milk. Therefore, when making pudding with uncooked rice cook it first in the milk (or other liquid) before adding the sugar, or be prepared for the rice to take longer to cook.

- Basmati rice makes a fragrant pudding, but will not be as creamy as pudding made with regular long-grain rice. Short- and medium-grain rices make the creamiest puddings.

- The soft texture of the rice in warm pudding will change when the pudding is chilled (see retrogradation, page 11). The hardness can be lessened by using soft cooked rice (cook it for a longer period of time) or reversed by reheating the pudding in a microwave, in a boiling water bath in a warm oven, or a double boiler.

Baked Lemon-Custard Rice Pudding

Makes 8 servings

This is my grandmother's recipe. Tender custard envelops each plump grain of rice. Use left-over cooked rice: 1½ cups cooked white rice yields a high custard-to-rice ratio; 3 cups cooked rice makes a stiffer but still creamy pudding; or adjust the amount between the two.

1 tablespoon unsalted butter, at room temperature

1½ to 3 cups cooked long-grain white rice (see headnote)

½ cup dark or golden raisins, optional

6 cups whole milk

1 vanilla bean or 2 teaspoons pure vanilla extract

6 large eggs, at room temperature

1 cup sugar

1 tablespoon grated lemon zest

Freshly grated nutmeg

1. Preheat the oven to 325°F. Generously butter a 13 × 9-inch baking dish with the butter. Set it in a larger baking pan. Set a kettle of water on to heat.

2. Spread the rice and raisins, if using, in the buttered baking dish. Pour the milk into a large saucepan; add the vanilla bean, if using. Heat the milk until small bubbles appear around the edges. Remove from the heat. If you used the vanilla bean, let steep, covered, for 10 minutes.

3. Beat the eggs and sugar in a large bowl until foamy. If using the vanilla bean, remove it from the scalded milk; carefully split the bean and scrape the soft center into the milk. Discard the pod. Gradually whisk the milk into the beaten eggs until blended. Add the lemon zest and the vanilla extract, if using.

4. Pour half the custard mixture over the raisins and rice in the baking dish; stir to distribute evenly. Place the larger baking pan on the center oven rack; pour remaining custard mixture into baking dish. Sprinkle the top evenly with nutmeg.

5. Carefully pour enough very hot water into the larger baking pan to come halfway up the sides of the baking dish. Bake for 1 hour and 15 minutes, or until the custard is almost set and the edges are golden. Let the pudding cool in the water bath. Serve at room temperature or chilled, cut into squares.

Turn Leftover Rice into Pudding

I get great satisfaction when I take a few cups of rice left over from a previous meal and with little effort and just a few extra-special ingredients turn it into a rather elegant dessert. The following three variations on the theme are each made with 2 cups leftover cooked rice. Use basmati, long-grain white, Arborio, or any medium-grain white rice. Then use the three variations as a springboard for further variations: Try raisins in place of the dried cherries or crystallized ginger, ground cinnamon instead of the cinnamon stick, grated lemon zest instead of the crystallized ginger. The egg and heavy cream mixture used in the dried cherry rice pudding and the chocolate rice pudding could also be added to the ginger rice pudding. Or, for a less rich version, they can be omitted from any of the puddings.

Crystallized-Ginger Rice Pudding

**Makes 4
servings**

2 cups whole milk, plus more if needed

2 cups leftover cooked rice, preferably basmati

⅓ cup chopped crystallized ginger or baker's-cut crystallized ginger chips

3 tablespoons sugar

½ teaspoon pure vanilla extract

½ cup (approximately) heavy cream, optional

1. Combine the milk and rice in a medium saucepan; heat, stirring, over medium-low heat until boiling. Stir in the ginger and sugar. Cook, stirring often, until thickened, 15 to 20 minutes. Remove from the heat and stir in the vanilla extract.

2. Serve warm or at room temperature. Add more milk or heavy cream as needed to thin the pudding, which will thicken as it stands.

Cinnamon and Sour Cherry Rice Pudding

**Makes 4
servings**

2 cups whole milk, plus more if needed

2 cups leftover cooked rice

1 cinnamon stick

⅓ cup sugar

⅓ cup dried sour cherries

½ cup heavy cream, plus more if needed

1 large egg

½ teaspoon pure vanilla extract

1. Combine the milk, rice, and cinnamon stick in a medium saucepan; heat to a boil. Stir in the sugar and dried cherries. Cook, stirring often, until thickened, 15 to 20 minutes.

2. In a small bowl, whisk the cream and egg until blended. Add a spoonful of the hot pudding to temper the egg, stirring to blend. Pour the egg mixture into the pudding and cook, stirring, until the pudding boils. Remove from the heat. Stir in the vanilla.

3. Serve warm or at room temperature. Add more milk or heavy cream, as needed, to thin the pudding, which will thicken as it stands.

Chocolate Rice Pudding

Makes 4 servings

Two all-time favorites, chocolate and rice pudding, in one dish.

2 cups whole milk, or more if needed

2 cups leftover cooked rice

¼ cup sugar

4 ounces semisweet or bittersweet chocolate, chopped

½ cup heavy cream, plus more if needed

1 large egg

1 teaspoon pure vanilla extract

1. Combine the milk, rice, and sugar in a saucepan; heat, stirring, over medium heat until the mixture boils. Boil gently over medium to medium-low heat, stirring often, until thickened, 15 to 20 minutes. Stir in the chocolate until melted.

2. In a small bowl, whisk the cream and egg until blended. Stir a little of the hot rice into the cream mixture to temper the egg. Stir the egg mixture into the rice and cook, stirring, until the pudding boils. Remove from the heat; stir in the vanilla.

3. Serve warm, with heavy cream, or serve cold. Add more cream or milk as needed to thin the pudding, which will thicken as it stands.

Rich Rice Pudding in the Style of *Riz à l'Impératrice*

Riz à l'Impératrice is a classic French extravaganza made with rice, custard, lots of cream, and candied fruits soaked in cherry brandy that is stiffened with gelatin so that it can be unmolded from an elaborate mold and stand regally on the platter. The following is a simpler, but equally rich and delicious, interpretation of this classic.

¼ cup golden raisins

¼ cup diced (⅛-inch) candied citron (see Note)

¼ cup diced (⅛-inch) candied orange peel (see Note)

3 tablespoons kirsch, brandy, or rum

1 cup uncooked long-grain white rice

2 teaspoons kosher salt

3 cups whole milk

½ cup sugar

One 3 × ½-inch strip orange zest

1 cinnamon stick

1 teaspoon pure vanilla extract

Custard

1 cup whole milk

2 tablespoons sugar

Pinch of kosher salt

2 large egg yolks, lightly beaten

½ teaspoon pure vanilla extract

¼ cup minced crystallized ginger

1 cup heavy cream, whipped

Optional Garnishes

Whipped cream

10 to 20 thin slices candied citron, cut into ¼ × ¼-inch diamond shapes, optional

1 tablespoon chopped dried sour or sweet cherries

1. Combine the raisins, citron, candied orange peel, and kirsch in a small bowl; stir to mix. Cover and let stand for at least 24 hours, stirring occasionally.

2. Combine the rice, 8 cups water, and salt in a large saucepan; heat to a boil, stirring frequently so the rice doesn't stick. Simmer, uncovered, until the grains are split and very soft, about 20 minutes; drain. Rinse out the pan.

3. Combine the cooked rice, milk, sugar, orange zest, and cinnamon stick in the pan. Cook, stirring frequently, over medium-low heat until the mixture is creamy, 15 to 20 minutes. Let cool to room temperature, stirring occasionally. Add the vanilla. Refrigerate until very cold.

4. *For the custard:* Combine the milk, sugar, and salt in the top of a double boiler and heat, stirring, directly on the flame. Whisk the egg yolks in a small bowl; gradually whisk in some of the hot milk mixture to temper them. Stir the yolk mixture into the remaining milk. Set the pan over the bottom part of the double boiler, filled with about 2 inches of simmering water, and cook, stirring constantly, until the custard thickens enough to lightly coat a spoon, 3 to 5 minutes. Pour through a sieve set over a 2-cup measure and let cool, stirring often. Add the vanilla and refrigerate, uncovered, until very cold.

5. To assemble the dessert, fold the cold custard into the (now very thick) rice mixture. Add the soaked fruits and the candied ginger; fold gently to blend. Gently fold in the whipped cream.

6. Spoon into a beautiful glass bowl and garnish with whipped cream, citron diamonds, and dried cherries, if desired.

NOTE: For best-quality candied fruits buy them in bulk at Italian, Middle Eastern, or other specialty food shops.

Saucepan Banana Rice Pudding

Makes 6 servings

If you are a banana fan, this pudding, bursting with the seductive taste and aroma of bananas, is for you. A halo of toasted coconut sprinkled on top is a nice accent.

4 large egg yolks

½ cup sugar

2 cups whole milk

2 cups cooked basmati rice

¼ cup heavy cream

1 teaspoon pure vanilla extract

½ cup mashed medium-ripe banana, plus 1 cup sliced medium-ripe bananas

Ground cinnamon

Toasted coconut, optional (see page 253)

1. In a large bowl, whisk the egg yolks and sugar until light in color. Meanwhile, heat the milk in a medium saucepan until small bubbles appear around the edges. Gradually whisk the hot milk into the egg yolks until thoroughly blended.

2. Pour the mixture back into the saucepan. Cook, stirring constantly, over low heat until the mixture thickens and begins to coat a metal spoon, about 10 minutes. Stir in the rice; cook, stirring, over medium-low heat until very thick, about 10 minutes. Stir in the heavy cream. Let cool, stirring frequently, for 5 minutes. Stir in the vanilla.

3. Pour into a bowl and refrigerate until very cold.

4. Just before serving, stir the mashed banana into the pudding until well blended. Then fold in the sliced bananas.

5. Spoon the pudding into small bowls. Lightly sprinkle with cinnamon and garnish with toasted coconut, if desired.

Brown Rice Pudding with Maple Syrup

Makes 8 servings

Sure to please even the most discriminating rice pudding aficionado, this heavenly but hearty dessert serves at least eight people.

⅓ cup golden raisins
2½ cups cooked medium-grain brown rice
4 cups whole milk
Pinch of kosher salt
½ cup pure maple syrup

1 teaspoon pure vanilla extract
Butter for the baking dish
¾ cup heavy cream
Ground cinnamon or freshly grated nutmeg

1. Place the raisins in a small heatproof bowl. Add boiling water to cover; let stand while you make the pudding.

2. Combine the rice, milk, and salt in a medium saucepan; heat to a boil over medium heat. Cook, stirring, over low heat for 30 minutes, or until very thick. Stir in the maple syrup; cook, stirring, for 15 minutes. Let cool for 15 minutes.

3. Preheat the oven to 350°F. Stir the vanilla into the rice pudding. Drain the raisins. Generously butter a shallow 1½-quart baking dish or deep 10-inch pie plate. Spoon the rice mixture into the dish; smooth with the back of the spoon. Pour the heavy cream evenly over the top.

4. Bake until the cream is browned and bubbly, about 30 minutes. Serve warm or chilled, sprinkled with cinnamon.

Wild Rice Pudding with Apricots in Vanilla Syrup

Makes 8 servings

Eat this wonderful mixture of chewy wild rice and soft cooked short-grain brown rice for dessert with heavy cream and the garnish of dried apricots plumped in vanilla syrup, or fresh sliced apricots in season, and a dusting of freshly grated nutmeg. For breakfast, eat it from a cereal bowl, sprinkled with a few raisins and broken walnuts, or with heavy cream and a sprinkling of cinnamon or nutmeg, or with fresh sliced apricots or peaches. For a more elaborate dessert, fold in a cup of heavy cream, stiffly beaten, before spooning the pudding into stemmed glasses.

½ cup uncooked wild rice, rinsed with warm water and drained
½ cup uncooked short-grain brown rice
½ teaspoon kosher salt
3 cups whole milk
½ cup packed light brown sugar

1 teaspoon pure vanilla extract
Freshly grated nutmeg or ground cinnamon
1 cup heavy cream, stiffly whipped, optional
Dried Apricots in Vanilla Syrup (recipe follows), optional

1. Combine the wild rice, brown rice, 3 cups water, and salt in a large saucepan; heat to a boil. Cover and cook over medium-low heat until almost all the liquid is absorbed, the wild rice has burst, and the brown rice is tender, 50 to 60 minutes.

2. Stir in the milk; heat to a boil. Cook, stirring, adjusting the heat as necessary to prevent sticking, until the pudding is very thick, about 30 minutes.

3. Stir in the brown sugar and cook, stirring, until dissolved, about 5 minutes. Let cool slightly; stir in the vanilla and nutmeg or cinnamon.

4. Serve the pudding warm, topped with the whipped cream and the apricots in syrup, if desired.

Dried Apricots in Vanilla Syrup

¼ cup sugar

½ cup packed dried apricot halves

1 cinnamon stick

½ teaspoon pure vanilla extract

1. Combine 1 cup water and the sugar in a small saucepan. Heat to a boil, stirring to dissolve the sugar. Add the apricots and cinnamon stick. Simmer, uncovered, over medium-low heat, until the apricots are plump, adding more water if needed, until the syrup is thickened, about 15 minutes. Let cool.

2. Stir in the vanilla extract.

Creamy Yogurt and Mango Rice Pudding with Toasted Pistachios

Makes 6 servings

If mango is unavailable, use sweet ripe peaches or nectarines. Garnish the pudding with finely chopped toasted pistachios or sliced natural (skin-on) almonds. An optional garnish of toasted coconut adds crunch, sweetness, and that addictive flavor.

1 cup uncooked long-grain white rice

½ teaspoon kosher salt

1 cup whole-milk yogurt, plus more if needed

½ cup heavy cream

⅓ cup sugar, or to taste

1 teaspoon pure vanilla extract

⅛ teaspoon pure almond extract

½ cup flaked sweetened coconut, optional

¼ cup chopped peeled pistachios or sliced natural (skin-on) almonds

2 cups diced peeled and pitted ripe mango, peaches, or nectarines

A little milk if needed

1. Preheat the oven to 325°F.

2. Combine 2½ cups water, the rice, and salt in a medium saucepan. Heat to a boil over high heat; stir once. Reduce the heat to low; cover and cook the rice until very soft and tender but still moist, about 25 minutes. Let stand, covered, off the heat for 5 minutes.

3. While the rice is cooking, whisk the yogurt, cream, sugar, vanilla, and almond extract in a bowl. Let stand at room temperature, stirring occasionally to dissolve the sugar.

4. Spread the coconut, if using, at one end of a baking sheet. Spread the pistachios at the other (or in the center). Bake until lightly toasted, 4 to 5 minutes. Let cool.

5. Add the hot rice to the yogurt mixture. Fold in the fruit. Serve warm or at room temperature, sprinkled with the toasted coconut and/or the pistachios. Add additional yogurt thinned with a little milk if the pudding gets too stiff upon standing.

Basmati Rice Pudding with Coconut Milk and Golden Cream

Makes 6 servings

A pudding that is reminiscent of everything exotic and seductive about India. Use imported basmati rice or a miniature basmati called *Kalijira* (or sometimes *gobindavog*).

Golden Cream

¼ teaspoon crumbled saffron threads

1 cup heavy cream

1 tablespoon sugar

3 whole cardamom pods

1 cinnamon stick

1 whole clove

½ teaspoon kosher salt

⅔ cup imported basmati or Kalijira rice
  (see glossary) or Texmati or Kasmati rice

¼ cup dark raisins

1 cup canned unsweetened coconut milk (see box)

1 cup whole milk

2 tablespoons packed light brown sugar

½ cup flaked sweetened coconut

¼ to ½ cup heavy cream, or as needed

3 tablespoons chopped pistachios

1. *For the cream:* Place the saffron threads in a small heavy saucepan; heat just until the saffron takes on a slightly darker color, about 10 seconds. Add the cream and granulated sugar; heat until the cream boils. Immediately remove from the heat. Cover and let steep for 15 minutes.

2. Strain out the saffron and refrigerate the cream until chilled.

3. Combine 1½ cups water, the cardamom, cinnamon, cloves and salt in a medium saucepan; heat to a boil. Stir in the rice. Reduce the heat to low; cover and cook until the rice is tender, about 15 minutes. Drain off any excess liquid.

4. Meanwhile, combine ½ cup boiling water and the raisins in a small bowl; let stand for about 15 minutes.

5. When the rice is cooked, stir in the coconut milk, whole milk, and brown sugar. Drain the raisins and add to the rice; heat to a boil. Cover and cook over low

heat, stirring occasionally, until the pudding is very thick, about 20 minutes. Remove from the heat.

6. Add the coconut to the pudding. Add heavy cream as needed; stir gently to blend. Serve warm or at room temperature. The pudding will stiffen as it cools; add more heavy cream or milk, 1 tablespoon at a time, to thin it to the desired consistency. Spoon into dessert dishes and drizzle each serving with golden cream. Sprinkle with the chopped pistachios.

Coconut Milk

Buy good-quality imported unsweetened coconut milk, available in the Asian sections of supermarkets. When you open the can, the milk will be separated into a solid cream layer and a more liquid layer underneath. Scrape the contents of the can into a bowl and gently whisk to blend the two together before measuring the amount needed.

Baked Coconut Rice Pudding

Makes 8
servings

This baked pudding uses cooked rice, canned coconut milk, and dried coconut. Don't confuse unsweetened dried coconut (sometimes called desiccated coconut) with the sweetened flaked or shredded coconut sold in the baking section of the supermarket. They are very different. Dried coconut is available in health-food stores and in markets where Asian ingredients are sold. Likewise, for the coconut milk. Buy unsweetened canned milk, used for making curries and other Asian-style dishes, not the cream of coconut milk used for making tropical drinks. Almost any type of rice can be used, although I prefer the aroma and texture of basmati or jasmine.

⅔ cup uncooked basmati, jasmine, or long-grain
    white rice (see Note)
1 cinnamon stick
1 slice (¼-inch-thick) fresh ginger
½ teaspoon kosher salt
One 14½-ounce can unsweetened coconut milk
    (see headnote)
1½ cups (approximately) half-and-half (or half milk
    and half heavy cream)
2 large eggs
⅓ cup sugar
1 teaspoon pure vanilla extract

½ cup unsweetened dried coconut (see headnote)
Ground cinnamon

Coconut Cream Topping, optional
One 14½-ounce can unsweetened coconut milk
½ cup heavy cream
½ teaspoon pure vanilla extract

1 to 2 cups diced, pitted (or seeded), and peeled
    mango, papaya, nectarines, or peaches, for
    garnish, optional

1. Heat 1½ cups water to a boil in a wide saucepan or deep skillet. Add the rice, cinnamon stick, ginger, and salt; stir once. Cover and cook over low heat until the water is absorbed and the rice is tender, about 15 minutes. Uncover and let cool.

2. Preheat the oven to 350°F. Set a 1½- to 2-quart shallow baking dish inside a larger baking pan. Set a kettle of water on to heat.

3. Empty the can of coconut milk into a 4-cup measure. Whisk to blend the top cream into the liquid coconut milk. Add enough half-and-half to measure 3 cups. Add the eggs, sugar, and vanilla; whisk until blended.

4. Remove the cinnamon stick and ginger from the rice. Spread the rice in the baking dish. Sprinkle the coconut evenly over the rice. Pour the egg mixture over the rice. Stir gently just to combine. Sprinkle the top evenly with ground cinnamon.

5. Set the larger baking pan in the oven on the center rack. Pour very hot water into the baking pan to come halfway up the sides of the baking dish. Bake until the pudding is set, about 1 hour.

6. *Meanwhile, make the optional topping:* Whisk the coconut milk, cream, and vanilla extract in a bowl until smooth. Cover and refrigerate until ready to serve.

7. Remove the baked pudding from the oven; let cool in the water bath. Serve warm or at room temperature. If desired, drizzle with the coconut cream topping and garnish with the fruit.

NOTE: If using leftover cooked rice (about 1⅓ cups), add 1 teaspoon grated fresh ginger with the vanilla in Step 3.

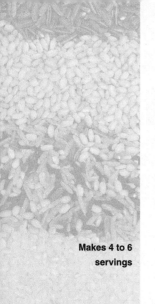

Creamy Black Rice Pudding with Toasted Coconut and Mango

Makes 4 to 6 servings

The black bran on black rice turns the water it is cooked in a deep purplish black, or milk a lovely shade of lavender gray. For this pudding, begin with soft-cooked black rice. Not all black rice needs to be soaked before cooking. If you use the Chinese Forbidden Rice from Lotus Foods (which is less sticky than some black rices and available in better supermarkets) or some brands of Thai black rice, it will be tender in 35 minutes and very soft in 50 minutes without soaking. Sticky black rice, found mostly at Asian grocers, may need to be soaked for several hours before cooking. Cooking black rice might seem like a lot of trouble, but this exotic rice, with its haunting aromatic flavor, is worth it—especially when used to make this irresistibly creamy pudding.

One 14½-ounce can unsweetened coconut milk
   (see page 249)
¾ cup (approximately) half-and-half or heavy cream
½ cup sugar
½ teaspoon kosher salt

2 cups soft-cooked black rice (see Notes)
2 ripe mangoes
½ cup unsweetened dried coconut, toasted
   (see Notes)
2 tablespoons brown sesame seeds, optional

1. Pour the coconut milk into a 2-cup measure; whisk to blend the solid coconut cream with the liquid coconut milk. Add enough half-and-half to equal 2 cups. Whisk to blend.

2. Combine the coconut milk mixture, sugar, and salt in a deep saucepan; heat to a boil. Boil for 5 minutes, stirring to prevent scorching. Ladle out 1 cup and reserve to serve as a sauce.

3. Add the rice to the saucepan; heat to a boil. Reduce the heat to medium-low; cook, stirring often to prevent sticking and adjusting the heat as necessary to maintain a steady simmer, until the pudding is very thick, about 10 minutes or more depending on the rice. Add more cream, if needed. Transfer to a bowl and let cool to room temperature.

4. Cut the mangoes just to the left and the right of the flat center pits. Peel the skin from the two cheeks. Place the cut sides down and cut crosswise into ½-inch-wide slices.

5. To serve the pudding, spoon a mound onto each dessert plate. Fan the mango slices and arrange on the side of each plate. Sprinkle with toasted coconut and/or sesame seeds. Pass a pitcher of the reserved sweetened coconut milk mixture to drizzle on top of the pudding, if desired.

NOTES: To cook black rice, first place it in a large bowl. Add tap water to cover, swish it around, and drain in a strainer. Repeat at least twice. If the rice needs to be soaked before cooking, return the rice to the bowl, cover with cold water, and soak for 4 hours. Drain.

Put the rice either soaked or unsoaked in a large saucepan. Cover with plenty of water and cook, uncovered, until the rice is plump and tender, anywhere from 30 to 50 minutes. Drain and let cool. Alternatively, to steam the rice: Place the soaked rice in a large bowl and add just enough boiling water to cover the rice. Place the bowl in a steaming basket set over gently boiling water. Cover the steamer and cook until the rice is tender and fluffy, 30 to 50 minutes, adding more boiling water to the rice if necessary. (One cup uncooked black rice will yield approximately 4 cups cooked black rice. Use leftovers in salads or stir-fries, or use ½ cup uncooked black rice.)

CREAMY WHITE RICE PUDDING WITH COCONUT MILK AND MANGO. Substitute 2 cups cooked Thai jasmine rice for the cooked black rice.

Toast coconut in a pie pan or small baking sheet in a preheated 350°F oven just until it begins to brown, 3 to 4 minutes, stirring once. Watch carefully: the coconut will toast very quickly. It can also be toasted in a small skillet on top of the stove. Stir constantly over medium-low heat until golden, about 3 minutes.

Sweet Endings

Cooked rice, rice wine, and rice flour inspire a unique assortment of sweets from cookies to poached fruits. Many are straightforward recipes that are made by stirring rice into a batter or poaching fruit in sweetened and spiced rice wine.

But baking with rice flour presents more of a challenge, because it is gluten-free. Baked goods need gluten to hold moisture and form a crumb that stays together. The following recipes use a combination of rice and wheat flours, resulting in cookies that are tender, crisp, and buttery with a slightly sandy texture. I use both plain rice flour from my Asian market and the boutique rice flours made from ground Bhutanese red rice and black rice in these recipes. The black rice flour gives the cookies an unusual pale lavender color, and the red flour lends a pale pink color. Otherwise, there is no discernible difference among the different rice flours.

Ground Walnut and Rice Flour Balls

Makes 5 to 6 dozen cookies

Ground walnuts go into the cookie dough and coat the cookies after they are shaped. Handle carefully, as cookies made with rice flour are very tender. These will keep about a week stored in an airtight container.

½ pound (2 sticks) unsalted butter, softened
½ cup sugar
1 teaspoon pure vanilla extract
¼ teaspoon salt

1½ cups all-purpose flour
½ cup white, black, or red rice flour
3 cups walnuts, finely ground in a food processor
2 large egg whites

1. In a large bowl, beat the butter, sugar, vanilla, and salt with an electric mixer until very light and creamy, about 10 minutes.

2. Combine the all-purpose flour, rice flour, and 1 cup of the ground walnuts in a medium bowl; stir to blend. Add to the butter mixture; beat on low speed just until the dry ingredients are incorporated, about 1 minute. Cover and refrigerate the dough for 1 hour, or until firm enough to form into small balls.

3. Preheat the oven to 325°F. Place the egg whites in a shallow bowl and whisk until foamy. Place the remaining 2 cups walnuts on a sheet of wax paper.

4. Shape the dough into ¾-inch balls. Coat the balls with the egg white, then roll in the walnuts. Place on ungreased baking sheets about 1 inch apart.

5. Bake one sheet at a time until the bottoms of the cookies are golden brown, 20 to 25 minutes. Cool on cookie sheet for about 10 minutes before carefully removing cookies from the baking sheet to a rack with a thin metal spatula. When the cookies are completely cooled, store in an airtight plastic container. Will keep one week. Cookies freeze well.

Coconut and Rice Flour Shortbread

Makes 5 to 6 dozen cookies

Delicate and buttery, these cookies are made with wheat flour and white rice flour, or one of the specialty rice flours made from red rice or black rice. Dried unsweetened coconut (see page 250) adds a nice crunch and extra richness.

½ pound (2 sticks) unsalted butter, softened
½ cup sugar
1 teaspoon pure vanilla extract
¼ teaspoon salt

1½ cups all-purpose flour
½ cup white rice, black rice, red rice flour
½ cup unsweetened dried coconut, plus ½ cup for coating

1. In a large bowl, beat the butter, sugar, vanilla, and salt with an electric mixer until very light and creamy, about 10 minutes.

2. Combine the all-purpose flour, rice flour, and coconut in a medium bowl; stir to blend. Add to the butter mixture; beat on low speed just until the dry ingredients are incorporated, about 1 minute.

3. Lay a sheet of aluminum foil on the counter. Turn the dough (it will be very soft) out onto the foil. With floured hands, shape the dough into an oval and divide in half. Gently roll each half into a log about 12 inches long. Roll up in foil. Refrigerate until firm, at least 1 hour. (If the dough becomes very firm, it will crumble when cut. Let very cold dough stand at room temperature for about 10 minutes before slicing.)

4. Preheat the oven to 325°F. Lightly brush the outside of the dough logs with egg white. Spread the remaining ½ cup coconut on a sheet of wax paper; roll the logs in the coconut, pressing lightly to coat evenly. Using a sharp, thin-bladed knife, preferably serrated, cut the dough into ¼-inch-thick cookies. Place on ungreased cookie sheets about 1 inch apart. Bake one sheet at a time until the edges are golden, about 20 minutes. Cool on cookie sheets for 10 minutes before removing from baking sheets to racks with a thin metal spatula. When the cookies are completely cooled, store in an airtight plastic container. Will keep one week. Cookies freeze well.

New Orleans Rice Fritters
Calas

**Makes
20 to 24
fritters**

"Belles calas tout chaud" was once a familiar cry on the back streets of the New Orleans French Quarter. Sold from carts by street vendors, *calas* were a popular breakfast food—and a practical way to use up leftover cooked rice from the night before. This recipe, from cookbook author and food writer Terry Thompson, is made with a yeast dough and produces a light airy fritter, similar to a doughnut, that is hard to resist. Plan ahead: the rice sponge (see Step 1) needs to stand overnight.

2 tablespoons granulated sugar

1 package active dry yeast

1½ cups cooked long-grain white rice

3 large eggs, beaten

1½ cups sifted unbleached all-purpose flour

½ teaspoon salt

½ teaspoon pure vanilla extract

¼ teaspoon freshly grated nutmeg

Vegetable oil for deep-frying

Confectioners' sugar or warm honey

1. Combine ½ cup warm water (105° to 115°F) and 1 teaspoon of the sugar in a large bowl; sprinkle the yeast over the water. Cover with plastic wrap and let stand until the yeast is dissolved and foamy, about 10 minutes. Stir in the rice and let stand, covered, in a warm place overnight.

2. The next day, the rice will be swollen; stir just to blend. Add the eggs, flour, salt, vanilla, nutmeg, and the remaining 1 tablespoon plus 2 teaspoons sugar; beat with a wooden spoon just until smooth. The batter will be the consistency of cookie dough or stiff cake batter. Cover and place in a warm place until the batter doubles in bulk, about 1 hour.

3. Heat 3 inches of oil in a deep heavy saucepan or a deep-fryer to 350° to 375°F. Stir the batter gently to blend. Scoop up rounded tablespoonfuls and drop into the hot oil; fry 3 or 4 at a time, tapping the fritters occasionally with the back of a spoon (they will puff up slightly), until golden, about 4 minutes.

4. Drain on paper towels. Serve hot, sprinkled with confectioners' sugar or drizzled with warm honey.

Orange Rice Torte with Grand Marnier

Makes 10 to 12 servings

In Bologna, Italy, *torta di riso*, or rice torte, is a specialty. This recipe is a favorite inspired by a recipe from Biba Caggiano, a wonderful cook, restaurateur, and cookbook author from Sacramento, California, whose food I greatly admire. The torta has the texture of a cheesecake and the flavors of a pudding. The quality of the candied orange peel is critical to the success of this torte. If you must rely on supermarket candied peel, be sure it is a fresh supply (usually available around the holidays), but I buy it in bulk at Italian, Middle Eastern, or other specialty food shops.

¾ cup uncooked medium-grain white or Arborio rice
4 cups whole milk
1½ cups sugar
1 tablespoon grated orange zest
1 cup finely ground natural (skin-on) almonds
1 tablespoon unsalted butter, melted
5 large eggs
½ cup finely chopped candied orange peel

¼ cup Grand Marnier
¼ teaspoon pure almond extract
Confectioners' sugar

Optional Garnishes
1 pint raspberries or strawberries, hulled and sliced
1 cup heavy cream, stiffly beaten
Minced candied orange peel

1. Heat 6 cups water to a boil in a large wide saucepan. Add the rice; cook, uncovered, until partially cooked, about 12 minutes. Drain.

2. Combine the rice, milk, and sugar in the same pan; heat to a boil. Simmer, uncovered, over medium-low heat, stirring frequently, until the mixture is thickened and the rice is very tender, about 30 minutes. Remove from the heat; let cool to room temperature. Stir in the orange zest.

3. Preheat the oven to 350°F.

4. Spread the ground almonds in a baking pan. Bake, stirring once or twice, until evenly toasted, about 10 minutes; let cool. Brush the bottom and sides of a 10-inch springform pan with the melted butter. (Make sure the seal is tight so that

the cake batter will not leak out during baking.) Evenly coat the bottom and sides of the buttered pan with approximately ¼ cup of the ground almonds. Reserve the remaining almonds for the torta.

5. In a large bowl, beat the eggs with an electric mixer until light in color. Stir in the cooled rice mixture, the candied orange peel, the reserved ground almonds, 2 tablespoons of the Grand Marnier, and the almond extract until thoroughly blended. Pour into the prepared pan; smooth the top.

6. Bake for 1 hour and 5 minutes, or until the cake is well browned and the sides are beginning to pull away from the pan. While the cake is still warm, make holes in the surface with a wooden pick and drizzle with the remaining 2 tablespoons Grand Marnier. Cool the cake on a rack.

7. When the cake has cooled, run a thin spatula around the edges and remove the rim of the pan. Serve sprinkled with confectioners' sugar, with a few fresh raspberries or sliced strawberries on the side, if desired. Or, cover the surface of the torta with tiny rosettes of whipped cream, using a pastry bag with a star tip; sprinkle the cream with minced candied orange peel.

Frozen Sake with Summer Fruit Salad

Makes 4 to 6 servings

A refreshing adult iced dessert with the consistency of a slushy Italian granita. Serve with any combination of seasonal berries or other fruits, such as blueberries, raspberries, and strawberries, peeled peaches, and raspberries or blueberries.

1 cup sake (see page 46)
1 cup plus 1 tablespoon sugar, or more to taste

4 cups mixed fruit (1 cup blueberries, sorted and rinsed, ½ pint raspberries, and 2 cups sliced strawberries, or 2 cups peeled and thinly sliced peaches plus 1 cup berries)

1. Combine the sake, 1 cup water, and 1 cup of the sugar in a medium saucepan; heat to a boil. Boil, stirring, until the sugar is dissolved. Reduce the heat and simmer for 5 minutes. Let cool.

2. Pour the sake syrup into a shallow 9- or 10-inch square baking pan or dish and place in the freezer. Freeze, stirring every hour or so, until the mixture is partially frozen. Scrape the solid edges toward the center with a fork, until evenly frozen, about 2 hours. Scoop or spoon into a plastic container. Cover tightly and freeze until ready to serve.

3. Combine the fruit and the remaining 1 tablespoon sugar in a bowl; toss to combine. Cover and let stand at room temperature for about 30 minutes so the fruits give up their natural juices.

4. To serve, with an ice cream scoop or server, scrape the sake mixture into bowls or stemmed glasses. Top with the fruit. Serve at once.

Tangerines Poached in Sake-and-Ginger Syrup

Makes 6 servings

Tangerines and sake make a refreshingly light dessert. Perfect served after a seafood supper.

1½ cups sake (see page 46)

1 cup sugar

1 slice (¼-inch-thick) peeled fresh ginger

1 tablespoon slivered mandarin orange, tangerine, or other small orange zest

6 seedless tangerines, or mandarin oranges or other small seedless oranges

One half-pint raspberries or blueberries

1. Combine the sake, 1 cup water, and the sugar in a saucepan. Heat to a boil, stirring to dissolve the sugar. Add the ginger and orange zest. Boil gently over medium-low heat until reduced to 2 cups, about 20 minutes.

2. Meanwhile, with a sharp thin-bladed knife, cut the peel and white pith from the mandarins. Cut crosswise in half. Remove seeds, if necessary. Place in a large bowl, cut side up.

3. Pour the hot syrup over the fruit. Refrigerate, covered, until very cold, at least 3 hours, or overnight.

4. To serve, add the berries, if using, to the tangerines. Using a perforated spoon, distribute the fruit evenly among six shallow soup plates or deep dessert dishes. Ladle the syrup over the fruit. Serve with a knife and fork to cut the tangerines, and a spoon for the syrup.

Breakfast Rice and Apple Hot Cakes

Makes 12 pancakes; 4 servings

Delicious little pancakes perfect for a lazy Sunday morning breakfast. Serve with ham or sausage, applesauce, and/or maple syrup.

1 cup cooked medium- or long-grain white rice
1 cup whole milk
1 tablespoon unsalted butter, plus more for the griddle
1 teaspoon pure vanilla extract
1 large egg, separated

½ cup all-purpose flour
1 teaspoon baking powder
Pinch of kosher salt
2 teaspoons sugar
1 cup diced (⅛-inch) peeled apple
Warm applesauce or maple syrup

1. Combine the rice and milk in a saucepan; heat, stirring, until boiling and the rice is softened, about 5 minutes. Stir in the butter until melted. Remove from the heat; cool to lukewarm. Add the vanilla and egg yolk; stir to blend.

2. Stir the flour, baking powder, and salt together in a large bowl. Add the rice mixture; stir just to combine.

3. In a small bowl, whisk or beat the egg white until foamy. Gradually add the sugar and beat until soft peaks form. Add the apple and beaten egg white to the batter and gently fold to combine.

4. Melt a thin film of butter on a griddle or in a skillet over medium heat. Add the batter by one-third-cupfuls; flatten with the bottom of the cup. Cook until there are small bubbles all over the surface of the cakes and the bottoms are golden, about 5 minutes. Turn and brown the other side. Serve with warm applesauce or maple syrup.

Sources   ·

AG Ferrari
14234 Catalina Street
San Leandro, CA 94577
(877) 878-2783
www.agferrari.com
Premium Italian rice.

Chefshop.com
1435 Elliott Avenue West,
P.O. Box 3488
Seattle, WA 98114-3488
(877) 337-2491
www.chefshop.com

Gold Mine Natural Food Company
7805 Arjons Drive
San Diego, CA 92126
(800) 475-FOOD
www.goldminenaturalfood.com
Excellent selection of rice, many organic.

Kalustyan's
123 Lexington Avenue
New York, NY 10016
(212) 685-3451
www.Kalustyans.com
*Wide assortment of imported and
domestic rice.*

Lotus Foods
El Cerrito, CA 94530
(510) 525-3137
info@lotusfoods.com
*Exotic rice from Bhutan, China, and
Bangladesh.*

Lowell Farms
El Campo, TX 77437
(888) 484-9213
www.lowellfarms.com
Organic brown and white jasmine rice.

Lundberg Family Farms
Richvale, CA 95974-0369
(530) 882-4551
www.lundberg.com
Premium natural and organic rice.

Made in France
San Francisco, CA 94107
(415) 861-2196
www.levillage.com
Red rice from the Camargue.

Martin Rice Company
22326 County Road 780
Bernie, MO 63822
(573) 293-4884
www.Martinrice.com
Baldo and other premium rice.

Pacific Rim Gourmet
Clipse, Inc. (headquarters)
4905 Morena Boulevard, Suite 1313
San Diego, CA 92117
(800) 910-WOKS
www.pacificrim-gourmet.com
Premium Asian and other rice.

Pasta Shop at Market Hall
Oakland, CA 94618
(888) 952-4005
www.manicaretti.com
Premium Italian rice.

Spanish Table
Seattle, WA 98101
(206) 682-2827
www.spanishtable.com
Premium Spanish rice.

Index